Ashgate Studies in Architecture Series

SERIES EDITOR: EAMONN CANNIFFE, MANCHESTER SCHOOL OF ARCHITECTURE, MANCHESTER METROPOLITAN UNIVERSITY, UK

The discipline of Architecture is undergoing subtle transformation as design awareness permeates our visually dominated culture. Technological change, the search for sustainability and debates around the value of place and meaning of the architectural gesture are aspects which will affect the cities we inhabit. This series seeks to address such topics, both theoretically and in practice, through the publication of high quality original research, written and visual.

Other titles in this series

Symbolic Houses in Judaism
How Objects and Metaphors Construct Hybrid Places of Belonging
Mimi Levy Lipis
ISBN 978 1 4094 2104 7

Neo-historical East Berlin
Architecture and Urban Design in the German Democratic Republic 1970–1990
Florian Urban
ISBN 978 0 7546 7616 4

Forthcoming titles in this series

Generating Typologies
An Analysis of Residential Plans
Frank Edward Brown
ISBN 978 0 7546 7933 2

An Architecture of Ineloquence
A Carmelite Convent by José Luis Sert
J.K. Birksted
ISBN 978 0 7546 7801 4

African Identity in Post-Apartheid Public Architecture

White Skin, Black Masks

Jonathan Alfred Noble
University of the Witwatersrand, South Africa

ASHGATE

Published by
Ashgate Publishing Limited
Wey Court East
Union Road
Farnham
Surrey GU9 7PT
England

Ashgate Publishing Company
Suite 420
101 Cherry Street
Burlington, VT 05401-4405
USA

www.ashgate.com

British Library Cataloguing in Publication Data
Noble, Jonathan Alfred.
  African identity in post-apartheid public architecture :
  white skin, black masks. -- (Ashgate studies in architecture)
  1. Public architecture--Competitions--South Africa--
  History--20th century. 2. Public architecture--
  Competitions--South Africa--History--21st century.
  3. Architectural design--South Africa--History--20th
  century. 4. Architectural design--South Africa--History--
  21st century. 5. Architecture and society--South Africa--
  History--20th century. 6. Architecture and society--South
  Africa--History--21st century.
  I. Title II. Series
  725'.07968-dc22

Library of Congress Cataloging-in-Publication Data
Noble, Jonathan Alfred.
  African identity in post-apartheid public architecture : white skin, black masks / by
Jonathan Alfred Noble.
    p. cm. -- (Ashgate studies in architecture)
  Includes index.
  ISBN 978-0-7546-7765-9 (hardback) 1. Architecture and race--South Africa.
 2. Architecture and society--South Africa. 3. Public architecture--South Africa. 4. Public
buildings--South Africa. 5. South Africa--Social conditions--1994- I. Title.

  NA2543.R37N63 2011
  725.0968'09049--dc22

2010027829

ISBN 978 0 7546 7765 9

FSC
www.fsc.org
MIX
Paper from
responsible sources
FSC® C018575

Printed and bound in Great Britain by the
MPG Books Group, UK

Contents

This book is dedicated to my parents, Alfred Henry and Christine Elizabeth Noble, for years of unfaltering love and support

List of figures

4   'We the People', Part 1

Foreword

In this remarkable study of five architectural projects, Jonathan Noble opens up for us a whole set of architectural questions, ranging from issues of methodology to the practice of architecture globally today. At the heart of the book rightly rest the five projects themselves, and indeed one of the most welcome aspects of this study is the way in which these projects are excavated in considerable detail. We learn at length not only about how they have been designed and constructed, about how they look and about what they might mean, but also about the way in which they have been produced as part of processes of debate, discussion and participation. Architecture emerges here not as the projected image of a single mind, but as it most often is, that is as the product of a hugely complex intersection of ideas, individuals, groups, thoughts, intentions and propositions.

Yet this book is far from being simply an extended exegesis of the workings of five projects. Also notable is the way in which the ideas of Frantz Fanon – and particularly those from *Black Skin, White Masks* – are brought into subtle interplay with the architecture. Here, notions of skin, mask, authenticity, subjectivity and postcolonial identity are introduced not to provide some kind of decorative categorisation, nor to provide some kind of *a priori* understanding, but as interrogative tools by which to question architecture, and to open it up to further speculations. As Fanon said, 'make of me always a man who questions.' Architectural history emerges here as a future-oriented enterprise, one concerned as much for the possibilities for lives yet to be lived as it is with the establishment and understanding of histories that have already occurred.

In general terms, therefore, for architecture and architectural history there are two important dynamics within this highly political trajectory. The first is perhaps implied rather than being explicitly stated, and that is the need to uncover the ways in which architectural modernism has constructed its 'exclusionary purity', and how this purity has operated over many decades. This is a challenge which others may choose to follow. The second is more explicitly stated, and that is to conceive of an architecture that involves at once inclusion and appropriation, that recognises both authenticity and inauthenticity, that both provides solutions and opens up new possibilities. For the five projects investigated here, the book does a fine job of disclosing a focus on types, patterns, figures, symbols and other architectural devices that have been brought into play with African contexts of landscape, tectonics and climate. But perhaps of wider significance is not the precise nature of these particular propositions themselves, but their underlying relation to different histories, time-scales, narratives, images, spatial types and forms of participation. This is an architecture which is composed not from rules, codes and types, not from categories, prescriptions and proscriptions, but from attitudes, intentions and relations, from politics, culture and people.

However imperative and difficult might be the contemporary situation of South Africa today, such architecture, of course, is far from being confined to the context of that country. Indeed, in today's world of increasing urbanisation, hybridisation, multiculturalism and globalised cultural connections, such an approach to architecture offers welcome relief from, for example, the highly reductive focus on aesthetics offered by the opposition between iconic, signature architecture on the one hand and everyday, normative architecture on the other. What this study of five buildings in one country ultimately offers, therefore, is an approach, an attitude to architecture that is more cultural, participatory and transparent. Like the book itself, this is an architecture that is provocative, open and, above all, questioning.

Iain Borden

Acknowledgements

A special thanks to Professor Iain Borden (Bartlett School of Architecture, University College London) for his solid advice and scholarship, friendship and encouragement, and for writing the foreword to this book. Thanks are also due to Professor Murray Fraser (School of Architecture and the Built Environment, University of Westminster) and Dr Adam Sharr (Welsh School of Architecture, Cardiff University) for their insightful criticism and comment. On a personal level, particular thanks are due to my wife, Kirsty McLean, for her loving support, companionship and understanding over the past years, indeed while completing her own PhD and book.

I am indebted to everyone who participated in my research, by way of interviews and through the supply of primary research material – be that in the form of documents, drawings or photographs – my sincerest thanks to you all. In the preparation of the material for this book, particular thanks are due to the following individuals: Henia Czekanowska who assisted with taking photographs of various large drawings, Patricia and Kirsty McLean for proofreading early drafts of the text, Samantha Brener for assisting with copyright requests, Michael Cornwell for assisting with image reproduction, Lia Marus for proofreading the final manuscript and Margot von Beck for indexing the book. I also wish to thank the kind and helpful people at Ashgate Publishing, UK – Valerie Rose, Sarah Horsley, Pamela Bertram and others.

Finally, thanks are due to my sponsors without whose generous support my research and writing would not have been possible: National Research Foundation Scholarship for Doctoral Studies Abroad; Universities UK, Overseas Research Student Award; Ernest Oppenheimer Memorial Trust; Wits University Appeal Fund Scholarship for Overseas Study; the SANTED teaching relief award; and to the School of Architecture and Planning at Wits University for facilitating my sabbatical leave, which allowed time for the completion of the final manuscript.

Introduction

In writing this book, I have wished to produce a reading of recent South African architecture in celebration of one of Africa's finest critical thinkers, Frantz Fanon. The title for this book, *On Questions of African Identity in Post-Apartheid Public Architectural Design, 1994–2009: White Skin, Black Masks*, was chosen with reference to Fanon's classic study of colonised subjectivity in his renowned book *Black Skin, White Masks (BS)*.[1] I contend that the metaphors of mask and skin – as gleaned from Fanon's title – are suggestive for architectural criticism in the context of post-apartheid public design. Fanon's non-essentialist theories of race, culture and identity provide a theoretical framework for dealing with the visionary quality of the new architecture and its relation to dominant versus repressed (African) forms of architectural expression – political and aesthetic themes that are central to the book as a whole. *White Skin, Black Masks* also recognises the fact that the new architecture of the last few years has mostly been designed by white architects – designers who have been asked to adopt an African persona in design.[2] And in most cases, these designs have initiated gestures that move architectural discourse in an appropriate direction. On this point, it may be noted that political/aesthetic questions as to what constitutes authentic (or inauthentic) African identity, authentic (or inauthentic) African expression in design are a recurring theme of the book.

Due to the destructive legacy of colonial and apartheid rule, the terms of reference for a new public architecture are far from clear. This circumstance, although tied to a bleak history, might also be seen as an important opportunity because it invites all South Africans to ask fundamental questions of their personal and collective belonging. In the absence of clear public or private grammars, recent public designs have begun to experiment with new forms of political imagination. Topical questions of African identity and imaginative dialogue with African landscapes, craft and indigenous traditions have inspired fascinating and impressive works of architecture. These projects represent a unique moment in the history of a nation and raise important political, social and aesthetic issues that warrant careful consideration.

Beginning with South Africa's first democratic election of 1994, this book considers public buildings that resulted from architectural design competitions. The prevalence of public design competitions, in the early post-apartheid period, is significant for it marks a departure from the past, where 'public matters' were controlled by the apartheid state and where design competitions were not common. Consideration of design competitions provides a useful way to study architectural and ideological debates, to ascertain why certain imaginations are selected and others rejected and may be used to inform interpretation of the buildings that evolve from this process.

A key question has concerned which projects to include in the book. Crucial in this regard has been the choice between covering a wide range of designs, or a select few studied in substantial detail. I chose the latter, opting to write detailed histories of five projects because this approach provides a better scope for the study of unique circumstances, particular dialogues and debates, and the architectural responses that result from these interesting processes. In each case, I consider various schemes that were submitted to the competition process, so the five case studies cover a fair number of designs. A positive feature of the new public architecture in South Africa today is its rich and diverse quality. The five case studies – spanning Chapters 2–6 – were selected for their political and architectural prominence, and showcase substantially different kinds of architecture, set in equally diverse locales. The book is attentive to the unique qualities of each case, but the narrative also raises more general, theoretical questions as to the representation of identities, culture and subjugated histories, and how these concerns impact on our conception of architecture.

Unfortunately, archival information for urban and architectural studies is virtually non-existent in South Africa. My research, of necessity therefore, has centred upon interviews with key parties concerned – architects, competition jurors, politicians, council and city officials, artists and crafters, and people who are involved in the day-to-day life of the buildings in question. During these interviews, I requested copies of documentary evidence and in this way, I began to build up a substantial archive of research documents – papers that are cited in this book. This approach has enabled me to position different subjectivities and to derive architectural interpretation from these perspectives.

Although there is a growing body of new literature on the subject of ethnicity – which includes wide-ranging social studies of ethnic and racial differences – scarce study has been made of the relationships that exist between architecture and racialised identity.[3] Lesley Naa Norle Lokko's edited book, *White Papers, Black Marks: Architecture, Race, Culture* has made a timely and unique contribution to the study of architecture and race.[4] It is worth noting that with respect to established architectural perspectives, Lokko states that 'blacks, either as Africans or as diasporic cultures, have historically had nothing to say about architecture – as a consequence, architecture has had little to say in response'.[5] Lokko furthermore maintains that working through the intertwined categories of race and architecture requires a stepping back from the 'traditional formal qualities' of architecture. My own work, however, moves in a different direction, in response to an emerging body of architectural design – works that warrant careful study of the aesthetics and materiality of buildings, the intentions of the architect and client, as well as a consideration of various forms of public reception.

We shall now proceed with a theoretical discussion of Fanon, and questions of postcolonial identity, to prepare a theoretical ground for the empirical case studies that follow in subsequent chapters.

Identifications

Questions of identity in design are commonly approached from the perspective of regionalist, contextual study, or in terms of some assumed genus of the nation. These approaches are limited since a contextual study of the post-apartheid city often fails to acknowledge that 'urban context' was produced by the dominance of colonial and apartheid practices, and therefore risk repeating what should be questioned while a preoccupation with nationalism places overly institutionalised restrictions upon the wider issues pertinent to a cultural politics of identity. This book has sought to resist these approaches and, instead, has taken its lead from theories of postcolonial subjectivity.

What is subjective identity, and how does it feature in questions of cultural politics? The French political philosopher, Etienne Balibar, is helpful when he suggests that we should not so much speak of identity, but rather of the more fluid processes of identification:

[i]n reality there are no identities, only identifications: either with the institution itself, or with other subjects by the intermediary of the institution. Or, if one prefers, identities are only the ideal goal of processes of identification, their point of honor, of certainty or uncertainty of their consciousness, thus their imaginary referent.[6]

Identifications are always performed in relation to others. The politics of identity involves motions of solidarity, through which we imaginatively construct the 'we' of political participation. Balibar emphasises the positioned, plural and participatory nature of this undertaking – a point that requires identifications to be studied in their contextual specificity. Identities are also inter-subjective and linguistically constituted, and are mediated through various types of media, including works of architecture.

I take it as given that architecture today is required to operate within the highly differentiated field of modern – or, if you prefer, postmodern – society. And for which reason, I have wanted to resist homogenising concepts, such as the idea of an 'African style', or of some unified conception of 'African architecture'. Not all buildings are equally suited for raising questions of cultural identity, and when issues of cultural identity are raised, the terms of reference are bound to differ from one building type to the next. Public buildings, such as the projects studied in this book, are loaded with explicit symbolic significance. As Norberg-Schulz explains: 'public building embodies a set of beliefs or values, it ought to appear as an "explanation," which makes the common world visible.'[7] In presenting recent public designs, I have sought to uncover the particularity of each case. And in doing so, my research has not so much focused upon an 'objective' set of buildings, but rather upon *the social discourses that circulate these projects, and the varied forms of identification that have resulted from these circuits.*

Black Skin, White Masks

Born in 1925 at Fort-de-France, the capital of Martinique, Frantz Fanon grew up in a French-speaking, middle-class family. He studied psychiatry at Lyon Medical School, obtaining his thesis in 1951. After completing his studies, Fanon moved to Algiers where he took up a post at Blida-Joinville Psychiatric Hospital. His experiences there as a psychiatrist provided invaluable insights into the pathologies of the colonised black subject, insights which later fed his early work *Black Skin, White Masks* (*BS*).[8] By 1956, Fanon had given up his position with the hospital, and left Algiers. He became a full-time revolutionary, devoting many years of his life to the cause of the Algerian revolution. He also travelled to Ghana and Mali, with the hope of developing anti-colonial solidarity across the Sahara. He died on 6 December 1961, his thought steeped in the issues and revolutionary thinking of his time.[9] And yet despite this fact, I hope to show that Fanon's work speaks for today, and with remarkable clarity.

Fanon wrote two books of seminal importance, *BS* and *The Wretched of the Earth* (*TWE*).[10] *BS* discusses ambivalences of subjective identity and a sense of inferiority that is induced by colonisation. *TWE*, his later work, by contrast concerns violence and revolt against colonial rule. A different Fanon can be made to emerge, depending on how one relates these rather different works. An important methodological issue begins to emerge. Is *BS* merely a prelude to *TWE*, or may we choose to read these works on their own terms – an important question that cannot be wrestled with here. Suffice to say that in the context of this study, *BS* provides a helpful entry into questions of African postcolonial identity – this being the precise issue that recent public architecture has sought to address.

Fanon's Prose

We shall now move to consider a reading of Fanon's text, *BS*, one that will open useful avenues for architectural interpretation. First-time readers of *BS* will undoubtedly be struck by the unique character of Fanon's prose. His thought is dense and multilayered, energetic and rich. The text progresses in a somewhat jerky fashion as the reader is made to jump from one section to the next, a jump which often brings with it the surprise of a different voice. The many voices that appear to speak through his work provide momentary perspectives. There are moments of intense subjectivity, moments of sober calm, moments of humour, moments of philosophical reflection, as well as moments of detached analysis. As noted by Kobena Mercer, Fanon's writing traverses a wide range of registers: 'autobiographical, clinical, sociological, poetical, philosophical, political'.[11] The polyvalent character of Fanon's thought is derived from his attempt to confront the impossibility of the colonial circumstance. How to be free in a world where the *black man*[12] is blocked and choked by white rule: '[a]ll round me the white man, above the sky tears at its navel, the earth rasps under my feet, and there is a white song. All this whiteness that burns me.'[13]

Fanon is not afforded the luxury of choice: he is compelled to search for freedom down diverging avenues. His book is not some artfully staged eclectic mix of ideas, but rather a quest motivated by an ethical intention. Philosophical considerations are not treated as autonomous signs belonging to closed loops of thought, but as vehicles in an urgent search for freedom. Fanon's text is not free of self-contradiction, nor easily resolved into a singular coherence. This has, no doubt, been perplexing for many readers of *BS*. Yet if, as I have suggested, Fanon's philosophical resolve can be read as a commitment to work through momentary propositions, then we are surely relieved of the need to systematise his thought.[14] Indeed, does not Fanon explicitly tell us as much?

I do not come with timeless truths. My consciousness is not illuminated with ultimate radiances.[15]

I leave methods to the botanists and the mathematicians. There is a point at which methods devour themselves.[16]

I have not wished to be objective. Besides, that would be dishonest: It is not possible for me to be objective.[17]

Subjectivity and Colonial Rule

The fragmentary, indeed the aesthetic character, of Fanon's prose introduces the leading aspect of his thought that is of interest here: namely that of the fluidity of the self and of the curtailment of subjectivity that is imposed through colonial rule. Fanon speaks of humanity, but he cunningly avoids any attempt to define in idealising or essentialising terms what the human identity, or potential, ought to be. Fanon is all too aware of the desolate exterior that closed definitions maintain. Instead, Fanon's thought rests on a conception of man that is open and irreducibly spontaneous.

Man is motion toward the world and toward his like. A moment of aggression, which leads to enslavement or to conquest; a moment of love, a gift of self, the ultimate stage of what by common accord is called ethical orientation. Every consciousness seems to have the capacity to demonstrate these two components, simultaneously or alternatively.[18]

Man is a flow of desire. This flow is marked by moments of love and aggression. Fanon's thought suggests a seamless motion between a subjective interiority and the objective conditions of an external world. The subjective and the objective, as we are accustomed to call them, are no longer so clearly separated because flows of human desire describe webs of mutual interdependence. Man is a relation, a mode of motion towards his fellow men. The objective patterns of our human world are already the moving imprints of so many inter-subjective, inter-human relations. Presenting the human condition this way, Fanon is defining a fluid notion of the self, a self that is always and already entangled with the others and their world. It is a displaced conception of the self, which is always and already tangled with the self of the others. Their world is already ours, and ours theirs.

Yet in *BS*, Fanon also seeks to describe the severe strictures of the colonial order – and we may include apartheid here as well – a circumstance defined by the confrontation of two subjectivities, the colonialist and the colonised. It is a world where flows of desire are dammed up into static opposition, into static domination. White civilisation, black savagery. White science, black animality. White mastery, black slavery. The words *skin* and *mask* – introduced in the title of Fanon's book – are metaphors that help to unpack the complexities of these social confrontations. And indeed, a fair portion of *BS* attempts to lay bare the strange duplicities (of masks and skin), the complex, split and ultimately unresolved subjectivities of the colonised world.

At this juncture, it is helpful to consider Fanon's non-essentialising conception of the human subject. A black man among his fellow black men may not know that he is black. Why should he? He may well know that he is not white like the sand, but sand is not human, and for Fanon, we require a conception of a human difference, of a black *man* versus a white man in order to establish the human difference that is signified as black. A white man, equally, among his fellow white men, may not know that he is white, and once again, why should he? The question of whiteness and blackness, this question of the racial determination of a human difference by virtue of the colour of the skin is the social construct of a body of human practices and knowledge that emerge at the intersection of white and black society. For Fanon, it is not nature that determines the colour of a man's skin, but rather it is the colonial confrontation of white set against black that constructs our conception of the 'naturalised' essence of the skin:

I move slowly in the world, accustomed now to seek no longer for upheaval. I progress by crawling. And already I am being dissected by white eyes, the only real eyes. I am *fixed*. Having adjusted their microtomes, they objectively cut away slices of my reality. I am laid bare. I feel, I see in those white faces that it is not a new man who has come in, but a new kind of man, a new genus. Why, it's a Negro![19]

The moment of exchange between white and black, a moment captured in the meeting of the eyes, constructs a new awareness, a new categorisation of cultural otherness. The ensuing categorisation of black and white are inter-subjectively constituted, but the relation is one that lacks reciprocity. And it is here that we need to be clear about the severe inequity of the colonial circumstance. Colonialism subjugates local traditions, histories and communal languages. In South Africa, colonialism – and in its wake, apartheid – stereotyped, marginalised and at times even liquidated indigenous architectures and forms of urban life.

Every colonized people – in other words, every people in whose soul an inferiority complex has been created by the death and burial of its local cultural originality – finds itself face to face with the language of the civilizing nation; that is, with the culture of the mother country. The colonized is elevated above his jungle status in proportion to his adoption of the mother country's cultural standards. He becomes whiter as he renounces his blackness, his jungle.[20]

Architecture, Mask and Skin

Written side by side, the words 'skin' and 'mask' suggest an intuitive degree of difference. One's skin belongs to one's body. This skin is mine, given to me by nature, by circumstance. There is little choice in this matter of the colour of one's skin. A mask, however, is something I wear as a way to cover my skin. The mask suggests a different, a less-than-natural projection of the self. Mask and skin, when taken together, suggest a tension, a duality of being. The mask covering the skin, a deceptive play of willed versus natural identity. These intuitive distinctions – of nature and will, of truth and deception – are constrained by a reductive binary, and as such fall short of Fanon's more nuanced analysis of identity. By contrasting skin and mask in the title of his book, Fanon highlights the obvious duplicity, but his consideration of the complexities of identity also reveal the instabilities inherent within this opposition – *and which ultimately begs the question as to which is the authentic and which the contrived.*

The metaphor of skin, and the stylistic identity that this denotes, is widely elaborated upon by established architectural theory. Where European modernism, for instance, rests its faith on an aesthetic concept of 'purity in design' and 'honesty to materials', it privileges a naturalised conception of architectural skin. To be sure, functionalist discourses produced the 'authenticity' of modernist designs – an identity of skin. Yet this 'honest' and 'natural' conception of architecture invariably represses inauthentic play; the mask emerges as a return of repressed elements, those not deemed to be functional, that may lead to a subversion of dominant codes. We might also observe that the universality of functionalist necessity, as proclaimed by modern architecture, has tended to silence the more complex and particular qualities that may result from a play between skin and its mutations in the form of a mask. In any event, I hope to demonstrate in this book how post-apartheid public designs realise a play of skin and mask, given (indeed, dominant) and formerly excluded codes of architectural identity.

Fanon's attention to the play of identity – in the relation of mask to skin – provides a useful language for understanding complexities of the in-between. His diagnosis is understandably trapped within the negative angst of his existential circumstance and to be sure, his depiction of the masks of identity are not necessarily seen in a positive light. It is interesting to note, however, that black (British) artists and intellectuals such as Stuart Hall, Kobena Mercer and Paul Gilroy – interpreters of Fanon – have sought to mobilise cultural criticism that is consonant with these terms, that is relations between naturally given and subverted forms of identity. The work of these intellectuals, which features in subsequent chapters, demonstrates that the Fanon of BS may be appropriated in a more positive sense: in affirmation of the complex, plural and irresolvable dialogues that need to occur with questions of identity. This book hopes to show that post-apartheid public buildings give positive expression to the terms mask and skin, be they drawn together, split apart or hovering in between.

The Weight of Culture

Fanon maintains that to speak means 'above all to assume a culture, to support the weight of a civilization', and by this he no doubt makes an appeal to some positive affirmation of African culture.[21] We will want to ask what the normative content of this affirmation is. Surprisingly, Fanon devotes little attention to this question. Perhaps he means to say that an African life is nothing more and nothing less than the life of one who lives in Africa, and as such there is little point to tie the boundless possibilities of an African life to some reductive essence. This suggestion is certainly consistent with his ideas of the African subject. A culture is, after all, but the aggregation of many instances, a collection of many people living their lives within the plurality of a common world. Fanon is the philosopher who closes his book with a question: '[a]t the conclusion of this study, I want the world to recognize, with me, the open door of every consciousness. My final prayer: O my body, make of me always a man who questions!'[22] This assertion tells that Fanon supports an open-ended conception of humanity, and this implies an equally open conception of African culture. African culture is not something to be defended, as though it needs apologetic support. To the contrary, African culture is something that must be questioned because the questioning act keeps culture alive.

Fanon maintains a self-critical conception of African identity. He nevertheless retains a strong feeling for Africa's specificity. The open question of African cultural identity does not fold onto a flat field where lived differences are dissolved. To the contrary, Fanon's repeated demand is for recognition in the eye of colonial power. His point is not that the black man lacks subjectivity, lacks history, but rather that he lacks these attributes in the eye of the white man who rejects him. Fanon's wish is not so much to find the truth of his African existence, something about which he has little doubt, but rather his goal is to be recognised in the modern sense of the word, to be recognised as an African who can stake his claim in the contemporary world order. This recognition is not compatible with assimilation, and hence Fanon's metaphors of mask and skin provide a useful way to subvert dominant codes: I will wear the white mask, but I will never let you under my black skin. This play of identity, in the eye of power, contains a powerful strategy for self-actualisation. It should be apparent that such a strategy might inform architectural design. Contemporary South African architecture obviously must use modern materials and modern means. In this sense, contemporary architecture will be framed in relation to a modern, indeed Western, discourse on design.[23] Using Fanon's metaphor, we might say that contemporary architecture has a 'white skin'. But this white skin may be allowed to wear a black mask. Vital aspects of African life, material tectonics, climate, landscape, patterns of dwelling, long-surviving figures and types – including imaginaries of the precolonial, handcrafts (both modern and traditional) and metaphoric symbolisations of Africa – may be brought into dialogue with the white skin of modern design. The purity of the modern may be opened to form a new hybridity; White Skin, Black Mask.[24] A new architecture of identity requires an awakening to the surrounding environment. Identity in design should also develop sensitivity to the *longue durée,* the long duration of human life in Africa. The long duration of time demonstrates certain social patterns and ways of life that have persisted throughout the history of the African continent. Historical awareness provides a storehouse of symbols, types and figures that can be appropriated and reconfigured by contemporary design. It will be seen that contemporary South African design maintains a confident appropriation of the modern – or if you prefer, the postmodern – but it is also a unique kind of modern architecture, one that bears the more unique signs of difference.

Recognition requires that something be recognised, and this something is nothing if not the positive assertion of an African life. The weight of civilisation, which marks one culture off against another, is the accumulative effects of differential history. But the bare facts of these historical differences alone do not explain what is at stake in the call for cultural recognition. It is not simply that one has a history, but rather that this history positions the subjectivity of the self. History should be understood as a resource. History provides the public grammars with which we make our way known, a vehicle with which we confront the future. These collective grammars are important because they empower the way of life that is given to us by historical circumstance. Philosopher Iris Marion Young expresses it this way: '[t]he language and historical narratives of a group, its literature, symbols, modes of celebration, and so on give individuals both context and media for expressing their individuality and interpreting the world.'[25] When we find authentication in the 'historical narratives of a group', we also discover the freedom to make critical choices for the future. The relation between group affiliation and critical choice is eloquently captured by Anthony Appiah when he explains that '[w]e make up ourselves from a tool kit of options made available by our culture and society. We do make choices, but we do not determine the options among which we choose.'[26] From these observations, it becomes clear that our interest in cultural history is never merely academic because this interest always sits in relation to a set of ambitions; history may be read as an instrumental support to a political goal.

A further important issue for contemporary South African politics, one that has direct bearing on architecture, is the burden of race itself. I believe it is true to say that most South Africans wish to do away with the racial impositions of the past. Black people, coloured people and white people wish to find one another. Racial imposition of black versus white must be eroded. But the way forward is not so straight or so clear. We cannot, for example, as some maintain, merely erase the past because our past lives within us. Our past breaks through into the present and into the future as well. South Africa's racial history, indeed Africa's racial history, will continue to inform public thought and opinion. Besides, race is not something to shy away from: issues of race and ethnicity should not embarrass us. Fanon's thought on these matters is helpful. It will be remembered that for Fanon, black versus white is not a natural distinction that has to do with the colour of the skin per se, but rather it is a cultural and political construction that is formed at the intersection of black and white society. A postcolonial politics requires that we think through the very real constructions of racial identity. Fanon's category 'black' should not be read in a mere literal sense. Black is an identification, an identification that is required not by nature but by an act of political will. This means that white people can choose to identify with 'black', or at least can choose to stand in solidarity with the symbolic figure of 'black', and the inverse is also true. Parallel observation may obviously be made about architecture as well.

Concluding Remarks

In concluding this chapter, I wish to consolidate a few important points that have emerged from this study of Fanon. First, *BS* highlights the demeaning silence that was imposed by colonial rule. The implication for architectural history – and indeed, for all forms of history – is that where we have a silenced, marginalised subject, we must also have a virtual perspective, and a virtual history associated with this subject position: we have new perspectives and forms of artistic expression that deserve to be heard. Fanon's work requires us to position these virtual histories alongside the dominance of 'known' history. From this, we have a direct relationship between subjectivities and the status of historical/critical narratives – an observation that is suggestive for a creative, public discipline such as architecture, and particularly so with respect to public buildings in post-apartheid South Africa. A key question that emerges is how to open dominant forms of architectural knowledge/practice to perspectives that were formerly denied. This question is developed in the next chapter. Second, *BS* hopes to express the substance of a positioned perspective and to stand in solidarity with this marginalised identity. Fanon's approach on this matter is momentary, subjective and engaged, yet never blinkered or merely parochial. In writing about recent public buildings in South Africa, buildings that have raised situated and particular questions of African identity in design, I have wanted to learn from the creative and open-ended character of Fanon's thought. Third, Fanon's terms *mask* and *skin* are highlighted because they are rich in architectural association. These terms are used repeatedly throughout this book to interpret relations of 'natural' or dominant – in other words pertaining to skin – versus more playful or subverted – in other words pertaining to the mask – forms of architectural identity. The precise logic and political significance of this relation will be developed in subsequent chapters. Finally, a key aspect of Fanon's thought is the fluid motions of the self, a point that is aligned to his critique of the Hegelian narrative of the master and slave, the precise details of which need not concern us here.[27] The suspension of resolution in the formation of the subject, as entailed by Fanon's presentation of fluid subjectivity, must surely lead to a suspension of the grand narratives of history, politics and culture, and this has important implications for the study of aesthetics as well as the history of architecture. For instance, the category of architectural Style – written with a capital 'S' – in art and architectural history commonly performs the narrative function of historical synthesis, 'Style' and 'Movement' as the expressive fulfilment of an age, society or nation – expressive genus as definition of national identity. Similar observations may also be made with regard to architectural notions of 'given context', as subsequent chapters will show. Writing a postcolonial account of recent public designs in South Africa has required a suspension of totalising categories, and attention to the more fluid cycles of identification.

The Layout of Subsequent Chapters

Two interrelated, avenues of enquiry are explored in the case studies that follow. Firstly, on an architectural level, attention is paid to metaphoric content in design. In particular, I have been interested in examining how poetic imagination relocates architecture between and beyond established codes. This amounts to an internal critique of colonial styles and types, and the search for alternatives associated with Africa. Secondly, on a social level, I have wished to look at forms of participation and identification. In this, I have tried to include various perspectives, such as the aspirations of politicians and other leaders, competition results and discussion among the jury, design development and participatory processes, contributions from artisans and crafters, media and forms of public reception and, where pertinent, aspects of social history that are associated with building sites.

The first pair of case studies considers the Mpumalanga (Chapter 2) and the Northern Cape (Chapter 3) Legislature buildings, which make for interesting comparison. Mpumalanga and the Northern Cape are new – that is, post-apartheid – provinces, both of which lacked adequate building accommodation for their respective seats of government. Both projects spring from localised, pragmatic need and both raise similar questions of African identity in design. However, the identity in question may be understood mostly in the particular context of local aspiration rather than in terms of a wider concern for establishing 'national symbols'. Chapters 2 and 3 respectively consider the institutional history of these projects, the choice of site, the adjudication of the design competition, examine various competition submissions, document post-competition dialogue, discuss the process of detailed design and refinement, and provide comparative interpretation of the completed schemes.

Using Fanon's metaphors of mask and skin, these chapters argue that the two Legislatures fuse emblems of African identity – spatial, material and symbolic – with architectural order derived from modernised building technique. This propinquity of black mask (Africanised emblem) and white skin (modernised building technique) is resolved in various ways. The Northern Cape Legislature consistently plays with differences to liberate a multiplicity of heterogeneous orders. Registers of structure, surface, materiality, space, utility and fantasy are woven together while remaining distinct, complexly layered, and at times incommensurable with each other. The Mpumalanga Legislature, by contrast, attempts to downplay the tensions between mask and skin, emblematic sign and structural building technique. Through the cunning of detail and surface treatment, the design attempts a more singular and unified expression of iconic identity: this building is wearing a mask. The third chapter concludes by considering these seemingly opposed representational strategies.

The following pair of chapters investigates formations of the 'we' in relation to two heritage sites: Constitutional Hill (Chapter 4) and the Kliptown commemorative precinct (Chapter 5). The Constitutional Court is the highest court, presiding over the South African Constitution. The court is part of a larger precinct, Constitutional Hill, which has reoccupied the Old Fort, a Johannesburg prison complex where many political leaders and activists of the anti-apartheid movement were incarcerated, including Mahatma Gandhi, Albert Luthuli, Robert Sobukwe and Nelson Mandela. These spaces of confinement have been transformed into a living museum devoted to human rights. Kliptown, by contrast, is one of the oldest residential quarters in Soweto. An abandoned landscape at the heart of Kliptown was the site for the 1955 'Delegation of the People', an anti-apartheid gathering from across the entire country which inaugurated the declaration of human rights known as the 'Freedom Charter'. The site has been redeveloped as a civic monument to the principles of social freedom, as enshrined in the Freedom Charter and the South African Constitution.

The historic significance of these sites resonates with local memory, as well as with narratives of national liberation. Political questions emerge regarding mediation between local, professional and national interests. Both projects involve the creation of civic urban space, and both attempt to engage the wider community to participate in the narrative development of these heritage sites. Chapters 4 and 5 cover similar ground to Chapters 2 and 3, in other words the institutional history of these projects, the choice of site, adjudication of the design competition, various competition submissions, post-competition processes, and so on. In addition to this, Chapters 4 and 5 also highlight participatory aspects – especially the role played by ex-convicts at the Old Fort, public media, and the contributions made by artists and crafters that have influenced the design and the programming of these sites. The interpretive theme of mask and skin is also considered, set in dialogue with the previous chapters.

Chapter 6 follows a history of Freedom Park, a national heritage project dealing with political violence and reconciliation, a project that was associated with State President Thabo Mbeki's office. Sited at the crest of Salvokop hill, on the outskirts of Pretoria, this landscaped precinct includes a museum, monument and garden of remembrance. The choice of site is provocative. Adjacent to Salvokop, and on the other side of the M1 motorway that leads into Pretoria, stands the Voortrekker Monument, an infamous symbol of the old apartheid order; Freedom Park literally confronts this racist monument. A primary theme of Freedom Park concerns the commemoration of silenced voices and subjugated cultural practices. This chapter looks at Freedom Park's attempt to speak on behalf of those who were silenced by an oppressive past. In presenting these subjugated histories, however, the Park cannot but appropriate these voices. In this, the park is also implicated in a narrative of the nation state. The chapter unravels the interwoven relations between poetic appropriation of subjugated voices and the restriction on representation that are introduced by nationalism. As with prior chapters, attention is paid to the institutional history of the Park, the symbolic significance of the site, the adjudication of the Union Internationale des Architects (UIA) international design competition, which was unsuccessful, the study of various competition submissions, as well as post-competition discourses and processes that have informed the completed design. Once more, the central interpretive theme of mask and skin informs an interpretation of the Park.

The concluding chapter weaves some reflections on the five case studies in relation to the central themes: of mask and skin, authentic and inauthentic forms of expression, of dominant and repressed narratives; and the socio-political significance of the different modes of architectural representation that are encountered in the study. Key findings are summarised, and questions are opened for further enquiry.

Notes

1 Frantz Fanon, *Black Skin, White Masks* (London: Pluto Press, 1986), originally published in 1952.

2 Due to the legacy of apartheid, there are currently few practising black South African architects.

3 See, among others: Bruce Berman, Dickson Eyoh and Will Kymlicka (eds), *Ethnicity and Democracy in Africa* (Oxford: J. Currey, 2004); Steve Fenton, *Ethnicity: Racism, Class and Culture* (Basingstoke: Macmillan, 1999); Roxy Harris and Ben Rampton (eds), *The Language, Ethnicity and Race Reader* (London: Routledge, 2003); Anthony King (ed.), *Re-Presenting the City: Ethnicity, Capital and Culture in the Twenty-First Century Metropolis* (Basingstoke: Macmillan, 1996); Sinisa Malesevic, *The Sociology of Ethnicity* (London: Sage, 2004).

4 Lesley Naa Norle Lokko (ed.), *White Papers, Black Marks: Architecture, Race, Culture* (Minneapolis: University of Minnesota Press, 2000).

5 Ibid. p 15.

6 John Rajchman (ed.), *The Identity in Question* (London: Routledge, 1995), p 187.

7 Christian Norberg-Schulz, *The Concept of Dwelling: On the Way to a Figurative Architecture* (New York: Rizzoli, 1985), p 13.

8 Fanon, *Black Skin, White Masks*.

9 Nigel C. Gibson, *Fanon: The Postcolonial Imagination* (Oxford: Polity Press, 2003).

10 Fanon, *Black Skin, White Masks*. Fanon (trans. Constance Farrington), *The Wretched of the Earth* (London: Penguin, 1967).

11 Alan Read (ed.), *The Fact of Blackness: Frantz Fanon and Visual Representation* (Seattle: Bay Press, 1996), p 16.

12 Throughout this chapter, I have referred to the 'black man'. This choice is motivated by Fanon's text, which consistently speaks this way. Since my study closely follows Fanon's thought, it feels convenient to follow suit. Other chapters of the book, however, will be written in a more gender-correct way.

13 Fanon, *Black Skin, White Masks*, p 114.

14 Fanon's work may be read in different ways. A humanist interpretation, as represented by Gibson for example, reads *BS* as an ethical work in search of an emancipated, African humanism. Poststructural, postcolonial readings of Fanon, as represented by Bhabha, by contrast, have tended to emphasise Fanon's poetic descriptions of fluid subjectivity and of artifice, which, it is argued, showcases the irresolvable hybridities of the self and of culture. I have preferred to work with the latter reading because, in my view, it is the one that allows for a greater sophistication in critique. And yet, despite this interesting distinction from the scholarship on Fanon, his text speaks, regardless, in its own highly unique and complicated way, and the final verdict on these matters is not always so clear. Gibson, *Fanon: The Postcolonial Imagination*; Homi K. Bhabha, *The Location of Culture* (London: Routledge, 1994).

15 Fanon, *Black Skin, White Masks*, p 9.

16 Ibid. p 14.

17 Ibid. p 86.

18   Ibid. p 41.

19   Ibid. p 116.

20   Ibid. p 18.

21   Fanon, *Black Skin, White Masks*, pp 17–18.

22   Ibid. p 232.

23   A visit to an architectural library will quickly demonstrate the severe lack of published material on contemporary African architecture, or on contemporary African theory in design. In the face of this absence, the theoretical and historical knowledge that drives the daily practice of South African design is knowledge and theory taken from European experience. Coded African architectural knowledge – in South Africa at least – is severely lacking, which means we have to produce this knowledge.

24   This distinction of the 'modernised skin' versus the 'black mask' – as the return of otherness – is not intended as a rigid binary, but rather as an interpretive device – or heuristic – for studying different representations of architectural identity. A more nuanced consideration of the duality that is implied by the use of these terms is discussed in the concluding chapter of this book.

25   Iris Marion Young, *Inclusion and Democracy* (Oxford: Oxford University Press, 2000), p 101.

26   Charles Taylor et al. (ed. Amy Gutmann), *Multiculturalism: Examining the Politics of Recognition* (Princeton: Princeton University Press, 1994), p 155.

27   Hegel derives a conception of the modern subject in the resolution, or synthesis, of the conflict that occurs between the master and his slave in his infamous narrative of the master and his slave. *BS* provides a far-reaching critique of Hegel's narrative as a way to theorise the unresolved subjectivities of the colonised world. Fanon's fluid conception of the self is a logical counterpart to the suspension of Hegelian synthesis in the formation of the modern subject. Georg Wilhelm Friedrich Hegel (trans. J.B. Baillie) *The Phenomenology of Mind* (London: George Allen and Unwin Ltd., 1949). Fanon, *Black Skin, White Masks*. Jonathan Noble, 'White Skin, Black Masks: On Questions of African Identity in Post-Apartheid Public Architectural Design, 1994–2006' (University College London, 2007).

Imagination and Identification, Part 1: The Mpumalanga Legislature, Nelspruit

New Provincial Borders

In 1994 the map of South Africa was redrawn as an accompaniment to the country's first democratic election held in April of the same year.[1] The former four provinces – the Cape, Natal, the Transvaal and the Orange Free State – which had been in existence since the time of the Union of South Africa (1910) were reorganised into nine new provincial regions – the Eastern Cape, the Free State, Gauteng, KwaZulu-Natal, Mpumalanga, the Northern Cape, Limpopo (formerly the Northern Province), the North West Province and the Western Cape – as part of a new system of governance that involves local, provincial and national spheres (see Figure 2.1).

2.1 New map of South Africa. Courtesy of *The South African Geographical Journal*.

The move from four to nine provinces, from a highly centralised apartheid state to a unique kind of post-apartheid federalism, has resulted in the formation of five new political regions, each requiring new legislative and executive powers.[2] Architecture entered this geopolitical formation in response to the practical accommodation requirements of new provincial government institutions, as well as in response to symbolic needs. In the latter, architectural aesthetics have contributed to the construction of new territorial identities. The Mpumalanga and Northern Cape Legislatures, studied by this chapter and the next, are the most significant works of architecture to have emerged from this geopolitical process.

The Great Paint War

As a prelude to the story of these two Legislatures, it is instructive to consider the new Gauteng Provincial Legislature situated in central Johannesburg. The history of this development predates the democratic elections of 1994 and probably represents the first case study for the architectural design of a post-apartheid Legislature. A feature article on this project, which appeared in *The Sub Contractor* journal, explains how the Central Johannesburg Partnership had 'spearheaded' an early drive to ensure that Johannesburg would be chosen as the capital city of the newly formed PWV area – now called Gauteng – and with this came 'the need to either create, or restore, a building suitable for the Legislature'.[3] An area within central Johannesburg was defined, and eventually the city hall[4] was chosen because it 'proved to have many of the ideal features, having been purpose built for council meetings, being central, and being underused as office space'.[5] Architect Mira Fassler Kamstra explained in an interview that her firm, Fassler Kamstra and Holmes, was appointed to design the required renovation because her father, Professor John Fassler, had previously been commissioned to restore the building during the late 1960s and that her firm had thereby acquired rare drawings and historical documents pertaining to this protected building.[6] As at this early stage, appointees for the new Legislature had obviously not yet been selected, the architects were forced to work without input from the eventual users of the building. The design brief, according to Fassler Kamstra, was largely technical in character, the main requirement being less a restoration of the original building than a stated need to provide a specified area of grade 'A' office space for the new Legislature.

Since the building had fallen into a terrible state, realising the design brief required a fair amount of internal demolition and restoration, as well as extensive replanning for the accommodation of modern services. The architects nevertheless were conscious of the fact that their work was in effect an exercise in redressing an old colonial building in a manner befitting of a new democratic South Africa. The original interiors were somewhat sombre in colonial neoclassical manner, with white and cream walls, embellished ceilings, decorative timber wall panels and widespread use of Brescia marble finishes.[7] The architects wished to breathe new life into the old interiors, a design strategy they believed would be respectful of the past while presenting a joyful face in celebration of the new South Africa. The architects put their case as follows, 'rather than reverting to a former colonial colour scheme, we chose to go forward and present the PWV Parliament with an exciting and vivid African palette … We latched onto the ochres, earth reds and offset these with various greens and blues.'[8]

This seemingly innocent approach was soon to spark a heated political debate among politicians of the new Legislature. The architects' bold colours had the unexpected effect of highlighting the grandeur, and what some referred too as the 'opulence', of this old colonial interior. Incredible anger was unleashed against the architects for their apparently insensitive design, which was interpreted to be in celebration of colonialist values. The scandal was soon to make its way into the press. An article in The Sunday Times newspaper, entitled The PWV is seeing red over the colours of colonial opulence, sensationalised the political conflict that the strident colours had initiated.[9] The reporters scandalised the 'great paint war', which was being fought between Mr Fowler, speaker for the PWV, and his ANC legislators who wished the renovation to, quoting Fowler, '"reflect the transition from colonialism to the present" using a plain colour scheme', against the architect decorator, Fassler Kamstra and her colour-expert daughter, who had 'festooned the building's dour interior with sixty colours'.[10] If the bright colours could be interpreted in support of colonial values, then a counter position was equally possible. Jack Bloom, whip for the opposition Democratic Party, was quick to make political use of the concurrently popular notion of a multi-racial democratic South Africa as expressed through the idea of a 'Rainbow Nation', choosing to support the design and describing it as the 'rainbow building'.[11] The Star newspaper reported more directly, quoting statements made from both sides of the divide:

Mira Fassler Kamstra told *The Star*: "When we started, we had no client to give us input. So what you see there is very much my firm's interpretation of giving an old building a new life of hope, excitement and colour – especially of Africa." PWV speaker Trevor Fowler said the problem arose out of different interpretations of what captured the "Afrocentric Present". He felt the vivid use of colour in certain areas had had the opposite effect, "reminding people of the past and the cost of that past in human lives".[12]

The heated debate on questions of appropriate expression for the 'Afro-centric Present' was initiated, seemingly by accident.

From a critical perspective, one may take stock of the 'African' signifiers that are being articulated here. Colourful colours are of course, on their own terms, thoroughly abstract. Ordinarily, one may not assume that colour schemes are political in nature, and as such, one might take for granted the 'free' and open-ended nature of the signifier: one might assume that bright colours can sustain a near infinite opportunity for different association. However, in the social context of this particular architectural project it becomes clear how the use of colour as signifier for 'Africa' was mobilised in accordance with quite specific political and professional intentions. It can be noted how the architect in effect has appealed to the 'innocence' of colour. Colour, as a symbol for Africa, is a celebration of Africa, a positive Africa, submitted as hope for the future and one abstracted away from concrete reference to the particularities of South Africa's past. Furthermore, this abstracted Africa may be painted on the wall in a manner that respects the past while celebrating the future. The symbol is flexible, easily applied to existing types and figures, and provides a convenient conception of Africa from the designer's point of view. For the majority of politicians at the Legislature, however, this symbolisation proves offensive because it reanimates the old colonial interiors, bringing them back to life. The expressed wish that the colours be toned down suggests that the physical existence of this colonial building alone was not the real problem. The old building with its white and cream interiors perhaps appeared to exist as a relic from the past and thus was not in itself offensive. The old, after all, may be repossessed as a new symbol of power. The important issue here, however, is the way the contemporary politic appears to cope with the past, provided it is a past which has been overcome. This sense of overcoming, or of putting into the past, requires that the aesthetic presence of the old buildings and its associated colonial values are in some way distanced from the present while simultaneously given a new meaning by virtue of a new occupation. The architect's strategy, which celebrated the highly ornate interior, seems to have achieved precisely what was deemed least acceptable: the old was being repositioned into the present, and it is this that triggered the angry response. Or to put this logic another way, occupying an old colonial building is not a problem, whereas redesigning, or activating a new one is. This particular use of colour as signifier for 'Africa' also relies on a highly abstracted reference and is lacking in explicit political content. The symbolisation does not substantially refer to any socio-historically derived content, nor does it engage existing political forms. In the absence of any real content, the only substance that may come to the fore is the social content that is associated with the old colonial symbol itself. And for this reason, the design intent is interpreted as insincere, cheap if you will: the wrongs of the past cannot be remedied by painting them over, redecorating with a happy smile.

This conflict over colour schemes, sparked by the Gauteng Legislature, highlights some important questions which will resurface repeatedly throughout this book: how to make a new architecture which can accommodate modern needs, yet at once be expressive of an Afro-centric present and understood in relation to the specific condition of the South African experience? How to deal with the legacy of the past – especially in terms of existing urban and architectural precedent, which are all too often Western and colonial in origin? And what is the appropriate role for aesthetic abstraction in public symbolisation: is the abstract signifier a sufficient remedy for a troubled past?

With these questions painted into the background, we shall move on to consider the new Mpumalanga Legislature and Government Complex built between 1998 and 2001 on the outskirts of Nelspruit, capital city of Mpumalanga. This project represents what is probably the first major post-apartheid public building to have been built in accordance with a submission won in an open design competition. The decision to build was motivated by pragmatic need because at this time, the existing accommodation for Government Departments in the province was dispersed among more than fifteen different buildings across Nelspruit, many of which were being rented at high rates, meaning that '[t]he cost of the seat and the rendering of services to the people of Mpumalanga became a hotly debated topic'.[13] Building a new complex was an obvious way to address this need.

A Deal for a Site

The siting of government buildings has serious political implications, especially in terms of public accessibility. In the context of South African cities, these issues are further highlighted and problematised by the urban legacy of apartheid town planning. South African cities are invariably twin cities, one white and the other black, one privileged and the other marginalised, and for this reason the locating of a post-apartheid Legislature is doubly charged with political meaning. In the context of a design competition, the site chosen will obviously have substantial influence on the kind of architecture that results. An official account of the events that led up to the final choice of a building site for the Mpumalanga Legislature is given by a 'progress report' of September 1999 compiled by the Steering Committee for the development.[14] The report explains how the Nelspruit City Council was commissioned, in 1995, to help find a suitable site for the Legislature. Proposals were heard from interested parties, including various developers, and eleven possible sites were identified. In May 1996, an ad hoc committee, appointed by the Legislature 'tables its first report at the legislature and supported the development at Boschrand Farm (known as Riverside Park)'.[15] The Legislature adopted this recommendation on 23 May 1996, and the report mentions that this decision was motivated by the donation of 10.5 ha of land for the new Legislature. The land donated by H.L. Hall & Sons was valued at R21 million.[16] However, the report does not spell out the reasons for this kind gesture. Interviews conducted with the architect, Patrick McInerney[17] and chairperson of the jury, Herbert Prins,[18] alerted me to the view that a deal must have been struck, and allegedly behind closed doors between politicians of the province and Hall & Sons. This suggestion is supported by the fact that the donation of land has proven highly beneficial to Hall & Sons, and indeed formed part of a well-conceived business plan for their farm lands at Boschrand, situated to the north of Nelspruit. *The South Africa Quarterly Report* covered the Halls' business plan as follows:

2.2   A Google
Earth, aerial
photograph
that shows the
proximity of the
Mpumalanga
Legislature
(positioned
to the right of
Government
Boulevard) to
the Riverside
Shopping Mall
and Emnotweni
Casino
(positioned
to the right of
Emnotweni
Avenue).

so it is time to build the "new" Nelspruit, as HL Hall and Sons describe their
ambitious Riverside Park project. The renowned fruit company … has chosen land it
owns near the town as the site of a 71 hectare development which will accommodate
the new Mpumalanga legislature and government offices, a 45,000 square metre
shopping centre, an hotel which will probably host a casino, several commercial office
parks and residential areas.[19]

A key interview conducted with Francis Motha and Elsa Visser enabled
me to probe this important question further.[20] Motha and Visser both
agreed that a deal with the Halls had indeed been struck, that this was no
secret and that it had been a 'give-and-take' kind of situation. The Halls'
donation of land for the new Legislature, and provision of basic services,[21]
was exchanged in favour of commercial development rights for the Halls'
farm, Boschrand 283, for the Riverside Shopping Mall and the Emnotweni
Casino (see Figure 2.2).[22] And it is noteworthy that a shopping centre, casino,
hotels, residential and low-rise office blocks are given as the immediate urban
context for the new Legislature by the competition brief.[23]

Motha further explained that he had been part of the panel which had made
a submission to the Provincial Cabinet on behalf of the town of Nelspruit as
part of a bid to secure their status as the new capital city for Mpumalanga. This

bid for the new capital city was considered in relation to three potential areas: the Highveld region represented by the towns of Witbank and Middelburg, the East Vaal region represented by Ermelo and Secunda, and the Nelspruit region. In their adjudication, the Provincial Cabinet placed strong emphasis on the creation of developmental options. Cabinet was obviously aware that the new capital city would allow for a rapid influx of financial capital and that this would need to be directed toward social and urban development in the area. For this reason, Cabinet wanted to locate the new capital city in an area best suited to the task. Early on in the process, the Highveld region had impressed Cabinet with their proposal, which included donated land for a proposed new Legislature and government complex, as well as an urban strategy for merging Witbank with Middelberg. Motha explained that he and his colleagues representing Nelspruit were impressed by this idea and in attempting to better it proposed a developmental corridor along the R40 road linking Nelspruit with White River, a small town some 21 km north of Nelspruit. A development towards White River was appealing as it would effectively place Nelspruit at the intersection of two major development corridors: the east–west Maputo Corridor which has recently enabled new trade links between South Africa and Mozambique and the Port of Maputo on the Indian Ocean, as well as a north–south corridor linking through White River onto the Phalaborwa Mine further in the north. The site chosen for the new Mpumalanga Legislature flowed quite naturally from these considerations because it provided an opportunity for a key developmental initiative which could be used to help establish the White River developmental node.

The key issue highlighted by this history is the developmental approach which drove the decision to locate the Legislature north of Nelspruit on a site dislocated from the established centre of town, and in close proximity to a commercial development node. The nearby shopping centre and casino both do what insular commercial buildings are designed to do. They suck life into themselves and negate the urbanity which surrounds them and, as a result, the graciously designed open public space which fronts the new Legislature stands empty. The decision to site the complex here, although no doubt appealing at the time, has produced disastrous results and would appear to be a major contributor to the currently defunct public nature of the new Legislature complex. One cannot help thinking that an opportunity was missed. The existing centre of Nelspruit offers little in the way of urban character, being as it is the pragmatic child of a railway transit stop-over town. The new Legislature could have contributed something to the town; instead, the public space in front of the new Legislature is isolated and closed off, a matter which will sustain further comments when discussion turns to a consideration of the built complex itself. The jurors' report from the design competition repeats a similar criticism, stating that '[n]either the distance from Nelspruit nor the elevation of the site favours strong visual links with Nelspruit. This is exacerbated by its situation behind and below the shopping centre and casino which front directly onto the PI7–7 road.'[24] The jurors also point out that the remote location of the chosen site has resulted in extensive parking

2.3   The
Mpumalanga
Legislature in its
natural setting.
Photograph by
the author.

requirements, which are both costly and environmentally undesirable. On the other hand, it may also be noted that the traditional centre of town has always represented the interests of established 'white' capital, and as such the decision to build out of town probably represented a political desire, by politicians of the province, to break with the racially inscribed urban patterns of the past. It is rather unfortunate therefore, that the urban deal which has allowed for this opportunity has had negative consequences in terms of urban accessibility.

A Corporate Context

On a more symbolic level, the corporatist fantasies that underlie this developmental node are brought home by a Riverside Park Urban Design Framework, which principles enforce an aesthetics of the 'harmonious whole', a 'seamless development', and the creation of a 'strong identifiable image'.[25] The image, harmony and unity, of course, are that of the shopping centre itself. Entry into Riverside Park via Government Boulevard, which provides the grand route towards the new Legislature, is announced by a semi-circular entrance wall feature, where '[t]he words Riverside Mall is [sic.] inscribed as a cut-out in granite and affixed to the walls … [and a] series of five banner posts carrying banners with the Riverside Mall logo'.[26] Government Boulevard has become an exercise in corporate branding which aims to enforce the commercial interests of contemporary shopping centre and casino architecture through the maintenance of a strict urban code.[27]

Despite these endeavours, the Mpumalanga Legislature has transcended, stylistically speaking, the sterility of this commercial urban context. In contrast to the self-confident and regressive colonial references to Victorian, classical revival and Belle Époque styles that are touted by the Riverside Mall[28] and Emnotweni Casio,[29] the Mpumalanga Legislature has taken a more 'authentic' set of architectural clues in relation to the natural beauty of the surrounding landscape as well as a distillation of memories derived from indigenous African architecture and craft traditions (see Figure 2.3). Although architecturally distinct, the Legislature nevertheless complements the grand urban design for the precinct. Looking down Government Boulevard, one is presented with

2.4   The Mpumalanga Legislature as termination of Government Boulevard. Photograph by the author.

a dramatic perspective terminated by the Legislature (see Figure 2.4). The towering palm trees which lead down the boulevard appear as if to merge, via artful perspective, with the sweeping colonnade of the Legislature that swings around toward the large dome, nestled graciously off to one side. The flowing colonnade and domed Assembly inform a dignified space as the public entrance into the Legislature complex and are staged in response to the boulevard. The Legislature's contribution is both subtle and thoughtful, for on the one hand it compliments the urban design while on the other it carefully distances itself from the mock colonial architecture that surrounds it. Indeed, upon first encounter, the new Mpumalanga Legislature presents an architectural expression that is unique. It would seem that this special design has received widespread approval among leaders of the province, such that Sipho William Lubisi[30] has stated that '[t]his is a landmark to be proud of and it is a befitting inheritance for future generations.'[31]

Establishing a Design Competition

The originality of this design was, no doubt, facilitated by the design competition that highlighted the symbolic significance of this project and provided a space for architects to explore their creative visions for this site. In November 1996, the Mpumalanga Tender Board appointed a series of consultants to assist with assessing key environmental, geotechnical and urban planning aspects of the site, while B.I. Associates (BIA) were appointed to make a spatial analysis and to develop a detailed brief for the competition.[32] An executive committee was also appointed by Cabinet in February 1997 to steer the project and by May a professional team, including engineers and a quantity surveyor, was established to aid the design competition.[33] This process was conceived as a limited competition with a pre-qualification round to screen out inappropriate applicants prior to commencement of the design competition itself. Pre-qualification requirements were established in support of local enterprise, such that the involvement of local architects was privileged, and Reconstruction and Development Programme criteria for the empowerment of local Previously Disadvantaged Individual and Affirmable Business Enterprises were enforced.[34] This meant that aspiring architects from outside the province were forced to form consortiums with local design firms in order to qualify. Sixteen submissions were eventually made and thirteen qualified.[35] The thirteen resulted in ten actual design submissions, one of which was disqualified for being late, meaning that an eventual nine design schemes made their way into the adjudication process.[36]

The design brief documents, prepared by BIA, provide a clear and detailed account of the spatial, programmatic, structural and ecological requirements of the project.[37] Sensitivity is shown towards the natural beauty of the site, which overlooks the confluence of the Nels and Crocodile rivers. Careful attention is also paid to a fundamental east–west relation, which structures the site: the western edge of the site fronts onto the new urban development at Riverside Park, while the eastern edge offers splendid views over the nearby river valley and onto the hills beyond with their dense vegetation and domed rock outcrops. Proximity to the Nelspruit Botanical Gardens, which neighbours immediately to the north, is well considered, as is the need to preserve indigenous fauna and flora on the site.[38] These environmental concerns are further translated into a series of design criteria, in particular, a 30 m buffer zone from the river is specified, building heights are restricted to 'ground plus two-and-a-half' while building mass is to be broken down into six separate elements, measures chosen to ensure that the design does not dominate the site.[39] Views over the river are paramount, '[a]ll staff have a right to this view when seated at their workstations.'[40]

Yet despite these sensitivities, the brief remains consistently technical in nature, an orientation which mirrors the pragmatic mentality of the consultants who wrote it. Surprisingly, scarce attention is drawn to the symbolic significance of the Legislature. No 'vision statements' by politicians from the province are included. No political or aesthetic questions are presented. No guidance – barring issues of sensitivity to the natural surroundings – is given as to what may or may not be deemed an appropriate architectural response. Indeed, the central question of architectural aesthetics is avoided altogether and the brief provides little more than a technical tabula rasa, a context which possibly resonated with the pristine nature of the new province itself. The competition did initiate discussion on questions of African identity, yet to find the early signs of this discussion we must look beyond the written record.

Adjudicating the Competition

A series of interviews conducted with the jurors for the competition threw crucial light on these questions and helps to explain which design strategies were deemed to be successful, and why. As might be expected, the interviewees highlighted different aspects of the adjudication process, yet no important disagreements or inconsistencies between testimonies were found. A good working relationship was established among the mixed team of adjudicators, which included two architectural academics (Professor Julian Cooke and Herbert Prins), two practising architects representing the Institute of Architecture (Mira Fassler Kamstra and Khotso Moleko), and three civil servants from the local Department of Public Works (Piet Duvenhage, Homa Khalili and Lawrence Lebea). As may be expected, the architects took the lead in adjudication, with the members of the Department of Public Works participating in the process with their comments and concerns.

Prins, who chaired the jury, made few comments on the decision-making process, except to say that he felt the winning scheme was the only workable design solution.[41] The other jurors explained that Prins had been an excellent chair and tended to mediate discussion rather than enforce his own views. Cooke, an academic representative who was responsible for writing the final jurors' report, explained that he was looking for a scheme with a strong idea, and especially one that opened itself to the public.[42] The winning scheme by Meyer Pienaar Tayob Schnepel (MPTS, a consortium of Meyer Pienaar and Tayob Schnepel Architects) was remarkable for its use of materials, and this gave the design an 'African ambience' (see Figure 2.5–2.7). The offices had big wide and open eaves and this helped the building to merge with the surrounding trees. Another juror, Fassler Kamstra – the architect for the renovation of the Gauteng Provincial Legislature – pointed out that the question of a new African architecture was in the back of everyone's mind.[43] 'We were looking for something that could tell us that the building belonged to South Africa, and to our time.'[44] And for this reason, she maintained that a modernist design would not have been selected by the jury nor would a contemporary fashion statement. The winning scheme had to be something unique, and in this respect Fassler Kamstra felt the chosen scheme was the only design that made clear connections with African architecture. In particular, she referred to the domed roof of the Assembly, and the corbelled brick towers, prominent features of the winning design. When asked why these elements speak of Africa, she replied, 'I am not so sure why, there was just a feeling.'[45] These elements seem reminiscent of African forms, and quite strikingly so. With the domed Assembly, we have a connection with indigenous beehive domes while Fassler Kamstra mentioned that the corbelled towers are possibly a reference to Egypt or even Mali, 'but not in a literal way'.[46] These comments concur with the jurors' written report which states, '[t]he huge form of the Legislature space and tall entrance towers add vertical accents and textured surfaces in brick. These forms, without

2.5   Upper
ground-floor plan,
Mpumalanga
Legislature,
(1997). Courtesy
of Meyer Pienaar,
Tayob Schnepel
Architects
(MPTS).

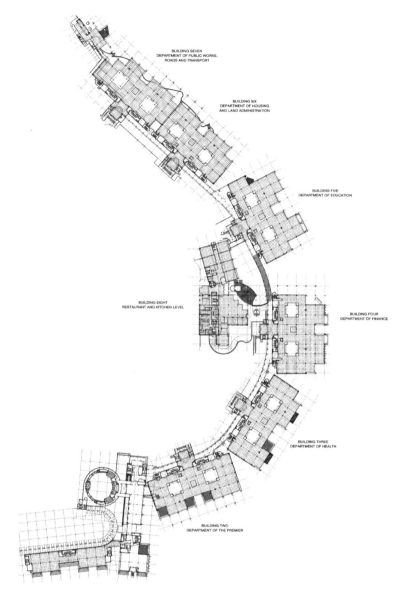

mimicry, contain a sense of the historical forms and building methods of the region, of traditional granaries and entrances.'[47]

But by far the most vivid memory was communicated during the interview with Moleko, the only black architect on the jury. [48] Moleko, representing the Institute of Architecture, explained how he had mentally arranged the various submissions into four fundamental categories: contemporary statements, grand or monumental ideas, domestic scale and more responsive designs. [49] Of the four, Moleko maintained that the least appropriate were the monumental and domestic kind. The grand and monumental schemes used bold, symmetrical geometries reminiscent of public designs from the colonial

WEST ELEVATION 1:200

2.6 Western elevation of the Assembly, Mpumalanga Legislature (1997). Courtesy of Meyer Pienaar, Tayob Schnepel Architects (MPTS).

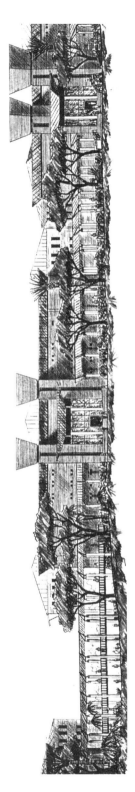

2.7 Part of long western elevation to offices, Mpumalanga Legislature (1997). Courtesy of Meyer Pienaar, Tayob Schnepel Architects (MPTS).

era as derived from classical prototypes. These schemes could not be chosen because they were far too colonial and Eurocentric in character. By contrast, the schemes with domestic scale, simple and ordinary buildings, failed to achieve an appropriate public stature. Widespread agreement quickly ruled against these grand and domestic designs. A sustained debate then began to develop between representatives of contemporary versus more responsive types of design. I use these terms in the loose sense of their meaning because we are referring here to differential shades of emphasis. A design can be more contemporary (fashionable) or more responsive. The distinction is certainly not clearcut and yet the specific choice of words that are used here favour an aesthetic sensibility informed by local forms and experience. We may go further by observing that the exact substance of precisely what constitutes a responsive design is not provided. After all, we only have vague references to Africa and local context, references which could be imagined in innumerable different ways. Thus, the defining difference only works because it is marked off against the other approach that is thought to be more fashionable and consequently less engaged.

Moleko expressed his concern for a new kind of responsive architecture by stating that 'this is going to be the capital of Mpumalanga, and therefore the design must break away from the past. We need a new language and a new form, but one that is easily identifiable by local people themselves.' He emphasised that the question of a new architectural language was foremost a political concern, and one which he himself had wrestled with in his final year BArch design discourse. The preamble to Moleko's design discourse maintains that 'it is an indictment that our knowledge of art, culture and architecture is restricted to a specific Eurocentric viewpoint, to the virtual exclusion of any other cultures'.[50] For this reason, his discourse set out to study the evolution of the Islamic mosque in Africa. His text demonstrates how the African mosque developed into a new hybrid type, with spatial and symbolic precedents taken from Islamic culture, merged with material tectonics derived from African building and craft traditions. During my interview, Moleko emphasised his belief that an approach of this kind would be productive in the given context, which required a modern Legislature complex for a post-apartheid Mpumalanga. Moleko also pointed to the decorative use of brickwork, the corbelled towers, and the domed roof of the Assembly as evidence of hybridised influences derived from African experience. And for these reasons, the winning scheme was strongly favoured by him because it was the only scheme that combined sensitivity to the natural landscape with explicit references to African history. He also explained that the runner-up was the best example of the more 'contemporary' designs he had referred to earlier. Moleko remembers the debate being heated at times because he had supported the winning scheme right from the start, whereas other members of the jury were impressed by some of the more 'contemporary' designs. I established that both Fassler Kamstra and Cooke were happy to accept the thrust of Moleko's four-way analysis, but Cooke was quick to add that he did not remember a heated debate. Nevertheless, the unanimous conclusion to this discussion was in favour of the winning scheme, which 'answered the conditions of the brief in a most appropriate and cost-effective way, while creating a group of buildings which would be unique, of a character linked closely to the region, and of a significance in keeping with dignified and democratic government'.[51]

Design Submissions

The Department of Public Works did not keep copies of the designs that were submitted for the competition, but fortunately a competition submission register obtained during my visit to the Legislature, names all the architectural consortiums who 'signed in' for their design submissions. With the aid of this list, I was able to make contact with all of the nine firms that submitted designs. In many cases the submissions had been lost, yet I did manage to obtain copies of the second-placed submission, as well as two further design submissions. And without doubt, the four schemes provide sufficient evidence in support of Moleko's interesting analysis.

A striking feature of the four is the similarity of their geometric parti, all of which embrace the landscape with an arc-like formation of separate building elements, joined by connecting walkways, while three of the schemes position the Assembly together with adjoining public space as a termination of the axis down Government Boulevard. These similarities are explained by the preliminary competition brief. This document details preferred site development requirements and calls for the sensitive siting of a series of interlinked buildings, with a centralised service block and in accordance with a site-zoning diagram which clearly hints at an arc-like arrangement.[52] But despite these similarities, these designs adopt different architectural postures. The project by Osmond Lange Mosinyane (OLM) demonstrates grand, classicising geometries (see Figure 2.8), while the projects by Taljaard, Carter, Ledwaba Tasker and Schuman (GOPAC) (see Figures 2.9–2.10) and Artech Association (see Figures 2.11–2.12) alternatively take on rationalist and loose sculptural themes, both of which fall within the earlier categorisation of 'contemporary statements' in design. Dietrich Ungerer, one of the principal designers for GOPAC who was awarded second place, explains that their approach to African architecture was a modern one, and therefore they decided not to refer to Africa in a literal way.[53] Instead, the African component of their design was established purely through relations with landscape and climate. According to Ungerer, 'Climatic and contextually sensitive design is Africa.'

The adjudication of these projects marks the emergence of a new architectural discourse in South African public design. The new discourse works with a conjunction of two important ingredients: a conventional architectural contextualism plus more explicit attempts to symbolise Africa.

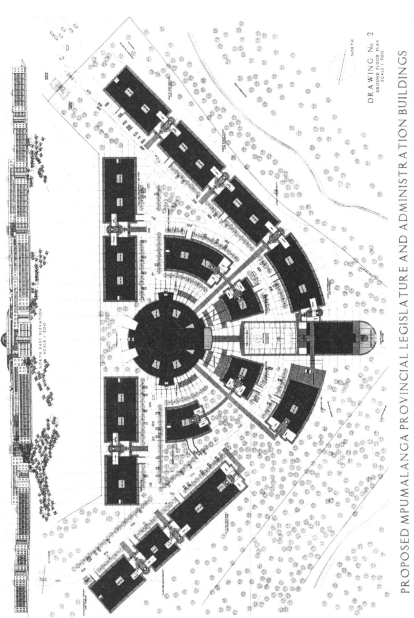

PROPOSED MPUMALANGA PROVINCIAL LEGISLATURE AND ADMINISTRATION BUILDINGS

2.8   Design submission by OLM, Plan and Elevation (1997). Courtesy of Osmond Lange Mosienyane.

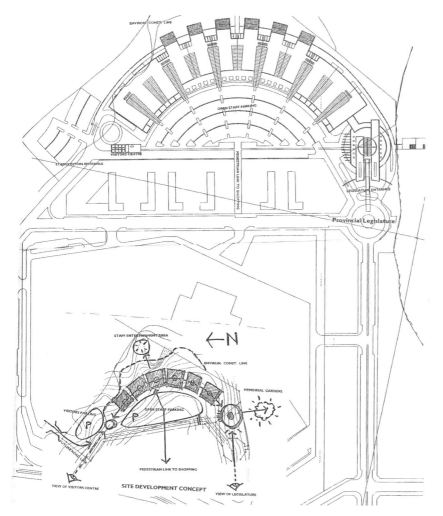

2.9 Design submission by GOPAC, Plan (1997). Courtesy of GOPAC.

Contextualism is, arguably, the dominant orientation in South African schools of architecture and has widespread support among vocal members of the profession. This conventional contextualism conceptualises questions of style and expression in relation to the character of a place: genius loci.[54] Expressions of genius loci can be derived from a wide range of sources, which may include urban morphology and spatial types, local building styles, the natural landscape and climatic conditions, as well as highly imaginative adaptations of these sources in keeping with a commitment to modernistic innovation in design. However, this contextual approach seldom raises more explicit questions of cultural identity because the question of identity that this contextualism sees operates mostly on a material level in relation to existing forms and patterns. But in many cases, these forms and patterns, and especially in the case of actual architectural forms, are hugely implicated in modes of cultural domination that issue from the past. And

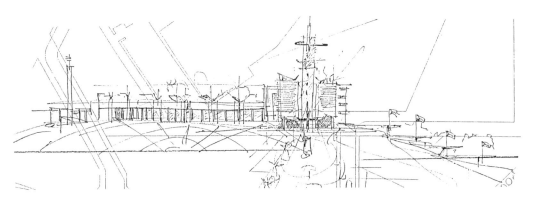

2.10   Design submission by GOPAC, western elevation (1997). Courtesy of GOPAC.

for this reason, design contextualism does not provide a sufficient remedy for post-apartheid public design because it lacks the visionary commitment to establishing a break with the past and the retrieval of subjugated cultural histories and practices. Indeed, identification with Africa is not sufficiently facilitated by contextual imagination. The new discourse in public design attempts to remedy this failing by adding further sources of imaginative and symbolic reference to the more limited ideas of working from existing context. The discussion generated at the adjudication of the Mpumalanga Legislature clearly demonstrates that symbolic identification with Africa is a necessary ingredient for success. This pattern continues across all the design competitions that are covered by this study, and this book will demonstrate the gradual development of this new motion.

A Commercial Type

In identifying this new discourse, we have not specified the kinds of symbol, nor the modes of aesthetic representation, that are deemed to be appropriate in any one case. For instance, at the competition stage for the Mpumalanga Legislature, we only had vague and generalising comments from the jury, for example with reference to the dome roof and corbelled brickwork, forms which provide an aestheticised sense of 'Africa'. As the project developed we find a gradual refinement of terms, and it is this history of design development that must now be studied.

The architects' first written report, which was submitted as an accompaniment to their competition entry, surprisingly makes scare reference to questions of African identity. The report explains how a 'conceptual framework' for the design was established which 'aimed at marrying functional requirements, subtle symbolic gestures and environmental sensitivity'.[55] Environmental and climatic considerations take centre stage in an attempt to ensure 'that nature and architecture are blended harmoniously'.[56] Architectural symbolism is either considered on a

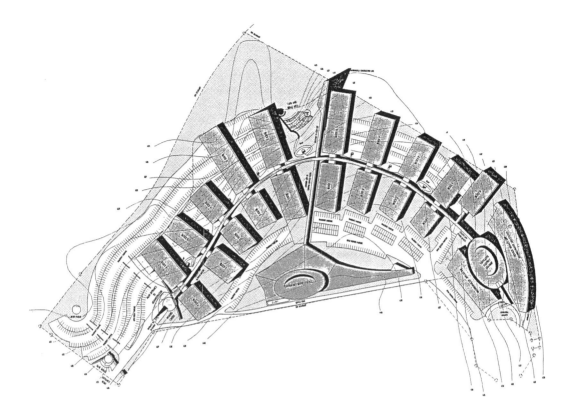

functional, pragmatic level, '[t]he parliamentary chamber is located literally in the pivotal position between the two main components of the total complex, between the legislative and the executive',[57] or in more generalising and universal terms such as with the major public space in front of the Legislature which is described as the 'archetypal forum for democratic activity'.[58] No reference is made to African spatial traditions. In fact, the only explicit reference to African architecture is made through the use of the word 'beehive', where this term is used to designate the large dome of the Assembly.[59] But this word just floats in the context of a single short sentence, and the cultural and political significance of this word is not developed. Instead, the text immediately continues with technical justification for the domed form: '[i]ts parabolic shape is the purest expression of structural forces distributed through a dome.' Then a more functionally derived symbolic argument follows: '[t]he desired effect is that of a sculpted expression of the buildings anchoring function', and finally we are presented with a return to ideas of universal symbolic significance because the dome is said to have 'mystic connotations, as archetypal expression of centrality'.[60] The cultural implication of this 'beehive' signifier is mute. The closing sentence of this report confirms the conventional, contextual approach adopted by the designers: 'the parliamentary complex has been infused with the qualities of an architecture inspired by the very spirit of

2.11 Design submission by Artech Association, Plan (1997). Courtesy of Artech Association.

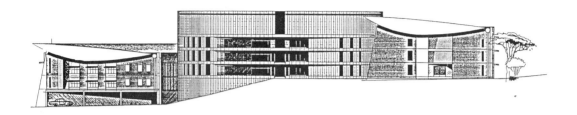

2.12   Design
submission
by Artech
Association,
Elevation
(1997). Courtesy
of Artech
Association.

place of a lovely African setting'.[61] These statements are in marked contrast
to the overt African references that are made in subsequent reports.

The success of this design hinged upon the jurors' ability to read cultural
significance into its suggestive forms, but crucial questions of an African
identification seem to be missing from the architects' original conceptual
framework. Indeed, the African themes so strongly evident in the built
design, and which shall be discussed shortly, were not far developed at
the early competition stage. Despite the jurors' kind criticism, a different
interpretation of the winning design is possible. A rendered perspective,
which was included among the competition submission documents, gives
the distinct impression that we are observing a commonplace speculative
development (see Figure 2.13). The perspective shows a repetitive beat of
standardised pavilion buildings which sweep around a sea of parked cars.
The arced motion is terminated at one end by the large domed Legislature
Assembly. The pavilion buildings are marked by towers and demonstrate
neoclassical-like symmetries complete with 'villa-style' pitched roofs. The
overriding spatial type thus seems remarkably close to that used for open-air
shopping centre designs. Indeed, the Crossing shopping centre in Nelspruit
provides an enlightening comparison as the Crossing would appear to
repeat all the salient features highlighted by this aerial perspective (see
Figure 2.14): repetitive arc of pavilion-type buildings, with pitched roofs
and towers, a wrap-around walkway, a sea of parking trapped at the centre,
and a large anchor tenant (the Legislature) which terminates the arc.

A series of interviews conducted with the principal design architect for the
project, Patrick McInerney, helped to clarify these questions and provided
some fascinating insights into the process of careful design development that
occurred subsequent to the competition award. [62] McInerney explained that
his firm, Meyer Pienaar Architects (MPA), which entered the competition
as part of MPTS consortium, have many years of commercial architectural
experience. If the design submission demonstrates standard aspects of
commercial architecture, then the reasons are the obvious ones, and this
aspect is hardly a source of embarrassment for the firm. Nevertheless, the
symbolic significance of this project was approached by the architects with
utmost seriousness, and it would seem the design process that unfolded
demonstrates an attempt to 'Africanise' an efficient, modern and indeed

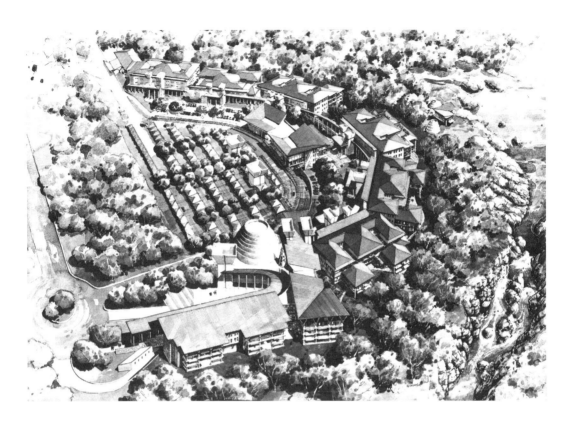

a commercially derived spatial type. The process of design development emerged as an attempt to hybridise established architectural patterns with elements derived from material, cultural and historical contexts.

2.13 Rendered perspective, Mpumalanga Legislature. Courtesy of Meyer Pienaar, Tayob Schnepel Architects (MPTS).

Soon after winning the competition, MPTS was required to make a presentation to Cabinet to explain the new design to the politicians of the province. McInerney remembers his surprise at the comments levelled against his scheme by a young ANC member at parliament. During his presentation, McInerney had termed the design an 'African building'. His critic proceeded to ask what was so African about this building, and how it differed from a commercial office design. McInerney had to agree that the building was indeed a conventional office, but argued the completed project would be African by virtue of its respectful relationship with the site. The reply initiated an extended argument. McInerney's preconceptions were beginning to be challenged. Soon after, a friendship developed between McInerney and Motha, the project manager for government on this project, allowing for further discussion on questions of African architecture and traditional cultural practices. McInerney began to learn many poetic aspects unique to African experience, and the knowledge gained informed the choice of material, detailing and decorative features of the final design.

2.14   The
Crossing
Shopping Centre,
Nelspruit.
Photograph by
the author.

Incommensurable Symbols

McInerney explained to me that the 'beehive' dome, as it was named in the original design report, was never intended as a replica of indigenous domed huts. Instead, the primary reference and inspiration for this form had come from the surrounding landscape, with its domed rock outcrops. McInerney had felt confident that this metonymic form gave the design a distinctly African, or at least 'local' identity. However, Motha explained that he was not entirely convinced by this approach and that he sought to challenge McInerney about his contextual assumptions.[63] The dome in question spans the Legislature Assembly, which is the pivotal space of the entire scheme, both functionally and symbolically, because it is here that the leaders gather to discuss issues of governance. And in fact, this pivotal locality of the dome, which unites the two arced wings of the executive and the Legislature, was a primary sketch design concept (see Figure 2.15).

In Motha's imagination, however, these design intentions were missing an essential element because they failed to refer to historical patterns of African governance. In precolonial times, and indeed continuing long into the colonial era, African elders would meet outdoors under a tree to debate political concerns and to administer justice. A village would always have this designated space beneath a tree where the elders would gather, and this provides us with a spatial type for the traditional African 'court'. This spatial practice has been well documented by anthropological and archaeological study of African society.[64] Motha felt that McInerney's celebration of the Assembly by virtue of the monumental dome, and its resonance to the dome rock outcrops that surrounded it, did not engage with an African imagination. Instead, it privileged Western

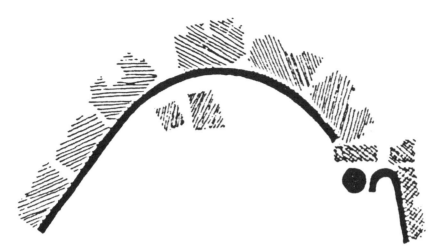

2.15   Conceptual sketch for the Mpumalanga Legislature. Courtesy of Meyer Pienaar, Tayob Schnepel Architects (MPTS).

histories where a political gathering is often held indoors, for which reason the internalised Assembly hall itself contained Western connotations. Motha was quick to point out that he and his fellow Africans from the province were obviously most content to meet and discuss indoors, but that in addition to this modern way, some symbolic reference to the old African ways should also be recognised, if only to facilitate a dialogue with the cultural roots of an African democratic consciousness. This difference of interpretation was remedied by the final design for the public space which fronts the Assembly. The civic square of the Legislature includes trees – as a symbol of an African court – with nearby stepped seating that descends into the square and the comforting sounds of a trickling water feature (see Figure 2.16).

2.16   Public square in front of the Assembly, Mpumalanga Legislature, (MPTS). Photograph by the author

The exchange between McInerney and Motha has resulted in the juxtaposition of a pair of incommensurable figures – dome and tree – that issue from the racially divided history of South Africa. The proximity of dome and tree is a form of hybrid representation, the significance of which will be theorised in subsequent chapters where it will be seen that the tree repeatedly features as an African symbol of governance.

Forming an African Discourse

A further area of discussion between McInerney and Motha, and which warrants consideration here, concerns tectonic sensibilities derived from African building and craft traditions. McInerney explained that, like many white South Africans, he had had limited prior knowledge or experience of indigenous African architecture. By contrast, Motha had grown up in a rural area and had vivid memories from his childhood years when he decorated walls with his fingers pressed into wet clay. Motha's knowledge of the old 'African ways' of building and of forming space was not learned from books but was from lived experience. In fact, the project had prompted him to reflect upon his childhood experience. McInerney and Motha together began to imagine ideas and strategies for understanding and artistically representing African tectonic practices, and McInerney explains how Motha helped him to appreciate African tectonic aesthetics. McInerney indicates that indigenous African architectures grow from the earth, and this poetic principle is key to an appreciation of the aesthetic charm of traditional building structures. In stark contrast to this organic principle, Western architecture primarily imagines itself in the lineage of rationalist, classical design – we can obviously include modernism here – and concerns the poetic order and logic of the building frame, an order which is imposed upon the site. In Africa, however, building is imagined as a prayer to the ancestors, and this respectful attitude is linked to a cyclical use of materials. Buildings are constructed from the immediate material that surrounds the site, and the ensuing natural cycle of building and decay from soft natural materials metaphorically translates a cyclical conception of architecture and nature: the purposes of this life and respect for the elders who observe from the other, the living and the dead. From his new-found appreciation of this poetic principle, McInerney began to cultivate a more respectful approach towards indigenous materials. A strategy was developed for the incorporation of local finishes, in ways both material and metaphorical, through a conscious establishment of three themed categories, which the architect describes as: '"Earth" i.e. finishes that are derived from or denote rock, mud or clay … "Grass" woven fabrics or patterns derived from weaving … "Reed" posts – angled or vertical elements on the edge of space'.[65] Wall surfaces, for example, are realised with earth colours taken from the surrounding landscape, in ochres and reds, set off against deep sky blue, and at times are rendered by hand with smeared, mud-like textures (see

2.17 a–c: Wall finishes derived from 'Earth', Mpumalanga Legislature, (MPTS) (left to right, top to bottom) d–f: Finishes derived from 'grass'. g–i: Finishes derived from 'reeds'. Photographs by the author.

Figure 2.17 a–c). Woven stainless-steel mesh is tensioned to form sunscreens, suspended as a ceiling feature beneath the Assembly dome and wrapped around concrete columns of the interior (see Figure 2.17 d–f). Continuing this strategy, memories of reeds are captured by the many vertical and angled poles on the eastern façade, timber balcony slats and are expressed in the fluting of wooden wall panels (see Figure 2.17 g–i).

Previous discussion of the architects' written report submitted at the time of the competition revealed that architectural identity was initially understood with reference to place rather than through political identifications with Africa. In marked contrast to this, subsequent design reports written by the architects make more explicit reference to Africa. For example, whereas previously the civic square in front of the Legislature was described as an 'archetypal' symbol for democracy, a later report emphasises instead that 'the spreading umbrella-thorn [the tree] symbolically marks the traditional gathering space of the leaders', while the symbolic significance of the 'beehive' dome is now said to refer to 'vernacular precedents'.[66] In another report, the pivotal centrality of the dome, an idea which was a fundamental concept for the early design sketch plan, is no longer derived from functional symbolism alone – as was the case with the competition report – but now additionally symbolises the fact that '[f]or centuries, African people have gathered in a similar fashion providing a spatial framework for the provision of a centre of power.'[67] The same report also uses an African title, Isigcawu, for the civic square plaza in front of the Legislature.[68] Mention is made of architectural references derived from 'Zimbabwe, Ethiopia, and South African indigenous architecture specifically in respect to texture, colour, pattern, contrast, repetition and attitude to light and shade'.[69] The report also maintains that '[i]f Great Zimbabwe can be considered parliamentary this would be the closest to a really conscious model.' (see Figure 3.6).[70]

The written content of these reports leads on to the book published by the architects themselves, entitled: *The Making of an African Building: The Mpumalanga Provincial Government Complex*. By this stage, the architects' mobilisation of African signifiers takes on a more confident, if not romantic, tone. The foreword opens with a grand announcement, '[a]s South Africa enters the new millennium, it is appropriate that the first building representing the new democratic government is published, promoting the idea of an African Renaissance in architecture, building and art.'[71] At times, the text tends towards a sentimental nationalism, which conjoins naturalistic metaphors with authority derived from the father, or 'parent culture', and in a way that suggests an unquestioning legitimisation of power:

[i]t is easy to imagine earlier African societies settled on this land, cultures living close to nature on fertile soil, near a river, subsisting off sorghum, millet and cattle. Walking over the virgin site, largely covered by a citrus orchard, one could be tempted to picture the council of tribal leaders meeting here long ago in their Kgoro, an open-sided thatched structure under a spreading tree, to exercise political and judicial governance over their people.[72]

These naturalisations attempt to synthesise nature, tradition and power, and when linked to the figure of political governance, mutate into counter democratic discourse.

Archaeological Finds

Reference to the ancient past introduces a new element into our discussion. The ancient past in question is a precolonial past, and it is one that has received scarce public recognition in South Africa. Indeed, the unearthing and mobilisation of precolonial signifiers is a prominent feature of the new political imaginary in South Africa, and it will be seen that various precolonial figures appear in all the projects examined by this book. Oddly enough, at Mpumalanga the precolonial discourse was sparked by accident. Unexpectedly, building works unearthed a series of important archaeological finds. Professor Tom Huffman, who led the 1997–98 archaeological digs in Nelspruit, explains that '[a] bulldozer cutting for a new road to the government offices [at Riverside Park] exposed storage pits, cattle byres, a burial and a midden on the crest of a gentle slope.'[73] One pit contained 'charcoal, cattle bones and pottery dating back to the eleventh century'.[74] A further cluster of five pits, some 30 m away, was found, as was the burial site of a young woman some 8 m north of the previously mentioned cluster.

These are very important finds, for as Huffman explains, 'the byre and cluster of pits – especially the two with dung lining – are diagnostic of the Central Cattle Pattern'.[75] The Central Cattle Pattern is a theoretical model, developed by archaeologists, which attempts to explain a spatial organisation that underlies the settlement patterns associated with Bantu-speaking peoples of South Africa. This settlement pattern privileges the safe position of cattle in an open yet secure space at the centre of the homestead, with individual dwellings surrounding it. The importance of this pattern, or so is it theorised, links to the practice of lobola (or, the preference for bride wealth in cattle) that was 'a defining characteristic of Eastern Bantu speakers in southern Africa'.[76] There has been some academic debate among anthropologists as to the correctness of this interpretive model, the exact details of which need not concern us here other than to point out that the recent discovery in Nelspruit now lends considerable scientific support to the Central Cattle Pattern hypothesis, meaning that '"[t]he diagnostic kraal and storage pits at the Nelspruit site show that lobola was an important principle of social organisation during the Early Iron Age in South Africa."'[77] More importantly for us, however, is the way this discovery captured local imagination, adding to the symbolic significance of Riverside Park and the new Legislature complex. The architects' book contains an early section, entitled 'Traces of the Past', which elaborates on the significance of this find. The section concludes by arguing that:

[t]he early inhabitants have left us only faint traces of their occupation of the site, yet an awareness of the spirit of their culture, and of historical continuity impresses itself on the mind. This, together with the sensuous nature of the immediate environment … adds to a very special spirit of place.[78]

2.18   Inner covered walkway, Mpumalanga Legislature, (MPTS). Photograph by the author.

Politicians from the province have also made political capital from these finds. At the official dedication ceremony for the Mpumalanga Provincial Government buildings and Legislature, the speaker for the Legislature, Lubisi, stated that:

[w]e are mostly elated by the historical significance that the building represents, in particular the fact that the building stands on the site where early inhabitants of our province had created a centre of government. The choice of this location as the seat of the democratic government is therefore a continuation of a legacy that was started by our forebears more than 1500 years ago.[79]

These statements mark a key moment in the architectural discourse at Mpumalanga. In each instance we have prose which links a poetics of place, of 'natural harmony', to associations or identifications with precolonial history. No doubt, we have an attempt to synthesise nature with history, material context with precolonial identity, architecture with authenticity derived from the 'parent' culture which was lost in the mists of time. The archaeological finds established a moment where the physical site became both the material repository and the symbolic referent for identification with precolonial history. Identifications of this kind involve imagined connections built across space

and time: the political 'we' is formed between the self and the others, mediated through narratives of historical time. The authenticity of the precolonial is used as an anchor to support a new collectivity in the present. These identifications seem cogent where they form a dialogue with subjugated histories. However, it must be said that where these identifications are linked to governance – be it the province or nation – we also have the unfortunate possibility for an unquestioning and romantic legitimisation of power, a move which would be thoroughly counter democratic in character. This question, of the relation between subjugated history and power is an important issue that resurfaces in the last case study chapter on Freedom Park.

2.19 Inner covered walkway, Mpumalanga Legislature (MPTS). Photograph by the author.

The Completed Design

The built complex is formed from a series of discrete elements, each with their own distinct spatial and structural order, which combine to form the greater whole. For instance, one has the repetitive beat of the office block building, each with corbelled entrance tower, double-volume entrance foyer spaces and internalised courts. One also has the covered connecting walkway,

2.20   Eastern façade, Mpumalanga Legislature, (MPTS). Photograph by the author.

which runs through the entire complex and joins all the entrance foyers together as they arc around the site. And finally, one has the Legislature itself, with its domed Assembly and external colonnade holding the civic space of the Legislature. Entry into the complex is via a security-controlled *porte cochère* on the northern side, leading into the centralised parking area. Exterior walkways lead from each office to the next, running around the large arc, but one can also enter any of the departmental office blocks, pass the security point at the entrance lobby, and gain access to the inner covered walkway which connects all the offices together. This inner covered walkway leads from one office foyer to the next, and one is able to walk through a series of indoor–outdoor spaces. Passing from the indoor foyer space to the outdoor covered walkway is facilitated by glass sliding doors and the abrupt change heightens awareness of the hot and humid climate outdoors. The walkway is covered by an exposed lean-to timber structure, with low-lying side walls providing ample opportunity for experiencing the dense vegetation flowing up into the gaps between the office blocks which radiate around (see Figures 2.18–2.19). Moving from indoor to outdoor and back again sets up a regular beat which is dramatically interrupted near the centre of the complex by the large open space behind the central service block (building no. 8) which provides a welcome relief. Here, the covered

walkway changes from a bricked surface to a timber deck bridging over the uninterrupted vegetation which breaks through on either side. The floor is made from timber slats – slightly separated so that rain can fall through – such that one has the sudden sense of being in the air, with the sound of twittering birds and dramatic views down toward the riverside. Lush vegetation is in close proximity on either side, with the river on one side and a cantilevered timber deck behind the service block on the other where lunch is served. Continuing, one will experience a further three indoor–outdoor sequences before arriving at the entrance lobby and security checkpoint for the Legislature Assembly itself. This well-conceived sequence of events helps to merge the otherwise hermetic and internalised environments of the departmental office blocks into open dialogue with the dramatic beauty of the surrounding natural landscape, and ensures a charming experience for all who visit.

2.21   Western façade, Mpumalanga Legislature, (MPTS). Photograph by the author.

The repeating office blocks, on their own terms, are speculative office buildings, with all the regular features of this generic type: a concrete frame grid with highly rationalised vertical services and circulation cores clustered around double-volume entrance lobbies. The interiors are open plan with flexible office partitions and internalised courts. This highly rationalised plan is aestheticised by interior finishes which follow the architects' triple theme of earth, grass and reed, as previously explained. At the same time, external façades develop their decorative themes in relation to the surroundings: the eastern façades facing the river have large glass windows and a series of balconies and projecting eaves which filter light (see Figure 2.20), whereas the

2.22a: Early Iron Age Pottery, archaeological finds at Nelspruit (1997–98) (left to right, top to bottom). Courtesy of the Archaeology Department, University of the Witwatersrand. b–h: Decoration derived from Early Iron Age Pottery, Mpumalanga Legislature (MPTS). Photographs by the author.

western façades are activated by the twin corbelled towers which pronounce the entrance as well as decorative brickwork motifs (see Figure 2.21).

In both cases, the African references are a matter of dress, a fact which no doubt followed from the design process itself where an attempt was made to Africanise a commercial, modern building type. It is in this sense that the offices demonstrate a distinct duality, a unity of structure, building type and space, versus the ornate yet tasteful surfaces which make reference to themes derived from African building material and craft traditions.

Decorative Themes

Careful study of the decoration reveals theme and variation developed from ornamental chevron-like shapes. I questioned McInerney about this, and he explained that the decoration was inspired by Early Iron Age pottery that was unearthed during the archaeological digs at Riverside Park. A detailed drawing of these pots, provided by Huffman, shows a variety of patterns derived from zigzag or chevron shapes, which is a distinctive feature of Bantu pottery (see Figure 2.22 a).[80] Notably, patterns of this kind are realised across a wide range of materials. For example, a typical entrance foyer has chevron patterns carved into the wooden reception desk, etched into a glass notice board forming a frame, and incised by hand into a 'mud'-like, wall-mounted cornice frieze (see Figure 2.22 b–d). Chevrons also inform patterned brickwork, especially high up on the western façades of the office buildings and as decorative brick paving along the covered walkway and around the colonnaded civic space of the Legislature (see Figure 2.22 e–f). The widespread nature of these decorative themes, derived from a single motif, emphasises the fact that the patterning is *applied*. The pattern possesses its own order, one that is layered upon the material which bears its mark. It is therefore not tectonically specific to any one material – or perhaps we might say this is an imaginary rather than a purely material tectonic. The abstract motif is a mark of identity, operating like a signature, stamp or seal. I was interested to learn, during a discussion with Professor Huffman, that repetitive decoration of this kind is a recurring feature of African craft. He explained that where an archaeologist finds a series of bumps, for example on a carved headrest associated with a particular group, then there is every chance of finding the same bump-like motif in the textiles, pots and even the body adornment connected with this group. Huffman refers to this phenomenon as the 'wide design field'. The design at Mpumalanga establishes a dialogue with this sophisticated idea, and in so doing produces a decorative logic that is incommensurable with modernist imagination which has mostly privileged more literal and utilitarian ties between materiality and surface.

The project showcases at least three levels of decoration: decoration associated with building materials, decoration applied by craft and adornment derived from art. Examples of the first kind have already been identified and include brick work patterning, textured wall finishes and wall panelling, as well as decoration applied to building elements such as built-in furniture, windows, doors and so on. In addition to this, further decorative elements were added as special features, applied by skilled or semi-skilled craftsmen and women, and in many cases provided much needed employment opportunities for local people. Economic empowerment through the incorporation of handicrafts is a strong feature of post-apartheid architecture, and one that will be considered more carefully in later chapters. Craft decoration includes exquisite floor mosaics, with patterns derived from African baskets, woven wall hangings in the Legislature Assembly, as well as protruding 'mud' reliefs which adorn wall surfaces (see Figure 2.22 g–h and Figure 2.17 c). The reliefs are the work of Tineke Meijer, a potter who has developed special techniques derived from her work with clay, for incising and carving patterns into wet cement.[81] Oxides are added to the sand to form earth tones and textures reminiscent of mud walls. Meijer has successfully marketed this technique and has worked on numerous recent buildings in South Africa, including Nelson Mandela's house.[82] At Mpumalanga, Meijer implemented her craft with the aid of three previously unemployed women whom she selected, trained and supervised. It should be noted that women have commonly been responsible for the decorative wall motifs that adorn traditional African designs, so it seems appropriate that the three women selected should be empowered in this way.

Interiors for the offices and Legislature are also richly adorned by works of art. McInerney explains that no budget was initially set aside for the purchase of art, so strategic moves were made to save on internal finishes and to use this money for the procurement of art. An art acquisition committee was established under the leadership of John Anthony Boerma, then Director of Visual Arts and Crafts for the province. Boerma explains that he wanted to put together the first democratic collection of art in South Africa.[83] His thinking on this matter led him to privilege works produced locally, to blur the boundaries between art and craft, and to favour curatorial inclusivity over censoring critique. These principles are crystallised in an art procurement policy which unfolds a pragmatic approach aimed at economic and symbolic upliftment of local people.[84] His thinking was informed by national policy of the time, which speaks of empowerment through 'craft industries'.[85] A further key feature of the procurement process was a roadshow, taken across the entire province, ensuring that works were canvassed from disadvantaged communities. Boerma informed me, with great delight, that in many cases he was able to purchase almost everything that was offered. The curatorial policy has meant that expensive works of art are exhibited alongside the 'cheap and lowly', resulting in some astonishing price differentials: for example, William Boshoff's Umhlabathi cost R55,000 while a mono print by Jop Khunicke cost a mere R250.[86] This radically inclusive approach is both postmodern and democratic because it deliberately obscures arbitrary aesthetic boundaries, placing high art alongside commercial craft. The display of work, however, does little to challenge the autonomy of the art objects themselves, a point to which we will return when discussing artworks at the Northern Cape Legislature in the next chapter.

The Dome of the Assembly

Having discussed the internal walkway, the office blocks and their interiors, we shall now conclude by considering the Legislature itself. Almost everything observed about the office blocks and their interiors is replicated in the Legislature building, and especially the duplicity of structure, space and form versus surface elaboration. Once again, African signifiers are layered onto the surface, yet here we also have an attempt at expressive form. The sweeping colonnade and civic space provide a welcoming entrance to the Legislature, and, as explained earlier, complements the grand axis down Government Boulevard. The combined effect of dome, colonnade and civic space is reminiscent of Herbert Baker's Union Buildings in Pretoria but, crucially, the composition here at Mpumalanga avoids neoclassical symmetry, relying instead on an artful balance of shifted elements. Unfortunately, the graciousness of this civic design has been marred by local politicians who have chosen to close the doors leading from the civic space to the foyer of the Legislature, which in turn leads on to the foyer of the Assembly where some of the most important artworks are displayed. Only card-carrying members can enter here from the civic space in front of the Legislature.[87] Regular members of the public are forced to enter the complex at the *porte cochère* on the far northern side and to walk the entire circumference of the arc before arriving at the Legislature. Even here, access to the 'democratic art collection' in the foyer of the Assembly is prohibited unless prior, indeed special, consent has been granted. The official reasons given for the closure of these spaces predictably are concerns over security, yet the architects' design carefully addresses these problems with a series of control points which were designed to give public access to the art collection while securing private areas. The decision to close entry in this way is disastrous for the civic space which stands empty because there are no adjacent functions to activate its use.[88] Counter-democratic action has turned democratic art into a form of authoritarian possession and civic space into cynical ideology, yet one hopes that the good intentions of the architecture can outlive this temporal politics.

We previously noted that the dome form was introduced as a symbolic gesture in celebration of democratic Assembly and in response to the domed rock outcrops of the surrounding landscape. Reference to South African beehive huts was also implied. Consequently, the dome was conceived as a formal and a symbolic device but naturally, as the project developed, it was necessary to solve the complex structural and spatial implications of this form. The architects were hoping to build a brick dome in the manner of

2.23   Dome of the Assembly under construction, Mpumalanga Legislature. Courtesy of Meyer Pienaar, Tayob Schnepel Architects (MPTS).

Hassan Fathy, but the span proved to be too large. Practical considerations of how to build this dome eventually resulted in a beautiful concrete structure, designed with the help of Ove Arup Engineers (see Figure 2.23). McInerney explains that the clarity of order and beauty of this structure introduced an unexpected crisis because the question was now raised as to whether the dome should gain expression as a symbolic form in relation to landscape and themes derived from tectonic sensibilities, or whether the expression ought to be tied to the implicit order of the structure itself. It is important to appreciate here that Willie Meyer, the principal of Meyer Pienaar Architects, studied under Louis Kahn, and that Kahn's thought has had an enduring influence on the work of this firm. Kahn's design philosophy postulates that metaphysical order is inherent in form, and that this form must be resolved through the honest expression of structure. Here then, we have the classical, platonic unity of order and truth. However, at Mpumalanga the dome soon developed a disturbing duplicity because the symbolic nature of the dome called for tectonic association with stone, mud or earth, and this seemed at odds with the 'natural' order which was introduced by the pragmatics of modern structural design. Not surprisingly, symbolic intention won the day. The concrete structure for the dome is completely concealed beneath brick panels hung on the exterior, and decorative, woven triangular panels, reminiscent of motifs taken from African baskets, adorn surfaces of the interior (see Figures 2.16 and 2.24).

The resolution of the dome demonstrates an extreme case for the modes of duplicity and disguise that inform this design. Throughout this chapter, we have seen that the design process was one where generic formal types,

2.24 Interior of the domed Assembly, Mpumalanga Legislature, (MPTS). Photograph by the author.

as well as conventional spatial and structural means, were hybridised by decorative and tectonic features derived from African experience. And yet, this fundamental duplicity is not well considered by the architects' own discourse. Instead, their design emphasises aesthetic ideas of order and unity, of harmony and synthesis, and the means of discursive representation, its rhetorical form, gives preference to tropes of tradition and authenticity. The African signifiers, although pragmatically linked to modern needs, nevertheless rely upon realist representation of traditional themes. But this chapter also highlights the fundamental asymmetry that exits between an architectural discourse of realist authenticity and the layered complexities of surface and form that complete this work. The Legislature may appeal to 'authenticity', but the means for realising this project have required numerous tactics of disguise. The Mpumalanga complex demonstrates duplicity despite itself, a publicity of disguise – this building is wearing a mask.

Concluding Remarks

By way of conclusion, I wish to theorise this duplicity of the mask. We may recall Fanon's metaphors of *mask* and *skin* – as discussed in the introductory chapter – and his description of the complex, split subjectivities that are produced by colonial rule. Consideration of subjective states is relevant for an understanding of architecture because architecture and subjectivity alike are discursively constituted. This means that where we have a subjugated subject position, we also have a subjugated history. And from this, any serious attempt to listen to these silenced histories will have implications for our understanding of architecture because architecture itself is a historical, discursive construct. Indeed, dominant histories and theories of architecture are already implicated in the colonial project, and it is precisely for this reason that we should wish to raise issues of marginality and subjugation in the context of architectural theory and design.

Fanon's use of the terms 'mask' and 'skin', in the title of his book, can be understood on at least two distinct levels. On the one level, we have an ontological claim as to the lived condition of colonised subjectivity. Fanon wishes to show the inauthentic duplicity of the colonised subject, a subject who finds herself torn between incommensurable worlds. Interestingly, this ontological theme has been developed by other black intellectuals.[89] In particular, a notion of simultaneous inside–outside relations with modernity is developed by Paul Gilroy in *The Black Atlantic*. Gilroy traces Du Bois' idea of double consciousness across the work of various intellectuals of the black diaspora in Europe and America. Du Bois' double consciousness is that of a black subjectivity spilt between two disjointed worlds, two disjointed histories, two disjointed imaginations. In the case of Du Bois, however, duplicity of the subject position does not necessarily result in alienation. A subject who perceives herself to be simultaneously in and outside of Western modernity, may discover unique and valuable perspectives. Why settle for one subjectivity when given the advantage of having two? The implications for architecture are that where we raise questions of African identity in design, we are immediately confronted by the fact that African architectures were largely destroyed, or at least severely marginalised, by colonial rule. This has meant that the only practical way to proceed is to work from within existing theories and practices of architecture, that is to say, to work from within the Western discourse of architecture but to do so by interrupting it with imaginations, and practices that were previously denied. This chapter has considered numerous instances of this practice, such as the thoughtful elaboration of decorative themes associated with African experience and traditions, the incommensurable relation between dome, tree and dressage of the domed structure. These exercises in the imaginary allow for the inclusion of what I wish to term 'foreign elements', elements that are brought into the operative realm of architecture. These foreign elements are brought in from the outside, that is, from a space on the exterior of the dominant practise of architecture. And in this way, the new architecture appears to inhabit an ontological duplicity, of inside–outside relations with regard to the dominant discourses of contemporary design. This effect may also be understood as a form of hybridity which, according to Bhabha, hinges upon 'a problematic of colonial representation and individuation that reverses the effects of the colonialist disavowal, so that other 'denied' knowledges enter upon the dominant discourse and estrange the basis of its authority – its rules of recognition'.[90] In most cases, what I have termed 'foreign elements', or hybrid effects, are formal fragments, details, surface treatments, signs and tropes derived from African experience, and not necessarily architectural elements as such. The story of this Legislature demonstrates key aspects of this process, and the next chapter will demonstrate that the Legislature at Kimberley continues in a similar vein.

On a second level of understanding, we may also focus upon the metaphoric content of Fanon's title, *BS*. The metaphor has spatial and material implications because the purpose of a mask is to hide ones skin. Fanon's choice of words is suggestive for architecture. At the most literal level, we might say that architectural skin, where related to the 'deep' order of structure and space, is a term commonly associated with authentic, honest expression – at least within the discourses of Western classical and modernist design. Whereas the term mask suggests a layering of the skin, a form of duplicity which complicates relations between structure and façade. Now, of course, there are many ways to read a metaphor, and a direct translation between Fanon's terms and the architectonics of surface treatment in design may not be the only, or even the best, way to proceed. But as it so happens, a 'direct' translation of Fanon's terms is productive for the study of the Legislature at Mpumalanga, as well as for the Legislature at Kimberley (Chapter 3). Both Legislatures showcase complex duplicities of structural order versus façade, and study of these relations helps us to analyse representational devices that are pertinent to questions of African identity in design.

Lastly, we need to distinguish between the intertwined levels of significance that I have discussed here. Fanon's ontological claim as to the duplicity of colonised subjectivities should not be equated with architectural relations of structure and façade per se, at least not in the sense of some deep ontological structure for postcolonial architecture. But rather, it happens to be the case that with these two Legislatures, relations of structure and façade indeed do play a significant role in the formation of African identity as presented by these buildings. And so, it would seem that Fanon's metaphor may be used to analyse these modes of layered composition, but this observation should not be conflated with his deeper claim as to the split duplicity of colonised subjectivity.

Notes

1   The history of this process and its incumbent geographic considerations is provided by: Meshack M. Khosa and Yvonne G. Muthien, 'The Expert, the Public and the Politician: Drawing South Africa's New Provincial Boundaries', *The South African Geographical Review*, 79, no. 1 (1997): pp 1–11.

2   Thabo Rapoo, 'Reflections on Provincial Government in South Africa since 1994', in Yvonne G. Muthien, Meshack M. Khosa and Bernard M. Magubane (eds) *Democracy and Governance Review: Mandela's Legacy 1994–1999* (Pretoria: Human Sciences Research Council, 2000).

3   'An Ancient Beauty Revived', *The Sub Contractor: The Official Journal of the Federation of Associations of Sub Contractors of South Africa*, 6, no. 6 (1994): p 21.

4   The city hall of Johannesburg, designed in a neoclassical manner by W. Hawke and W.N. McKinlay, was completed in 1915.

5   'An Ancient Beauty Revived', p 21.

6   Interview, Johannesburg (February 2005).

7   'An Ancient Beauty Revived', p 23.

8   Ibid.

9   Ray Hartley and Linda Shaw, 'The PWV Is Seeing Red over the Colours of Colonial Opulence', *The Sunday Times*, 30 October 1994, p 7.

10 Ibid.

11 Nornavenda Mathiane, '"Rainbow Building" to Be Toned Down', *Business Day*, 25 October 1994, p 1.

12 Jo-Anne Collinge, 'Tone Down City Hall, Designers Are Told', *The Star*, 25 October 1994, p 2.

13 Sipho William Lubisi, 'Official Dedication of the Mpumalanga Provincial Government and Legislature Buildings' (Nelspruit: Mpumalanga Provincial Government, 2004), p 2.

14 Steering Committee, 'Progress Report 01/10' (Nelspruit: DPW, 1999).

15 Ibid. p 3.

16 Ibid. p 4.

17 Interview, Johannesburg (August 2004).

18 Interview, Johannesburg (October 2004).

19 'Down by the Riverside', *The South Africa Quarterly Report*, January/March (1997): p 49.

20 Francis Motha served as project director, and Elsa Visser as chief of finance for Government for the duration of the project. Interview, Nelspruit (January 2005).

21 BIA, 'Detailed Competition Brief for Mpumalanga Provincial Legislature and Administration Buildings' (Johannesburg: BIA, 1997), p 5.

22 Documented history of this initiative, as well as future intensions for the White River developmental node, can be read from local town planning documents, in particular the Integrated Development Plan for Nelspruit and the Riverside Park Phase 2 Precinct Plan.

23 BIA, 'Detailed Competition Brief for Mpumalanga Provincial Legislature and Administration Buildings', p 2.

24 'Assessors Report on the Architectural Competition of the Riverside Government Complex' (Johannesburg, 1997), p 1.

25 Taljaard Carter Ledwaba Architects, 'Riverside Park Urban Design Framework for Phases 1 (Government Boulevard) and 2 (Along North South Boulevard)' (Johannesburg: Taljaard Carter Ledwaba), section 1.

26 Ibid. section 4.

27 Ibid. section 9.

28 Marian Giesen, 'Riverside Mall, Nelspruit', *Planning*, November (1998): pp 42–5. MDS-Architects, 'Riverside Mall: Nelspruit, Mpumalanga' *Architect and Builder*, December (1998): pp 10–13.

29 'Emnotweni Casino, Nelspruit', *Planning*, March/April, no. 168 (2000): pp 56–9. 'Fifty Two Million Rand Emnotweni Sun Hotel Opens in Nelspruit', *SA Builder*, November/December, no. 945 (2002): p 45.

30 Speaker of the Mpumalanga legislature, 2003.

31 Lubisi, 'Official Dedication of the Mpumalanga Provincial Government and Legislature Buildings', p 1.

32 Steering Committee, 'Progress Report 01/10', p 4.

33 Ibid. p 5.

34 BIA, 'Consultants Practice Information Requirements: Mpumalanga Provincial Legislature and Administration Buildings' (Johannesburg: BIA, 1997), pp 1–2.

35 Steering Committee, 'Progress Report 01/10', p 5.

36 A submission record, obtained during my visit to the Mpumalanga Legislature, lists fourteen design consortiums, ten of which bear the signature of a local representative who, presumably, submitted a scheme.

37 BIA, 'Detailed Competition Brief for Mpumalanga Provincial Legislature and Administration Buildings'.

38 Ibid. p 4.

39 Ibid. pp 4–5.

40 Ibid. p 25.

41 Interview, Johannesburg (October 2004).

42 Interview, Cape Town (December 2004).

43 Interview, Johannesburg (February 2005).

44 Ibid.

45 Ibid.

46 Ibid.

47 'Assessors Report on the Architectural Competition of the Riverside Government Complex', p 2.

48 Interview, Johannesburg (October 2004).

49 The term 'contemporary statement' used here, signifies a building that is influenced by contemporary architecture, but one that does not attempt a unique affinity with symbolism derived from African experience. Moleko actually used the word 'deconstruction', yet in further discussion, it was apparent that his use of the word 'deconstruction' does not reflect my own, and I believe 'contemporary statement' better captures the essence of what Moleko was saying.

50 Khotso Moleko, 'Seven Heavens: A Jumma Masjid in Maseru' (University of Natal, 1991), p 2.

51 'Assessors Report on the Architectural Competition of the Riverside Government Complex', p 5.

52 BIA, 'Preliminary Competition Brief: Mpumalanga Provincial Legislature and Administration Buildings' (Johannesburg: BIA, 1997), p 14.

53 Telephone interview between Johannesburg and Nelspruit (February 2005).

54 See Christian Norberg-Schultz, *The Concept of Dwelling: On the Way to a Figurative Architecture* (New York: Rizzoli, 1985).

55 MPTS, 'Mpumalanga Provincial Legislature and Administration Buildings: Design Report' (Johannesburg: MPTS, 1997), p 4.

56 Ibid. p 5.

57 Ibid. p 11.

58 Ibid. p 11.

59 Ibid. p 12.

60 Ibid. p 12.

61 Ibid. p 19.

62 Interviews, Johannesburg (September 2003, November 2004, February 2005).

63 Interview, Nelspruit (January 2005).

64 For example, with respect to the Tswana, see Isaac Schapera, *A Handbook of Tswana Law and Custom* (London: Oxford University Press, 1955). This custom of the court beneath the tree is not restricted to the Tswana, but is in fact wide spread across Southern Africa.

65 MPTS, 'Mpumalanga Provincial Legislature' (Johannesburg: MPTS), p 1.

66 Ibid. p 1.

67 MPTS, 'Riverside Government Administration Complex and Legislature: Report' (Johannesburg: MPTS, 2000), p 7.

68 Ibid. p 9.

69 Ibid. p 10.

70 Ibid. p 11.

71 Malan and McInerney (eds), *The Making of an African Building: The Mpumalanga Provincial Government Complex*, p 9.

72 Ibid. p 11.

73 T.N. Huffman, 'Presidential Address: The Antiquity of Lobola', *South Africa Archaeological Bulletin*, 53 (1998): p 59.

74 Ibid. p 60.

75 Ibid.

76 Ibid. p 57.

77 T.N. Huffman, 'Cattle for Wives', *Arena* 5, no. 16 (1998): pp 4–5.

78 Malan and McInerney (eds), *The Making of an African Building: The Mpumalanga Provincial Government Complex*, p 12.

79 Lubisi, 'Official Dedication of the Mpumalanga Provincial Government and Legislature Buildings', p 1.

80 Huffman, 'Presidential Address: The Antiquity of Lobola', p 60.

81 Interview, Pretoria (February 2005).

82 'Carved Plaster Shines in Prestigious Projects', *Concrete Trends: Official Journal of the Cement and Concrete Institute*, 8, no. 1 (2005): pp 14–15.

83 Interview, Nelspruit (January 2005).

84 Department of Sport, Recreation, Arts and Culture, 'Purchasing of Art Works for the Riverside Government Complex and Legislative Assembly' (Nelspruit: Department of Sport, Recreation, Arts and Culture, 2000).

85 DACST, 'Cultural Industries Growth Strategy: The South African Craft Industry Report' (DACST, 1998).

86 Legislative Assembly Art Committee, 'Artwork Procurement Budget' (Pretoria: MPTS, 2000).

87 As much was obvious from my visit, and this fact was verified by Sbongile Redebe, private secretary for the Deputy Speaker of the Legislature. Telephone interview between Johannesburg and Nelspruit (February 2005).

88 McInerney informed me that the South African Police, who are responsible for security at the Legislature, recently called him to ask that a fence be designed and positioned in front of the civic space of the Legislature to bar entry. McInerney declined this request. Interview, Johannesburg (February 2005).

89 Sandra Adell, *Double-Consciousness / Double-Bind: Theoretical Issues in Twentieth-Century Black Literature* (Chicago: University of Illinois Press, 1994). William E.B. Du Bois, *The Souls of Black Folk* (New York: Bantam, 1989). Paul Gilroy, *The Black Atlantic: Modernity and Double Consciousness* (London: Verso, 1993). Samira Kawash, *Dislocating the Color Line: Identity, Hybridity, and Singularity in African-American Narrative* (California: Stanford University Press, 1997).

90 Homi K. Bhabha, *The Location of Culture* (London: Routledge, 1994), p 114.

Imagination and Identification, Part 2: The Northern Cape Legislature, Kimberley

A Colonial Town

Kimberley lies at the centre of South Africa on the border of two biomes represented by the Great Karoo and Kalahari deserts. The climate is incredibly hot and dry in summer while cold in winter, with temperature extremes in the range of -8 to 40°C. The semi-desert conditions of the surrounding landscape – with its parched soil, near-infinite horizon and expansive blue skies – possess a special quality: intense, still and sublime. But the arid beauty of the land is not the reason for this town. In 1871, diamonds were discovered near Barkley West and shortly after, in the same year, a further discovery of diamonds by Esau Demoense, a black labourer, led to the establishment of the world's richest diamond mine at Kimberley. It was not long before the British Government of the Cape Colony decided they needed to own this great wealth, and so annexed the Zuid Afrikaanse Republiek (ZAR)[1] diamond fields in 1871, an action which helped trigger the South African War.[2] Present-day Kimberley sprung to life as a British colonial mining town, with diggers rushing there from across the world. But few of these early miners found their fortune. Instead, 'many diggers met their death in mining accidents. The unsanitary conditions, scarcity of water and fresh vegetables, as well as the intense heat in summer also took their toll.'[3] Ultimately, the great wealth of Kimberley fell into the hands of a small elite of white businessmen – most notably, Cecil John Rhodes, Alfred Beit and Barney Barnato – who worked to consolidate the many early mines and control diamond supply.[4] The De Beers Consolidated Mine of Kimberley was formed in 1888 and the 'Big Hole' positioned at the centre of the town is all that remains of that infamous mine. By 1914, when digging stopped here, the mine had yielded some 2,722 kg of diamonds.[5] The big hole is 'reputed to be the largest handmade cavity on earth … [with] a diameter of 500 meters and a maximum shaft depth of 1,100 meters'.[6]

Unlike Nelspruit, Kimberley is a town rich in architectural heritage, with many beautiful museums, galleries and monuments. For this reason, it is worth picking out some of the key architectural layers that inform this town. The Honoured Dead Memorial that was commissioned by Cecil John Rhodes,

3.1
The Honoured
Dead Memorial,
Kimberley,
Sir Herbert
Baker (ca 1904).
Photograph by
the author.

designed by Sir Herbert Baker and dedicated in 1904 is a fine example of the various neoclassical monuments of Kimberley (see Figure 3.1). Seen from one of the approaching roads, the solid and weighty mass of the base supports a doric peristyle surround which dematerialises the block, filtering light into the deep blue sky beyond. Plain and stark with its pure cubic geometries, the monument stands in silent commemoration of those who died defending British Kimberley against its siege during the South African War. The Richmond Pharmacy building in Jones Street, designed by D.W. Greatbatch (1906) provides a fine example of city retail architecture of this time (see Figure 3.2). Simple pitched roofs in corrugated iron are hidden by gabled parapet walls that front the street, and gracious covered walkways

span the pavement supported by decorative cast-iron columns. Kimberley also has some impressive modern icons, especially the Miesian, black-glass Trust Bank (1971) (see Figure 3.3), and Harry Oppenheimer House designed by Hentrich and Partner in association with Hentrich-Petschnigg and partner KG of Dusseldorf (1974).

3.2   The Richmond Pharmacy, Kimberley, D.W. Greatbatch (1906). Photograph by the author.

Finding a Suitable Site

Our quick tour reveals a wealth of architectural precedent associated with the apartheid and colonial legacy of the town. It is not surprising, therefore, that the new legislature complex for the Northern Cape, in Kimberley, has sought to bypass the established architecture of the town. The Northern Cape Legislature is certainly not contextual in the common sense of the word. Instead, Luis Ferreira da Silva (LFS), the architects for this project, have opted for a unique and visionary expression. The architects explain, 'what was required was not … just a traditional building mimicking the familiar symbols of the past regime, but one that presented a statement of creative design', a design that would 'create a new identity, a new reality'.[7] This visionary expression is twinned with an equally visionary choice of site. Situated 4 km to the west of

3.3   Trust Bank,
Kimberley (1971).
Photograph by
the author.

the CBD, the new legislature stands in an open stretch of land between the city and Galeshewe township. This portion of land forms part of an old apartheid buffer strip, which was used as a physical and symbolic barrier between the black township at Galeshewe and the formerly white-owned centre of town. Briefing documents for the design competition are explicit about the visionary intentions that this choice of site entails in terms of new development aimed at integrating across old urban divides.[8]

Ethne Papenfus, the then Speaker of the House, explained that the choice in favour of Kimberley as capital city for the new province of the Northern Cape was made by the Provincial Cabinet and was passed through the legislature.[9] There were no bids between competing towns, as was the case with Mpumalanga. Nevertheless, the two contenders, Upington and Kimberley,

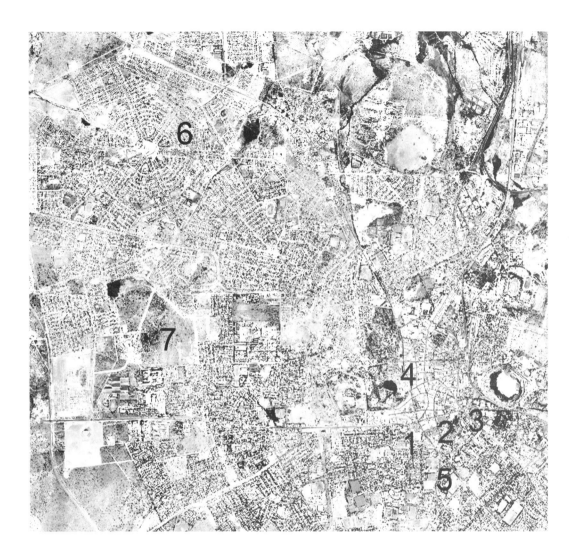

3.4   Map depicting six possible sites in Kimberley: 1) Piet Els property, 2) Oppenheimer Gardens, 3) west of municipal offices, 4) Kimberley Big Hole, 5) Northern Cape Technical College area, 6) Tshwaragano Centre. The figure 7) indicates the eventual location of the Northern Cape Legislature. Courtesy of Sol Plaatje Municipality.

were considered. Upington seemed ideal, geographically speaking, owing to its central location within the vast terrain of the province.[10] On the other hand, Kimberley has always been the most prominent town in the region, with a rich history and excellent infrastructure.

Initially, the new Provincial Cabinet was accommodated in old premises in the CBD of Kimberley, and was sharing the City Council Debating Chamber for sessions of the Legislature. The situation was not ideal; consequently, a representative building committee was set up, chaired by the Department of Public Works, to investigate opportunities for more suitable accommodation.[11]

The search for an appropriate site was initiated, with some debate as to whether existing in-town accommodation could be extended and renovated or if a new building was required. Potential sites were identified and a consulting firm of town and regional planners, Macroplan, was approached to help with assessment of these sites. A report by Macroplan initially considered ten sites, later reduced to six, ranked in preferential order – all but one of which are located near the centre of town (see Figure 3.4).[12] The first and last sites on this list disclose a noteworthy tension. Least preferred is the site named Tshwaragano Centre, which is located in Galeshewe township at the centre of a wheel configuration of housing lots, with radiating roads converging like spokes. This land belonged to the Kimberley City Council and could be acquired at a convenient price. Positioning the Legislature here would have placed it firmly on the black residential side of town – a symbol of empowerment – but would also have meant the Legislature being somewhat removed from the CBD. By contrast, the site most favoured by this list, named Piet Els Property, was a portion of open land in the centre of town near to a retail store. The central location had obvious advantages, but the land had to be purchased at a considerable cost. Willie Kruger and Ethne Papenfus confirmed, independently, that at one point in time this was the preferred site for the new Legislature, but ultimately cost considerations proved prohibitive and the decision-making process proved difficult to resolve.[13]

A crucial insight into this matter was provided by Hirsch Fish.[14] Fish was at this time an executive member of the Independent Development Trust (IDT). The IDT is a development agency which was set up under the old National Party, which gave R2.1 billion from the National Treasury, a sum that the trust manages for developmental projects aimed at poverty alleviation. Dipico, then Premier for the Northern Cape, had approached the IDT to assist with the development of the new Legislature. This was an unusual move because normally a public building of this kind would be procured through the local Department of Public Works. However, the IDT's earlier success with transforming the previously white Kimberley hospital led the Premier to ask for the IDT's input into this project. Fish says that he flew to Kimberley at Dipico's request, where he met the Premier to assist with the difficult question of the site. Dipico explained to Fish that he wished to position the building in or near to Galeshewe township, but this idea had received opposition from the City Council. Fish emphasised his understanding that this opposition was not merely a black/white political issue but was owing to pragmatic considerations because building out of town had cost implications in terms of the provision of new infrastructure and services, hence the Premier's dilemma. Fish proposed a compromise, suggesting that the building be located on the buffer strip separating Galeshewe from the town. The cost of servicing this site could be justified to the Council by the catalyst it would provide for new development bridging the white and black sides of town. Furthermore, this was Government land, and was subsequently donated to the Legislature.[15] A PowerPoint presentation, created with the help of the IDT, contains a diagram representing the developmental advantage of the buffer-strip site.[16] This presentation was shown to concerned parties, and helped to win the day in favour of this buffer-strip site.

Establishing the Competition

Although funds for the building were provided by the National Treasury, the IDT gave money for the competition and this appears to have been a key ingredient in the success of this project.[17] The competition was promoted by the local Department of Public Works which entered into a joint venture with the IDT, and the process was more inclusive than that at Mpumalanga.[18] Design submissions were called for in two rounds: an early conceptual stage, 'to identify rich and suggestive concepts',[19] and a second stage for resolving detail planning. The final outcome was announced in mid-April 1998.[20]

The 68-page competition brief, developed by Herbert Prins[21] and Hilton Schwenk,[22] is a significant document informed by careful research. The brief differs from that encountered at Mpumalanga as in addition to defining programmatic requirements, this document also elaborates on questions of political ambition, empowerment, public symbolism and architectural character. A wide range of contexts are considered, with sections that highlight the natural, cultural, political and historical heritage of the region. Specific reference is made to local fauna and flora, the archaeology of the area, precolonial settlement patterns, Stone Age heritage, rock engravings, vernacular architecture, as well as cultural and political leaders of the region. A total of 51 historical sites are noted.

The brief opens with Premier Dipico's vision for the new Legislature: '[t]he legislature project has enormous cultural and historic significance ... [it] will celebrate the leaders, artists, poets, prophets and philosophers who have originated in the Northern Cape and who have contributed to its cultural heritage'.[23] Being the first major public building of the Northern Cape, the new Legislature is required to have a 'distinctive presence, as befits its role', and to 'convey an atmosphere of balance, rationality, security, tranquillity and humanity. It should be dignified and serious, but have a welcoming, open and attractive character which makes everyone feel free to enter, safe and protected once inside.'[24]

The brief calls for a contextual approach to design and questions of public identity are raised in relation to this privileged category. But it must be stressed that this concern with context is neither literal nor singular in its scope. Instead, it provides the dispersed terms for an expanded conception of context. Contextual design must draw on the particularities of the region, such that 'the buildings should ... reflect the cultural aspirations and characteristics of the Northern Cape',[25] however, this particularity is understood to be richly layered and widely dispersed. Indeed, the idea of 'context' is allowed to operate on various levels – physical and imaginary, dominant and forgotten. Contexts are evoked in respect of the many, and are linked to the histories of different groups spanning different timescales, from the precolonial to the postcolonial and beyond. It will be remembered from the previous chapter where we identified the emergence of a new architectural discourse in South African public design, one that required an expanded conception of context; one which moves beyond dominant architectural forms and types to retrieve subjugated cultural histories and practice. The brief for the Northern Cape Legislature provides an exemplary articulation of this expanded contextualism.

Adjudicating the Competition

The jurors were treated to an aerial tour of the province on the first day of the adjudication. The airplane made a representative sweep across the vast expanse of the province, providing jurors with a feeling for the diverse landscapes that make up the Northern Cape. All interviewees expressed fond memories of this event and, it would seem, this experience influenced the decision-making process. The mixed panel of seven jurors was comprised of: three architects (Professor Lindsey Bremner, J. Forjaz who was replaced by Professor Pancho Geddes, and Mohamed Mayet), three political representatives from the Legislature (Ethne Papenfus), local government (R. Moses) and the Department of Public Works (E.V.G. Komane) respectively, as well as the chairperson of the IDT (Hirsch Fish), who is also an architect. The jurors confirmed that the adjudication was aided by a free-spirited collaboration between all parties and while the architects took the lead with architectural matters, no heated debates or politicised differences were encountered.

Seventy-two submissions were examined at the first round, from which five were selected for admission into the second.[26] The jurors' written report explains that the successful designs where distinguished by 'strong and evocative ideas', and that provided 'certain things were corrected, these concepts all had the potential to translate into unique and relevant buildings'.[27] The jurors were clearly concerned that certain issues needed to be addressed in the second round and in this regard, the report underscores a requirement of the brief that '[t]he building should be rooted both physically and culturally in the South African landscape … [and should] reflect the cultural aspirations and characteristics of the Northern Cape'.[28] And, '[t]he choice of local materials is deemed to be of great importance … because the sensitive and appropriate use of local materials could help to achieve the indigenous appearance'.[29]

Interviews conducted with the jurors for the Northern Cape Legislature competition proved less informative than was the case with Mpumalanga. Nevertheless, important insights were obtained. Papenfus remembers that the jury was looking for a unique and elusive quality, something that would signify that the winning design belonged to the Northern Cape.[30] She remembered the winning model, 'it looked like a flower in the desert', and went on to emphasise that this design was 'special' because it seemed to belong to the

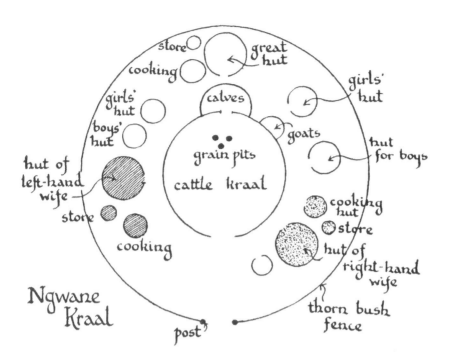

3.5 An Ngwane
homestead
and cattle byre.
Courtesy of
J.L. van Schaik
Publishers.

Northern Cape. Mention was made of the scheme's thoughtful use of open
space, the People's Square, which she understood to be modelled on African
spatial traditions such as the traditional homestead and cattle byre, which is
characteristic of the central cattle pattern (see Figure 3.5). She also referred to
the symbolic tower as the 'Zimbabwe Cone'. The ruins of Great Zimbabwe
feature a conical tower made from stone, and it would seem that the tower
at the Northern Cape Legislature is commonly associated with this iconic
precedent (see Figure 3.6).[31]

For Fish[32] and Bremner[33] alike, the winning scheme was marked by its
'originality'. The architects had captured a unique sense of 'fluidity', of
'plasticity', and Fish particularly felt this resonated with the flora and fauna
of the area. 'This building best captured the spirit of the Northern Cape', he
said. Mayet, an architect from Johannesburg, explained that the question of
an African architecture was in the back of everyone's mind at that time.[34] For
him, it was immediately clear, in the second round, that the two really good
schemes were those which were awarded first and second place – the designs
by LFS and Masabane Rose Associates (MRA) respectively. Mayet remembers
that MRA's modernist design was accomplished and very sophisticated, yet
lacked sympathy for the region: this design could be built 'anywhere' he said.
He referred to the tour made on the airplane, explaining that this experience
had given the jurors a feeling for the 'colours and textures' of the province
and, with this in mind, the design by LFS seemed to possess a unique sense of
empathy for the region. Mayet and others were clear to stress the substantial
difference between these two submissions in terms of design resolution and

3.6   The ruins of
Great Zimbabwe.
Courtesy
of Patrick
McInerney.

presentational competence. In many ways, the MRA design was a superior
submission and yet it failed to capture the imagination of the jury. Mayet
explains, 'We took a visionary approach, and were happy to support this [the
winning scheme's] poetic idea.'

Design Submissions

Design submissions from the first round were not kept by the Department of
Public Works, but fortunately, some of the drawings and models of the five
finalists were preserved and we shall now turn to study these five schemes.[35]

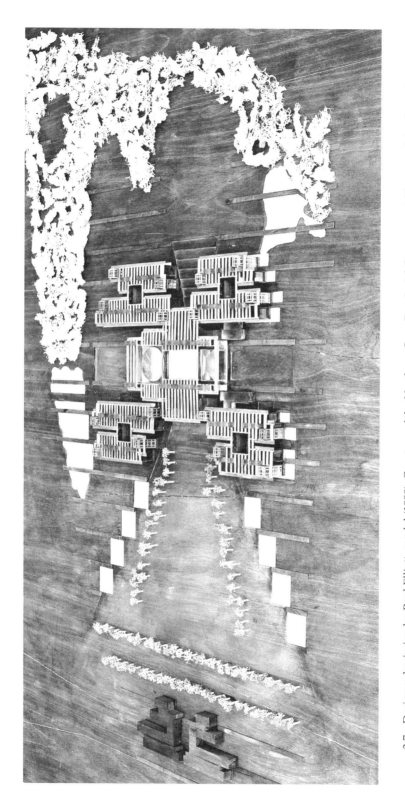

3.7   Design submission by Paul Elliott, model (1998). Courtesy of the Northern Cape Provincial Government. Photograph by the author.

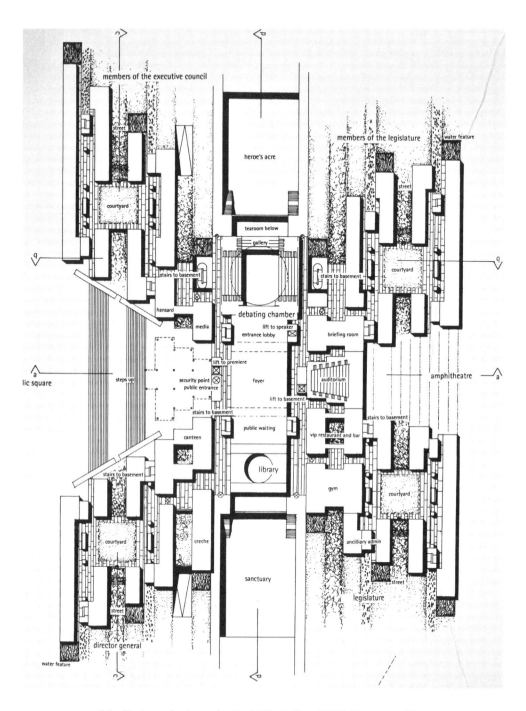

3.8   Design submission by Paul Elliott, Plan (1998). Courtesy of the
Northern Cape Provincial Government. Photograph by the author.

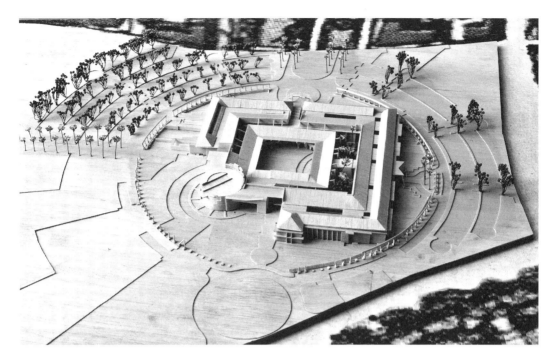

Working in reverse order, from fifth to first place, we shall first consider the design entered by Paul Elliott (see Figures 3.7–3.8). This design presents a series of ecological themes. Climatically, the building is intended as 'a thermal system, the idea of creating an oasis, "a preserve of moisture and coolness in a desert landscape."'[36] In plan, this theme is translated into an order of parallel lines or contours, which extend across the entire site, filtering built form into the surrounding landscape. This flexible arrangement allows blocks of accommodation to slide past each other, establishing relations to outdoor courtyard space. The architecture is said to be 'rational and organic', it 'acknowledges the strength of space between red earth and blue sky', and mimics the landscape with its horizontality 'in the form of low, spread out buildings, set on a stone plinth, or plateau, with a cloudlike pergola element and delicate towers which frame and celebrate the ends of the buildings'.[37] But the organic ideas which successfully inform both plan and section seem lost in the three-dimensional form, where the disaggregated parts are fused into a single dominating mass. The individual parts are connected into a megastructure with a head and four limbs, supported by a labyrinth of circulatory paths. The use of a continuous, over-sailing parasol roof structure, which shields against the harsh sun and allows for thermal cooling, is largely responsible for the unification of the building mass.

The jurors focus their criticism here, maintaining that the 'steel shade roof is costly and problematic', and furthermore that '[t]he wind towers' imagery is questionable. They are overpowering and industrial in character.'[38] The written report also makes numerous cultural and historical references to African

3.9 Design submission by AC, model (1998). Courtesy of the Northern Cape Provincial Government. Photograph by the author.

3.10 Design
submission by
AC, Plan (1998).
Courtesy of
the Northern
Cape Provincial
Government.
Photograph by
the author.

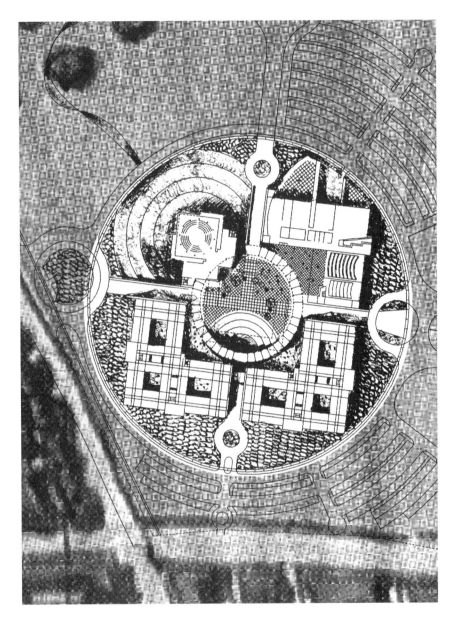

traditional wall patterns, to spatial patterns of African kraal and village, to
the sacred earth cosmology of the /Xam, rock art and so on. Yet these cogent
signifiers are not sufficiently translated into an architectural idiom, and do not
rescue this buildings from its somewhat awkward character. Unfortunately, it
would seem this design did not fulfil its true potential.

   The Architects Collaborative (AC) was awarded fourth prize for their design
which is imagined through homely and naturalistic metaphors, 'I think some
of the buildings should be like those trees next to the path, generous, cool,
welcoming and sheltering.'[39] But despite these words, the formalistic geometry

of circle and square that underpin this scheme conveys a rigid and defensive character (see Figures 3.9–3.10). The image and idea for this submission are reminiscent of the Secretariat for the Bophuthatswana Government in Mmabatho, designed by Bannie Britz and Michael Scholes (1978–83) for the new capital of Bophuthatswana, an apartheid Bantustan.[40] Britz and Scholes' response to President Mangope's request for a 'Tswana building' involved the creation of a large open space, or *khotla*, a form gleaned from Tswana settlement patterns.[41] The original design placed the Government building to one side of the central space, allowing open access into the *khotla*. This scheme was later redesigned following Mangope's request that the *khotla* be placed at the heart of the building complex. Britz emphasises that this contradicts the spatial logic of the *khotla*, which normally connects to a village.[42] The design by AC repeats the same theme, 'Our building must have a big *khotla*, a *werf*, a forum, a *lapha* in the middle which will be the symbol of that openness, where the ceremony of government takes place.'[43] Yet the dominant manner suggests otherwise: a pure form removed from its surroundings and fenced at its border by a circular colonnade. The overriding effect is heavy handed, and it is not surprising that the jury felt ambivalent towards this design, complimenting the bold and beautiful resolution of planning, but criticising the main weakness which they perceived to be the design's 'bureaucratic, government image'.[44]

In comparison with the submissions awarded fifth and fourth place, the other three schemes demonstrate more open and disaggregated geometries. Henri

3.11   Design submission by Henri Comrie, model (1998). Courtesy of the Northern Cape Provincial Government. Photograph by the author.

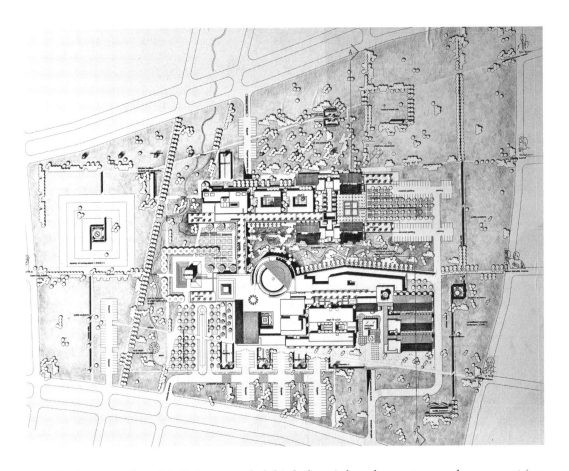

3.12   Design submission by Henri Comrie, Plan (1998). Courtesy of the Northern Cape Provincial Government. Photograph by the author.

Comrie's design, awarded third place, is based on a strong urban concept (see Figures 3.11–3.12). A set of four conceptual sketches, which are included on the competition submission drawings, shows how the design evolves from a cluster of climatically sensitive courtyard buildings arranged to facilitate linkages across the site in response to the supplied urban framework. The Debating Chamber is given a 'pivotal' position near the centre where the building splits in half, separating the Legislature from the executive and 'creating an enclosed public corridor that includes the public square exhibition of local art … The envelope of the debating chamber is peeled away and punctured at the interface with this public corridor.'[45] The surrounding spaces are beautifully landscaped with indigenous plants and enriched by a series of symbolic architectural interventions located in the landscape.[46] Detailed models, submitted in the second round, explore these symbolic interventions. Included are designs for a protected 'succulent garden', a 'reptile enclosure' containing engravings of tail patterns and footprints of reptiles associated with the province, a 'survival enclosure' which pays homage to the mammals of the province by presenting their footprints, a 'foot print enclosure' which 'captures images from the lion stories of Sol Plaatje',[47] an 'amphitheatre' to act as a focal point along Parliament Avenue and a grand entrance into the Hero's Acre featuring seated

3.13   Design submission by MRA, model (1998). Courtesy of the Northern Cape Provincial Government. Photograph by the author.

sculptures of 'the *Kimberley Eight* … forgotten heroes of early defiance against apartheid'.[48] These designs are infused with symbolism derived from the natural environment, vernacular architectures, San rock engravings, histories of anti-apartheid resistance and idealistic visions of future democratic governance. Yet despite these symbolic gestures, and the rustic, earthbound materiality of this design, the architecture remains stifled by static, monumental symmetries and solid geometrical forms – an architectural language insufficiently distinguished from the architecture of Kimberley's colonial past. As was the case with Elliot's submission, the indigenous references do not sufficiently translate into a new architectural imagination and consequently, this scheme lacks visionary appeal. The jurors complimented Comrie's submission for its 'considerable presence and monumentality', while their criticism is more pragmatic than my own, maintaining that the 'excessive reliance on elements such as colonnades, garden follies and landscaping which would give the scheme identity but might have to be omitted due to cost constraints'.[49]

The submission by Mashabane Rose Architects (MRA), awarded second place, possesses a pristine order, structured by a pair of axes, running east–west and north–south (see Figures 3.13–3.14). Entrance and primary circulation into the complex is provided by a north–south axis which traverses the site linking Kimberley with Galeshewe. This route leads from ground level, ramping up to the centre of the complex where stone 'blade walls' open onto a floating concrete deck, with the pure cubic form of the debating chamber dislodged on the western side. Open views to the east overlook the adjacent public space of gathering and onto the Hero's Acre which stretches eastward. Divided into six parallel bands representing the six regions of the province – the Kalahari, the Diamond Fields, the Green Kalahari, the Karoo, Hantam and the Namaqualand – the 'manicured garden' of the Hero's Acre contains plants from across the province, interspersed with 'walls of stone in carved relief and sculptures, creating a framework for a visual depiction of history'.[50] This east–west cross axis is symbolic of a timeline. The narration of time begins 'on the east edge of the site with Pre Colonial, moving westwards through time [along the Hero's Acre] to the announcement of our new democracy in 1994, in the form of the Debating Chamber',[51] which forms the termination and focal point of this cross axis. The more practical accommodation of office

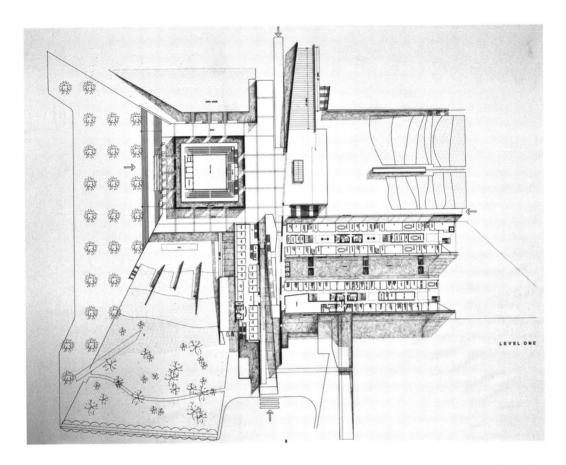

3.14 Design
submission
by MRA, Plan
(1998). Courtesy
of the Northern
Cape Provincial
Government.
Photograph by
the author.

space is neatly planned into three-storey linear blocks which reinforce the cross-axial design, being orientated in east–west and north–south directions. A careful play of levels informs the sectional development of the scheme, with buildings cut into the landscape to 'create a strong sense of place within the surroundings', and raised concrete platforms which hover above ground level, providing views of the landscape.[52]

The symbolic importance of the debating chamber is given architectural expression by virtue of its isolated form and monumental scale, creating an 'evocative image'.[53] A translucent inner chamber is raised above ground on a 3m-high base and surrounded by an outer wall made from,

local dressed stone … celebrating personalities and events from Kimberley and provincial history in the form of Stone age engravings, etched symbols and images made to touch allowing the individual visitor or tourist to interact and learn about the workings of our new democracy and the political struggle to achieve it.[54]

The stark geometry of this external form is softened internally by acoustic panels, suspended over the chamber in a cloud-like, spherical form. These panels, made from woven grass, make tectonic reference to '[t]he matjiehuis house form of the Khoisan and Tswana',[55] where mats of woven grass are

used to cover sapling building frames. This theme is later 'abstracted and mimicked' in office ceiling panels.[56] Further tectonic reference is also made by the widespread use of local materials, such as 'native stone', which is 'utilised on site for different purposes: large stones for cladding, flatter stones for retaining walls and paths, and finally very small pebbles for decorative stone beds in the gardens'.[57] In addition, traditional bi-lobial dwellings, which show a sequence of layered spaces mediating between public and private realms, are said to inform the creation of public–private thresholds and filters 'through which one must pass before entering the central chamber'.[58]

3.15 Winning submission by LFS, model (1998). Courtesy of the Northern Cape Provincial Government. Photograph by the author.

The immaculate drawings and 53-page written report, submitted at the second round, no doubt led the jurors to comment that this design is 'well handled and sophisticated. The models, drawings, etc. are beautifully presented.'[59] And yet, despite the incorporation of political narratives, and artful reference to African tectonic and spatial themes, this design failed to capture the jurors' imagination, with the jurors' report ultimately maintaining that this 'design lacks empathy for Northern Cape conditions and cultural aspirations'.[60] No further clarification is given, but the reason would appear to hinge upon the abstract nature of the architecture, its powerful and, at times, foreboding monumentality, an expressive language which does not appear to fit the new imaginary of the early post-apartheid era. Mayet's comment that this design could be built 'anywhere' is telling, especially when one considers the generic modernism that informs building façades.

3.16 Winning
submission by
LFS, Plan (1998).
Courtesy of
the Northern
Cape Provincial
Government.
Photograph
by Henia
Czekanowska
and the author.

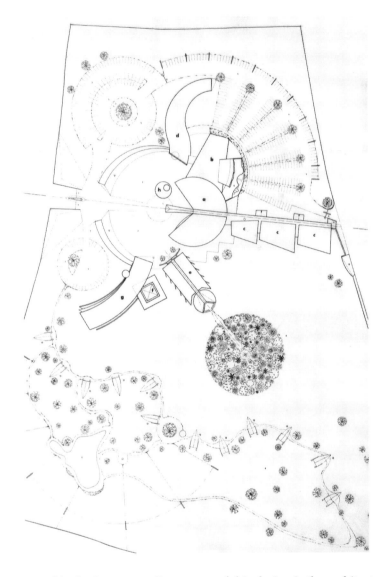

But possibly the least appealing aspect of this design is the architecture of the Debating Chamber, with its solemn order and mausoleum-like expression. One is mindful of Herbert Baker's *Honoured Dead Memorial* which emblemises colonial Kimberley, an unfortunate resonance, since it is precisely the legacy of this history that the new Legislature wishes to overcome.

The Winning Scheme

The contest between the first- and second-place submissions shows a similar pattern to that observed in Mpumalanga, where the successful design was distinguished by virtue of its more 'responsive' character, and this enabled

it to stand out against the second-place award which was understood to be 'merely contemporary' in character. The jurors' report states that LFS's winning submission was the one which:

3.17 The Northern Cape Legislature in its natural setting, LFS. Photograph by the author.

> most captured the spirit and aspirations of the people of the Northern Cape by its unique, evocative family of forms and the interrelation of volumes and spaces. Dynamic tension is created by the differentiated scales of the composition which tend to lend themselves to be landmarks rooted in local traditions and place.[61]

In marked contrast to the precise, rectilinear order of the MRA submission, the winning scheme, designed by LFS, presents a scattered array of building fragments, gathered together around a large, open public space, the People's Square (see Figures 3.15–3.16). LFS have not been vocal about their design, and their written report does not unpack the full significance of this highly original scheme. In presenting LFS's winning scheme, therefore, I shall intersperse my own interpretations of the completed project alongside noteworthy aspects of the architects' competition report.

Approach to the Legislature is currently via an extension of Nbengula Street and a new road, Parliament Avenue, which moves westward in the direction of Green Street before curving north for axial entry into the complex. Travelling down Parliament Avenue, one gets an early glimpse of the Legislature nestled amid long grasses and low-lying trees. The dominating forms of the tower and Assembly appear etched against the sky, with angled profiles not unlike the cactus plants that abound in the landscape (see Figure 3.17). One has the sense of a naturalistic expression, one that grows from the semi-desert landscape. Continuing with our approach, the road bends northward and we now get a sense of the primary axis that structures the scheme. Entry via a security checkpoint leads directly into the large circular space of the People's

3.18   The People's Square in front of the Northern Cape Legislature, LFS. Photograph by the author.

Square. The open circle is inscribed by two radiating wings of stepped seats on the south side to form an amphitheatre, which cunningly conceals ramps allowing cars to drive down to the basement parking, while the northern half of the circle is more loosely defined by three fragmented buildings (see Figure 3.18). The leftmost building accommodates the members of Parliament, central and largest is the Legislature Assembly, and to the right is the office of the Premier. Slightly offset to the left-hand side of the Assembly stands the conical tower that serves as a lectern, and to the right we have a grass mound with symbolic trees.[62] The spatial orientation of these three buildings is suggestive of an organic, loosely defined symmetry, with a central axis focused upon the assembly.

In Kimberley, the morning heat is absorbed by the parched earth, radiating back throughout the afternoon. One develops an acute awareness of the ground, its incredible mass and ability to store energy from the sun. The hard paved and barren surface of the People's Square captures this poetic sense of the scorched Earth, its mass and blurring haze as energy is released into the afternoon air. Wherever you are, big black ants traverse the hot Kimberley soil, moving with jerky crisscross patterns. If one could imagine the patterns that are formed by their hurried motion, then perhaps one would have the meandering paths that are tattooed onto the surface of the People's Square. Or perhaps the hierarchy suggested by primary, secondary and tertiary lines, which snake and encircle the ground plane of this space represent human paths trod into the bare soil. Central, yet offset to the right, sits a circular, grass mound, with newly planted trees, the significance of which will be familiar from previous discussion of the tree as the symbol for an African court. The overriding effect that is captured here by this public space is that of a stylised semi-desert landscape. This outdoor expanse is loosely formed and opens at its edges where space permeates around and in between the fragmented buildings and views are opened towards the barren landscape beyond. One has the foreboding sense of a dialectic of culture and nature, with the desert patiently waiting to reclaim her own; a confluence of two timescales, one human and urbane, the other natural, infinite and sublime. And in fact this is the sense one gets from the urbanity of the Northern Cape, where human intervention stands in stark contrast to the vast expanse of open land and sky. The fragmented architectural arrangement ensures integration 'with the surrounding landscape in an organic manner'.[63] The plan is also suggestive of the central cattle pattern, as previously noted, while the fluid geometries are possibly a sculptural way to reinterpret the soft tectonics of traditional African buildings, as, for example can be seen at Dithakong,[64] a prominent Tswana Iron Age settlement of the Northern Cape based on rounded forms (see Figure 3.19).

The architects' report prepared for the final round presents their design concept as 'attempting to interpret traditional responses to shelter, open space, ceremony and celebration through a language. African architecture developed along the same philosophy, rich in their three-dimensional

3.19   Tswana
Iron Age
Settlement at
Dithakong.
Illustration by
Tim Maggs, from
'Dithakong', in
*Archaeology in the
Northern Cape:
Some Key Sites*, ed.
David Morris and
Peter Beaumont
(Kimberley:
McGregor
Museum, 2004),
pp 38–9.

KEY
O   Monolith
(˙)   Stone ring
      ?hut
⚛   Stone pile/platform
      ?grainbin stand
▬   Lower grindstone
∴   Grey deposit
      ?cattle pen

0   100m

interpretation, while maintaining a consciousness of the local availability of materials.'[65] The architectural order is divergent and multiple, with each building being given its own, unique character. The buildings are suggestive of living organisms, and it does not take much imagination to interpret these forms in suggestive ways. So for example, we have the flower petals of the Legislature Assembly (see Figure 3.20a), the robust Premier's building, locust like with its high-security outer exoskeleton (see Figure 3.20b), the reptile like, and snaking meander of the Members of Parliament building (see Figure 3.20c), the caterpillar administration block poised on crawling legs located behind the Legislature Assembly (see Figure 3.20d) and finally the Premier's support building, added later owing to insufficient accommodation, which oddly combines many aspects of the others merged in a colourful and decorative manner. This building is located between the Legislature and the Premier's Building (see Figure 3.20e) The architects maintain that 'different buildings housing different activities not only emphasise the individuality of the different components making up such a divergent and highly charged group of political buildings but also offers the opportunity for varied and yet related architectural treatments (a common architectural language allowing an individual response to each building)'.[66]

Architectural language makes use of free geometry and playful surface treatments, which are populist, light hearted and thoroughly non-bureaucratic in character, an aspect which enables this design to challenge, more so than

others, the institutional image associated with Government buildings of the aparthied era. The architects' competition report develops some thoughts as to the 'metaphoric' treatment of building surfaces, 'finishes would include tinted plasters exploring the earthy tones of the top soil found on the site, hardy sun screens and hand crafted finishes as detailed in our drawings. Where possible these surfaces will make reference to indigenous craft and decorative traditions.'[67] And later, '[t]he introduction of artistic poetry in the form of mosaics, sculptural elements, detailed surfaces, and earthy finished colours, is hopefully reminiscent of beadwork, basket weaving and traditional

3.20 a–e: The buildings of the Northern Cape Legislature, LFS (left to right, top to bottom). Photographs by the author.

3.21   Profile
head sculptures,
Northern Cape
Legislature, Clive
van den Berg.
Photograph by
the author.

skin decoration (scarification).'[68] These intentions are consistent with other
competition submissions that follow what I have previously termed an
expanded contextualism, where cultural and political references, associated
with different histories are layered onto the façade. And once again, we
have poetic relations to landscape, tectonic memories of African crafts and
decorative traditions as well as anti-apartheid narratives, an aspect which
will be highlighted in due course. Yet LFS's design furthers these ideas in
at least three significant ways: with regard to the formation of new imagery,
through the interactive design of public space and through an exploration of
cosmopolitan narratives.

New Imagery

The first innovation concerns the creation of new imagery which seeks to
establish a visionary break from the past. This commitment is articulated
in the section describing the Hero's Acre, a public park with sculptures that
celebrate 'historically neglected heroes … we proposed an avenue of profile/
sculpture heads lining the meandering road as it moves towards the heroes'

acre situated along the eastern site boundary'.[69] The winding path, which connects to the park, is shown on the competition entry drawings, weaving to the right of the People's Square. A sketch of these 'profile/sculpture heads' demonstrates how they double as seats or picnic spots shaded by hair, in fact shade cloth, which blows away from the profiled heads. Heroic symbols are used as functional support for everyday recreational retreat. The architects explain, '[i]n this we do not wish to repeat the traditional styles and materials used for the deification of political heroes in the past. It is important to signal a political change with simultaneous change of imagery, materials, context and the spatial relations between citizen and representation of hero.'[70]

Unfortunately, owing to budget constraints, the Hero's Acre was not realised. Instead the few profile heads that were made for samples were salvaged as landscape sculptures (see Figure 3.21). But more importantly, this commitment to the creation of new imagery has influenced almost every aspect of this project. Early indications of what this imagery might entail can be seen from the cartoon-like drawings which illustrate the written report. These drawings have a popular, iconic quality, humorous and free (see Figure 3.22). Common people, iconic symbols and spaces appear as if in spontaneous dialogue with each other: bodies, spaces and icons seem interchangeable. A further instance of the new imagery can also be seen in the linear sequence of small images which frame the bottom edge of the design drawings submitted in the second round (see Figure 2.23) These representations are graphically presented in bold, black and white tones, and include images of indigenous plants, textures of grass and trees, cactus plants, traditional costume and headdresses as worn by African women, vernacular stone wall patterns, San rock art, informal township settlement patterns and local Earth and rock formations. Importantly, these images are interspersed with vignette sketches showing architectural surfaces and three-dimensional views of the intended project. Images of this kind can also be found on other design submissions, but the difference here is the way the textures and forms depicted by these images have been translated into the architectural idiom of this design. It is not always easy to pinpoint precise relations between any one image and its translation into architecture. Instead, the full sequence of images is suggestive of a visual language which is captured, in a loose and partially abstract way, by the organic manner of this design, and the rich texturing of its material surfaces.

The concern with new imagery is furthered by South African artist Clive van den Berg, who was appointed by the architects to design and procure artworks for the Northern Cape Legislature. Van den Berg explained to me that he did not wish to collect paintings, frame and hang them on a wall in the manner associated with colonial and modernistic practice.[71] And in this respect, his art policy differs from that followed at Mpumalanga, where arts and crafts are displayed on walls and in glass cabinets as in museum or gallery exhibits. Instead, he wished to challenge spatial limits set between fine art, handcrafts and architecture. Disciplinary boundaries, which protect the status of 'fine art', are mostly a product of Eurocentric preoccupation with

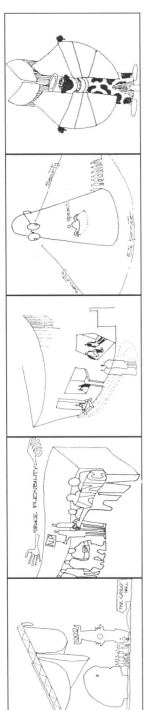

3.22　Drawings that illustrate LFS's competition entry report (1998). Courtesy of the Northern Cape Provincial Government.

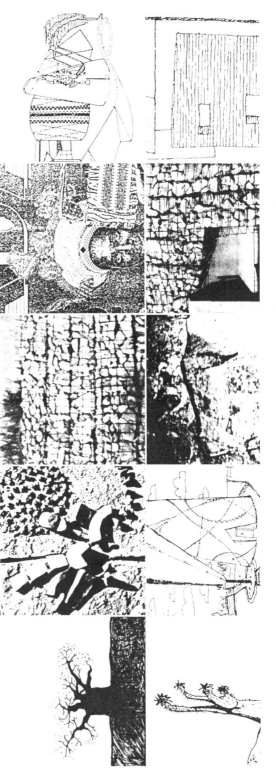

3.23　A selection of iconic images used to frame the bottom of LFS's competition submission drawings (1998). Photographs by Henia Czekanowska and the author.

3.24 a–h: Sculptural interventions and surface treatments at the Northern Cape Legislature, Clive van den Berg (left to right, top to bottom). Photographs by the author.

aesthetic autonomy, whereas African creative traditions have tended to be less differentiated from daily life. With this in mind, Van den Berg set out to establish a team of local artists and crafts people to help realise sculptural and decorative designs that could be worked into the architectural surfaces of the Northern Cape Legislature. Collaborating with the local Department of Arts and Culture, Van den Berg made a representative tour of the province in search of suitable candidates. Twenty individuals were selected and brought to Kimberley for intensive workshop training sessions, and finally ten were selected to work on the project. Van den Berg found he needed to take a lead in the design of mosaics, sculptures and other decorative motifs, but also allowed his co-workers room for improvisation. Material processes were selected with empowering skills transfer in mind, with an emphasis placed upon casting procedures, mosaics and welding.

Van den Berg wished to use art and design as a way of contributing to a new public language, a new identity for post-apartheid society. He wished to give 'echo to post-apartheid subjectivity', and therefore found it was necessary to look to material sources, expressive languages and human subjectivities that were previously denied. His visionary designs take clues from multiple sources, such as attitudes to landscape, glacial rock formations that feature in the province, fauna and flora of the region, San rock art, ways of moving through space, popular icons from the years of anti-apartheid struggle, symbolic reference to popular political sentiments and so on. His work has resulted in a variety of free spirited, and at times enigmatic interventions, which include wall protrusions, cast aluminium and brass plates, decorative screens, profiled heads, wall mosaics, incised figures, free-standing sculptural forms and wire frames (see consecutively, Figure 3.24 a–h). We shall consider some of these works where pertinent to the discussion that follows.

Interactive Public Space

A second innovation of this scheme is its careful, interactive consideration of public space. The complex is structured by an axial route that traverses the entire complex, from the main southside entrance at the end of Parliament Avenue, continuing onto the north-most side where the intention is for a future tram line to connect back to the CBD.[72] Upon entry, one gains immediate access to the People's Square and it is possible to circulate uninhibited on the outside, around the Assembly, along and under the administrative building which stands on *pilotis*. The original design intended a completely free and uninhibited public passage across the site but, unfortunately, entrance into the complex is restricted by security guards, a matter which displeases the architects.[73] Nevertheless, visitors are welcome, provided correct arrangements are made.

The intended north–south passage is facilitated by places to sit and various sculptural interventions adorn this route. For instance, we can see how the wall thickness of the assembly is hollowed out to allow for 'places to sit, relax,

3.25 a–c: Interactive public spaces and artworks at the Northern Cape Legislature, LFS and Clive van den Berg (left to right). Photographs by the author.

hide and watch other people' go by (see Figure 3.25a).[74] The wall protrusions seen here are by Van den Berg and were inspired by *mesems* – rock-shaped plants that are unique to the Northern Cape (see Figure 3.25b). Further along, under the administration building, a group of strangely enticing chair sculptures are waiting to be found, where one can sit and enjoy the shade. Once again, these are sculptural works by Van den Berg (Figure 3.25c). And as previously encountered, there is also the design for shaded picnic spots which 'will be provided in the greater site landscape, shaded secluded spots offering litter disposal points, and natural earth areas for recreation or the place to eat lunch'. However, by far the most successful interactive aspect of the scheme has proved to be the People's Square, with its semi-circular open-air seating arrangement, hard landscaped surface, symbolic trees and tower, and this space has successfully hosted numerous public events.[75]

Cosmopolitan Narratives

Finally, the third unique element that is introduced by LFS's design report – which in effect combines the implications of the previous – is a preference for cosmopolitan representation. This idea is first presented in relation to the Madiba Park,[76] which is 'envisaged as a formalised circle, a forest of indigenous trees and a selected collection of exotics, chosen as a representation of the cosmopolitan make up of our national community standing together, growing together'.[77] The park is positioned to the rear of the Premier's Building such that '[v]iews from the Speaker's office and the Premier's office are centred on the forest and in turn its focal point, the celebratory statue of Nelson Mandela.'[78] From this, we can see how cultural diversity is linked to a naturalistic metaphor of biodiversity and co-joined to the necessity for conservation of heritage, a cultivation of the many and the multiple. The competition report does not take these ideas any further, yet they reappear in a later report prepared by LFS for the occasion of the Dubai International Architectural Awards. In this second report, we read that '[a]n attempt to literally portray any single theme found in one's examination of the context, ran the potential risk of alienating some other equally valid ingredient. We, therefore, sought to create buildings that made allowances for all readings.'[79] And soon after, we are informed that 'it is dangerous to create a public building that expresses a single interpretation or vision as in this, many other valid histories would be disenfranchised or excluded'.[80] This scheme's reliance on a playful dispersion of building fragments and surface elements gives substance to this notion of a cosmopolitan narrative.

This concern with cosmopolitanism raises some important questions of democratic symbolisation. Democracy must go beyond an easy representation of the common will. Commonality is not merely given, it is achieved and produced, and the process of this production also needs to be democratised. The process needs to be as inclusive as it can be. Democratic culture must open itself to forms of difference and questions of otherness. Conflicting voices should not be silenced in favour of the comfortable totality. From this consideration, it may appear that singularity, totality and unity are forms ill-suited to democratic symbolisation, for singularity is dominance and dominance is counter-democratic. Now, I wish to suggest there are at least two fundamental ways to answer this problem of the dominant representation. We can either replace a dominant presence with a universal neutrality (an empty signifier), or with a cosmopolitan multiplicity (a saturated signifier). In the first instance, we have a signifier which attempts to stand above history and beyond the specificity of any one cultural position. The rationalist, internationalism of the modern movement in design would appear to be such an attempt at neutral universality, a mode of symbolisation, or at least of 'rational design process', which tried to be valid for all circumstances. Modernity, a condition of the contemporary, was written behind the back of each and every cultural particularity, while modernism, the 'authentic' expression of modernity, was by inference assumed to be valid everywhere. But the problem with this idea issues from the observation that architectural modernism is neither neutral nor transcendent, but rather is deeply entangled within the trajectories of European history. On a more philosophical level, we may assert the following: that the very notion of universality is itself a specific cultural production, that not all cultures have laboured to produce this transcendent ideal, and, furthermore, that colonial violence has been implicated in attempts to impose Western constructions of universal rationality upon others. So it would seem the neutralised, universal image, when read in the context of South Africa's early postcolonial and post-apartheid condition, does not provide what is required.

Another alternative is a cosmopolitan representation, one that recognises the multiplicity of cultural difference, and so attempts a representational strategy that takes this multiplicity into itself. In so doing, the dominance of the one is opened up and saturated by traces of the many. Of course, there are practical limits as to what can be achieved from this as every built representation must surely posses some particularity of its own. Yet this particularity, this unique character, can be pluralised. The Northern Cape Legislature attempts to do this through the use of multiple references, metaphoric layers and the loose play of fragmented elements. Some may argue that a cosmopolitan representation risks losing its specificity, and thereby the valid concern for an African identity in design will be relativised. Our attempts to empower the symbolisation of Africa will be diluted. But this need not be the case, and, besides, this begs questions of essence and authenticity for what precisely is the singular and the unique expression of an African way of life? A cosmopolitan conception of Africa, her multiplicity of differential histories, is the conception and the identity, or identities of Africa, which must concern contemporary democratic politics on the continent. What has been identified as the new discourse in post-apartheid design, an aesthetic dialogue, with expanded material and cultural contexts, is a move towards a more inclusive form of representation.

The Northern Cape Legislature shows the cosmopolitan implications of this new discourse and as such, it furthers our concern with an ethical orientation toward questions of difference.

Concept and Process

The two design reports referred to above are the only written contribution by the architects. My research interests led me to talk to the authors of the Northern Cape Legislature. Interviews conducted with Clara da Cruz Almeida and Kevin Johnston, project architects with LFS for the Northern Cape Legislature, revealed some fascinating insights into the design process which help to explain the originality of their approach.[81] The competition brief presented a clear description of planning requirements, structured around three functional zones, each with discrete blocks of accommodation: zone one accommodates the debating chamber with its ancillary facilities, zone two contains offices for members of the legislature and administrational staff, whilst zone three supports the executive wing, with offices for the premier, members of the executive committee and the director-general.[82] At an early conceptual stage, this division of accommodation was translated into separate buildings. The architects worked with Plasticine, creating an intuitive form for each building, and then threw these sculpted forms onto the ground. This idea was inspired by traditions of the *sangoma*, an African shaman whose divinatory practices involve the throwing of bones. The *sangoma* reads patterns formed by the bones in order to divine spirits and to know the will of the ancestors. Johnston explained that the initial arrangement created by throwing the Plasticine pieces didn't seem to work, so they threw the Plasticine pieces a few more times, sketched the patterns, studied the distribution, rationalised and rearranged the building parts. The loose geometry of the plan was formed from this attempt to capture these randomised effects, and indeed the Plasticine model submitted to the competition was created in this way. This fascinating approach has established a dialogue between incommensurable modes of thought: the rationality of a modern design process is hybridised with African divinatory practices. Da Cruz Almeida was clear to point out that the modern *sangoma* will often adopt modern objects, such as bottle tops and feather dusters, ritualise them and use them in conjunction with traditional emblems. The *sangoma* creates a hybrid mix of modern and traditional elements, a practice that informed LFS's design thinking for this project.

Johnston emphasised that at one stage in the detail design process, a concern developed as to the 'Eurocentrism' of their original design, with its preference for abstract, sculptural forms delineated by pure, clean lines – an unwelcomed sense of modernistic order.[83] As was the case with Mpumalanga, the architects sought ways to layer building façades with emblems and tectonic themes to further their earlier metaphoric intentions. Van den Berg's decorative artworks were extensively used to enrich the façades with social narratives and popular iconic motifs, while 'bad workmanship' added its own character, helping to break the formalistic purity of line.[84] The artworks were experimental, being directly applied to the building surface by Van den Berg and his team, without proofs or controls exercised by the architects. Johnston explained how Van den Berg would call them up by phone to ask them to come and take a look, and the next trip to Kimberley would be a wonderful surprise. The working relationship was one of friendly trust as LFS and Van den Berg had worked together on many occasions. The architects also began to explore surfaces, thickening the building skin and playing with materiality, earthy colours, and contrasting surface textures to particularise and differentiate architectural elements, allowing for better interaction with external spaces. Aesthetic decisions regarding surface treatment were commonly made on site in a thoroughly free spirited and experimental way, and in many respects this project captures a jazz-like aesthetic which has resulted from momentary improvisations.

Structural Type and Architectural Articulation

In the previous chapter, we saw how the Mpumalanga Legislature developed a duplicity of structure (plan type and structural system) and skin (decorative and surface treatments). This duplicity was theorised in relation to Fanon's metaphors of mask and skin, of a play between given (that is, 'natural', pertaining to one's skin) and subverted (that is, re-imagined or disguised, a form of mask) forms of identity. To facilitate a comparison between these two projects, we shall now move to consider the architectural games of structure and skin that richly inform this design.

From their intuitive experiments with Plasticine, the architects arrived at a dispersed set of unique building forms. Pragmatic dialogue with engineers enabled an appropriate technical means for the realisation of each building form, and we shall examine these formal and structural resolutions, one by one, to see what relations are implied. The Legislature Assembly and foyer make use of a complex concrete frame and a steel network to support sloping walls. The Premier's Building is a robust concrete frame with brick infill, the Members of Parliament Building is a simple lean-to roof with load-bearing brickwork, and the administrational block has a steel portal frame to accommodate open-plan offices. Architectural elaboration is resolved in relation to these different structural types, but in a playful way which emphasises material differences and complex dislocations. The only building which could be said to possess an 'honest' architectural expression is the administration block, where *pilotis*-like legs, open planning, a floating steel roof structure, *brise-soleil* style walkway screening the western façade and clear articulation of service cores, provide memories of modernist design. And yet the reliance upon contrasting material textures, and the wilful character of the façades, suggest a more earthy modernism, reinvented in response to

3.26   Interior
of the Assembly
foyer showing
repeated columns
and cavernous
space beyond,
Northern Cape
Legislature, LFS.
Photograph by
the author.

the semi-desert landscape. And, one has to admire LFS's sense of humour for housing the administration in an architecture derived from modernist design. The other buildings, by contrast, are less 'honest' and more playful with the geometric order that was derived from structural type.

The main Assembly, for the most part, has a regular concrete frame with brick infill, but the outward sloping walls proved difficult to resolve. Johnston explains that the original intention was for a 6° outward slope. The engineers preferred 3° and a 5° compromise was eventually built. An additional steel framework, with wire mesh, was required to prevent bricks from popping out from the sloped walls. This structure is briefly revealed on the inner west wall of the foyer, wrapping round to the southern side where the curved outer walls lean back to reveal a rectilinear framework of concrete and steel. The structure provides support to this interior's impressive spatial design (see Figure 3.26). Entering off the People's Square, we move via a fore-chamber and security checkpoint defined by an amorphous wall which curves to one side. Moving on, we approach the central section of the plan where the ceiling is lowered and a regular beat of columns create a forceful directionality informing a direct passage through the foyer and out to the administrative building at the rear. Slipping past the columns, on the left in order to enter the foyer, one is swept away by the cavernous foyer space where axial geometry evaporates into

fluid surfaces enlivened by contrapuntal, spatial inflexions. The architecture makes use of this dramatic contrast, directional order providing a perfect counterfoil to the dramatic floating space of the foyer beyond. This darkly moulded volume is punctuated by light which streams through seemingly deep reveals in the outer wall (see Figure 3.27). One has the sense of a natural cave-like interior. I was interested to learn about the archaeological digs at nearby Wonderwerk Cave, which demonstrate important signs of early human habitation.[85] This sense of the cave is highlighted by dark, stone textured floor tiles, and it is not long before one discovers a series of mysterious yet beautiful brass reliefs that are inserted into the floor (see Figure 3.24b). Van den Berg was inspired by San rock engravings, which are particularly prominent in the province. The seemingly random position of these inserts allows for the joy of discovery, mimicking actual rock art which is commonly happened upon by surprise, where found on rocks in natural surroundings.

The Premier's Building provides a counterexample to the fluid spatiality of the Assembly. Fulfilment of the high-security brief required solid construction, and for this reason a rectilinear concrete frame, with brick infill, was chosen. Structural frame and infill enabled the use of locally made bricks, which were of inconsistent quality, and therefore not well suited to robust load-bearing applications. A sequence of cast concrete wings line the long north and south

3.27   Cave-like interior of the Assembly foyer, Northern Cape Legislature, LFS Photograph by the author.

3.28 North façade of the assembly, Northern Cape Legislature, LFS. Photograph by the author.

sides of the building, providing bulletproof shields and filtering light for indoor offices. Internally, double-volume courts with water features open the space, adding a sense of tranquil calm. And finally, the Members of Parliament Building was designed as a linear, snaking form with a simple lean-to roof which changes pitch along its length, translating into a gentle curvature in elevation. The curving geometry prohibited the use of a concrete frame, in terms of cost. Instead, an elementary, load-bearing brickwork structure was chosen, making this the only load-bearing brick building in the complex. This simple, linear arrangement provides a flexible plan while allowing for shallow office space and the advantage this brings in terms of natural air and light. The long south façade is layered by planes of brick, glass and a floating *brise-soleil*, which provide degrees of translucency to filter the harsh natural sunlight.

Having described these different structural types and the architectural order which results from them, I now wish to consider façades which are attached to, and at times detached from, these supports. This elaboration is to further an understanding of the complex games of architectural identity that inform this design. For brevity, we shall consider the three elevations that

address the People's Square: façades of the Assembly, the Premier and the Members of Parliament buildings.

Johnston explains that the front elevations for these three buildings were 'humanised' with symbolic elements creating a face or mask which present their unique identity to the square.[86] In each case, façade treatment establishes a playful duplicity with the different structural types that provide support. For example, the main façade of the Assembly works with spatial themes set in dialogue with the powerful spatiality of the interior. A wedge is cut from the circular building mass to form a welcoming fore-space onto the public square. The butterfly roof translates into a pair of façades which rise with wing-like gestures. The left wing is attached to the building while the right wing façade has been cleaved free of the building, possibly a second slice into the circular form (see Figure 3.28). In so doing, the tension between built mass and façade is spatialised. The gap formed at this interface allows a ramped circulation which moves from the ground floor and occupies the space between building and winged façade, while the second half projects through the cleaved-out façade onto the outside where it can be seen climbing diagonally up to the balcony level above. Circulating along the ramp, it is possible to experience the full spatial duplicity of this play between building mass and winged

3.29   Cone structure with mosaic, Northern Cape Legislature, LFS and Clive van den Berg. Photograph by the author.

3.30   North
façade of the
Premier's
Building,
Northern Cape
Legislature, LFS.
Photograph by
the author.

façade. Spatial volumes and light intensity of the interior versus the exterior
are starkly differentiated and yet cunningly intertwine. Returning to the
exterior, the detached conic form of the tower stands to the left side, juxtaposed
against the almost blank, winged façade of the Assembly.[87] The relation is
one of spatial proximity and difference. The cone is richly textured by Van
den Berg's mosaic designs, depicting South African State Presidents Nelson
Mandela and Thabo Mbeki, while a blank space is provided for future leaders.
Van den Berg has made extensive use of blank spaces for the application of
future icons, attempting to create an open social narrative, one which can be
changed through time. This idea of an open narrative is an interesting feature

3.31   Winged north façade falls free of the Premier's Building, Northern Cape Legislature, LFS. Photograph by the author.

of post-apartheid public architecture, and one which features in the next chapter. Overhead, glass bulb sculptures hang from the tower glinting in the sun, which Van den Berg informs were inspired by the coloured beads that adorn traditional Xhosa blankets and an enigmatic mosaic of a head floats horizontally (see Figure 3.29). Van den Berg explains that this is the 'sleeping head' which looks upon the public square from another space and another time, a contemplative realm of spiritual reflection.[88] 'This sleeping head is a figure in the imaginary; a reminder to power.'[89]

The winged elevation of the Assembly, is mimicked by the façade of the Premier's Building, except that here the expression is more material than

3.32   North façade of the Members of Parliament Building, Northern Cape Legislature, LFS. Photograph by the author.

spatial, with façade planes that play against the block-like weight of the building mass. The front elevation is based on a metaphor of the Premier's body. A sketch included in the architects' written report shows the Premier standing with cape and outstretched arms welcoming people who are about to enter beneath his legs. The architects explain that this 'front elevation overlooks the People's Square in an all-embracing form, symbolising its role on behalf of the people'.[90] The façade is treated as dressage, firmly attached, yet gradually disassociated from the rectilinear order of the plan. Seen obliquely from one side, we see how the façade is layered by three separate planar elements, namely the front surface of the building block, the curved wings which peel off the building mass and the 'H'-shaped plane which pushes forward and through which axial entry is made into the interior (see Figure 3.30). Moving closer into the gap opened at the interface of these three planes, we can see the dramatic effect of these disengaged elements, which appear to free themselves from the solid mass of the building block (see Figure 3.31). The central 'H' plane, textured in mud brown, is richly decorated by Van den Berg. Two figures stand with outstretched arms to guard the door, their forms drawn by raised concrete bumps covered in mosaic tiles. Van den Berg explains that he was inspired by an African tradition where patterns are drawn from a sequence of bumps, as can be seen on sculptures of human

figures, especially fertility symbols. In some parts of Africa, bumps of this kind are worn as body adornment, or scarification, yet this particular practice is not widespread in South Africa. Cast aluminium plates are fixed to the façade, emblems of good governance, among which are included a book, a bowl full to the brim, a house, blocks that symbolise construction work, the head of a child, an HIV/Aids awareness ribbon covered with funerary crosses and so on. The towering figures and reflective emblems are intended as reminders to figures of power that the needs of the common people must not be forgotten.

3.33 Spatial volume behind the north façade of the Members of Parliament Building, Northern Cape Legislature, LFS. Photograph by the author.

And finally, the front elevation to the Members of Parliament Building displays the diagonal line of the lean-to roof such that expression is related to the structure (see Figure 3.32). However, the façade is dislocated from the main body of the building by a space that is carved out behind to form an empty volume at the entrance where steel roof beams are exposed. The dislocation is further facilitated by the use of contrasting finishes where the façade is textured in grey plaster with small circles embossed in a square grid pattern (see Figure 3.33). The elevation is composed of three distinct elements, the vertical cylinder, accommodating stairs to upper level offices, the primary façade plane which repeats a familiar, single wing-like motif and a free-standing column, positioned to the right (see Figure 3.32). Each of these three elements gain separate expression by virtue of careful detailing which preserves their separate identity.

Note the small strip windows which separate cylinder from façade plane, and a load-bearing pin which allows the façade plane to float free of the column.

When taken together, the three elements remain in line with each other. The column is centred on the wall plane flying above, while the cylinder, similarly positioned, appears as though sliced in half. We have a tight-knit proximity of separate parts that form an intriguing duplicity: on the one hand, the elements almost synthesise into a single totality but on the other, they assert their individuality, appearing as though to pull apart. This elevational play seems halfway between the full spatial dislocations of the Assembly and the bonded, yet layered, frontality of the Premier's façade. The large vertical cylinder mimics the cone tower which stands in front of the Assembly, only here the relation is embedded rather than spatially discrete. Thirty oval icons, by Van den Berg, adorn the shiny, white surface. The portraits are mosaics of 27 South African heroes such as Oliver Tambo, Chief Galeshewe, Robert Sobukwe, Olive Schreiner and Abraham Esau, while a further three remain blank for future representation.[91] The soft focus depictions appear to be framed as though mantelpiece portraits of a loved one. The representations capture a popular iconic quality, heroic memorabilia, nostalgic yet progressively so.

Concluding Remarks

Architecture enjoys a dense field of signification, which operates across multiple registers: material, iconic, ideational, spatial, functional and so on. No one interpretation can hope to capture all that is unique to the complexity of a single work. And why should this be otherwise? Criticism need not be definitive or complete. My own study of the two legislatures has been filtered through political questions of post-apartheid identity. At an elementary level, both projects resulted from similar pragmatic circumstances and evolved in accordance with similar cultural and political aspirations. More significantly however, both projects frame an expanded conception of context, one which includes dialogue with forgotten or subjugated histories, operating across different timescales from the precolonial to the postcolonial and beyond. Both projects accommodate incommensurable relations between different forms of knowledge and social practice. And both projects include what I previously termed 'foreign elements' (Chapter 2), material fragments, surface treatments, signs and tropes of identity, which are layered into the architectural object. This process of layering the architectural object with signs or codes of identity has commonly resulted in duplicities of structure and surface, which in turn were theorised in relation to Fanon's metaphors of mask and skin (given versus subverted forms of identity), at the conclusion to Chapter 2. And yet despite these similarities, there is a substantial difference between these two projects in terms of their respective strategies of representation.

In the previous chapter we saw how the architecture for the Mpumalanga Legislature made multiple references to African craft and tectonic traditions, but the means of representation that presented these relations relied upon aesthetic ideas of order, unity, harmony and techniques of compositional synthesis. In the concluding remarks to the previous chapter, I commented that the means of discursive representation, its rhetorical form, gives preference to tropes of tradition and authenticity. We also considered the unacknowledged duplicity that underlies this apparent synthesis. In most cases, cultural representations were applied to building surfaces, while the supporting architecture was one which followed more standard, pragmatic requirements. The Northern Cape Legislature, by contrast, consistently resists unity. Instead, the architecture plays with a multiplicity of fragments. Differences of structure and skin, of texture, materiality and colour, of plain wall and handcrafted surface are brought into close proximity but rarely synthesised. Differences are negotiated without the order of one dictating to the others. In particular, relations of skin and mask, structure and façade that were identified at the Mpumalanga Legislature, are now emancipated by the highly imaginative and playful architectures of the Northern Cape Legislature. The Northern Cape Legislature complicates literal or realist representation. We are seldom served an authentic image, a mere copy or correct depiction of African forms and traditions. Instead, the Northern Cape Legislature takes and makes, displaces and co-joins multiple references, transfiguring them via free imagination. Narrative remains open, totality unresolved. Using post-structural terms, we might say that where the Mpumalanga Legislature provides a predominantly 'centred' narrative of African craft and tectonic traditions, the Northern Cape Legislature, by contrast, is more 'decentred' and 'dispersed'.

The tension suggested by these contrasted modes of representation, as found at the Mpumalanga and Northern Cape legislatures, bear a striking resemblance to representational strategies adopted by black British artists, especially cinegraphic productions which deal with questions of black identity.[92] In his essay, 'Cultural Identity and Diaspora', a study of black British film, Stuart Hall identifies two modes of representation which correspond with two conceptions of cultural identity. It is useful to follow Hall's analysis for, I believe, it helps to clarify our conception of the two legislatures at Mpumalanga and the Northern Cape. Hall presents his contrasting accounts of identity as follows, '[t]he first position defines "cultural identity" in terms of one, shared culture, a sort of collective "one true self", hiding inside the many other, more superficial or artificially imposed "selves"'.[93] This notion implies that 'our cultural identities reflect the common historical experiences and shared cultural codes which provide us, as "one people", with stable, unchanging and continuous frames of reference and meaning, beneath the shifting divisions and vicissitudes of our actual history'.[94] A 'centred' presentation, such as the one we have encountered at Mpumalanga, is well suited for the portrayal of this notion of 'common identity'. But Hall also introduces an alternative conception of identity, stating that '[t]his second position recognises that, as well as the many points of similarity, there are also critical points of deep and significant difference which constitute "what we really are"; or rather … "what we have become"'.[95] And he continues, '[f]ar from being grounded in a mere "recovery" of the past … identities are the names we give to the different ways we are positioned by, and position ourselves within, the narratives of the past'.[96] Then later, '[c]ultural identities are the points of identification … within the discourses of history and culture. Not an essence but a *positioning*.'[97] From this conception, affirmation of the self is less a question of common ground and more a question of relative position within and across competing discourses of identity. From this perspective of the relative position, we do not require grand, sweeping narratives. We no longer require synthesis and totality, a 'true' recovery of the past or common origin, notions of cultural depth and singular essence. All we require are fragmentary points of identification. The 'we' of political identity is, after all, a wide dispersion, a constellation of differing positions, scattered throughout the social field. 'We' are the 'many'. A decentred representation, as we have encountered at Kimberley, is easily aligned to this more differential conception of identity – in the present South African context, that is.

An important question that emerges from this analysis concerns whether the critic has a right to judge between these two strategies of representation. Should we promote one against the other? Hall is subtle and engaging in that he treasures the necessary contribution that both forms of representation provide. The politics of cultural representation is a complex game, with many variables at stake. It is best handled pragmatically in response to unique circumstances and, as such, a politically conscious artist should be open to multiple tactics. For this reason, Hall argues in favour of a dialogic relation between what we have termed 'centred' and 'un-centred' modes of representation. These two modes operate along axes of similarity and difference, and we may choose to support a 'dialogic relation between these two axes. The one gives us some grounding, some continuity with the past. The second reminds us that what we share is precisely the experience of a profound discontinuity.'[98] In a separate essay, which follows an almost identical argument to the one presented by Hall, Kobena Mercer makes a similar point concerning opposed conceptions and strategies of representation, '[w]e are dealing not with categorical absolutes but the relative efficacy of strategic choices made in specific contexts of production and reception.'[99] The two legislatures demonstrate the importance of this point. But, however, the reader prefers to understand these questions of representational strategy. I think it is safe to say that the differences so defined demonstrate how similar projects, which raise similar concerns, can be answered, and appropriately so, in very different ways. A strength of the new post-apartheid architecture would appear to lie in its capacity to resist banal recipes of 'correct' style. Instead, we find a commitment to social dialogue – even if in some cases enforced by circumstances rather than goodwill – and an indulgence of the imaginative impulse, a desire to experiment, to create in new ways that were denied by the authoritarian politics of the recent past.

And one can only hope this creative engagement with questions of social identity will continue into the future as well.

Notes

1   The Boer ZAR Government was formed in 1858 in the Transvaal region.

2   Previously known as the Anglo-Boer War.

3   Judith Horner, *Kimberley Drawn in Time* (Kimberley: Kimberley Africana Library, 2004), p 16.

4   Ibid. p 9.

5   Johann van Schalkwyk (ed.), *Kimberley: The City that Sparkles* (Kimberley: JVS publication), p 7.

6   'Kimberley Mine: The Big Hole', in David Morris and Peter Beaumont (eds), *Archaeology in the Northern Cape: Some Key Sites* (Kimberley: McGregor Museum, 2004), p 67.

7   LFS, 'Northern Cape Legislature: Kimberley, South Africa' (Johannesburg: LFS), p 1.

8   IDT, 'The New Legislature Buildings or the Province of the Northern Cape: Architectural Competition Brief – Format, Rules and Information' (Kimberley: DPW, 1997), p 1.

9   Interview, Kimberley (February 2005).

10   The Northern Cape is geographically the biggest province in South Africa, containing approximately one third of the entire land mass of the country.

11   According to Papenfus (former speaker of the Provincial Legislature) and Kruger (Department of Public Works). Interviews, Kimberley (February 2005).

12   Macroplan, 'Evaluation of Additional Sites: On Which to Erect the Northern Cape Provincial Legislature Buildings' (Kimberley: DPW, 1995).

13   Papenfus also mentioned that rumours of a corrupt property deal, in relation to this site, had begun to circulate at this time, which would have made this choice somewhat contentious. Interview, Kimberley (February 2005).

14   Interview, Cape Town (December 2005).

15   Sandi Kwon Hoo, 'Govt Got Land for Free', *Diamond Fields Advertiser* 2003, p 11.

16   A copy of this presentation was supplied by Fish: IDT, 'Northern Cape Legislature Project' (Cape Town: Hirsch Fish). Herbert Prins confirmed that the buffer-strip development concept was established prior to the competition brief and the urban design for the site: Interview, Johannesburg (October 2004).

17   Prize money was allocated for competition finalists, which was not the case at Mpumalanga.

18   Entry requirements allowed anyone to enter, with the qualification that non-architects were required to form professional associations with registered architects. IDT, 'The New Legislature Buildings for the Province of the Northern Cape: Architectural Competition Brief – Format, Rules and Information'.

19   Ibid. p 3.

20   Ibid. p 9.

21   Interview, Johannesburg (October 2004).

22   Interview, Kimberley (September 2003).

23   IDT, 'The New Legislature Buildings for the Province of the Northern Cape: Architectural Competition Brief – Format, Rules and Information', p 1.

24   Ibid. p 8.

25   Ibid. p 19.

26   'The New Legislature for the Province of the Northern Cape: Report by the Panel of Judges on the Adjudication of the Competition' (Johannesburg: Herbert Prins, 1998), p 2.

27   Ibid. p 2.

28   Ibid. p 3. IDT, 'The New Legislature Buildings for the Province of the Northern Cape: Architectural Competition Brief – Format, Rules and Information', p 19.

29   'The New Legislature for the Province of the Northern Cape: Report by the Panel of Judges on the Adjudication of the Competition', p 4.

30   Interview, Kimberley (February 2005).

31   This association cropped up in numerous interviews.

32   Interview, Cape Town (December 2004).

33   Interview, Johannesburg (October 2004).

34   Interview, Johannesburg (December 2004).

35   Competition submissions are currently held by the Department of Public Works in Kimberley. Drawings by the five finalists – mostly from the first round only – have been preserved, as have models submitted to the second round, but written reports could not be found. Fortunately, I was able to obtain the reports from the architects concerned and where unattainable, written comments are gleaned from the drawings and models.

36   Paul Elliott, 'New Legislature Buildings for the Province of the Northern Cape: Report on Architectural Proposals' (Cape Town: Paul Elliott, 1998), p 1.

37   Ibid. p 4.

38   'The New Legislature for the Province of the Northern Cape: Report by the Panel of Judges on the Adjudication of the Competition', p 9.

39   *Building an African Icon* quotes selectively from the architects' written report, the original of which has since gone missing. See Christoph Malan and Patrick McInerney (eds), *Building an African Icon: The Northern Cape Provincial Government Complex* (Johannesburg: MPTS Architectural Library, 2003), p 21.

40   The Bantustans were four 'independent, self-governing territories' in South Africa, also known as the TBVC states, namely Transkei, Bophuthatswana, Venda and Ciskei. The South African Government established these 'states' during apartheid to provide a façade of self-government to the black population who were largely forcibly removed to these areas. These 'states' were not, however, recognised by any other country and have since been reincorporated into South Africa during the democratic transition.

41 'Government Square, Mmabatho', *Architecture SA* May/June (1984): pp 34–41.

42 Bannie Britz, 'Secretariat for Bophuthatswana Government, Mmabatho (1978–83)', *UIA International Architect*, no. 8 (1985): p 30.

43 Malan and McInerney (eds), *Building an African Icon: The Northern Cape Provincial Government Complex*, p 20.

44 'The New Legislature for the Province of the Northern Cape: Report by the Panel of Judges on the Adjudication of the Competition', p 9.

45 Henri Comrie, Submission Drawings (Kimberley: DPW, 1998), dwg. 1.

46 The competition brief mentions the possible inclusion of 'ancillary outside areas' which 'might include, inter alia: [a] sanctuary; hero's acre; amphitheatre; facilities associated with tourism', but no further guidelines are given. See IDT, 'The New Legislature Buildings for the Province of the Northern Cape: Architectural Competition Brief – Format, Rules and Information', p 43.

47 Solomon Tshekisho Plaatje (1876–1932), a renowned author, linguist and activist, worked as a journalist in Kimberley for some years. His book, *Mhundi*, is commonly regarded as the first English language novel by a black South African author. Sol T. Plaatje, *Mhundi* (Johannesburg: Penguin, 2005).

48 Henri Comrie, 'Detail Models' (Kimberley: DPW, 1998).

49 Technical criticisms are also levelled against the 'cumbersome', 'rigid' planning and acoustic problems associated with the debating chamber. See 'The New Legislature for the Province of the Northern Cape: Report by the Panel of Judges on the Adjudication of the Competition', p 12.

50 MRA, 'Northern Cape Legislature Competition: Architectural Competition Entry, Stage 2, Document A' (Johannesburg: MRA, 1998), p 28.

51 Ibid. p 4.

52 Ibid. p 3.

53 'The New Legislature for the Province of the Northern Cape: Report by the Panel of Judges on the Adjudication of the Competition', p 9.

54 MRA's competition report, first stage: MRA, 'The New Legislature Buildings' (Johannesburg: MRA, 1997), p 1.

55 MRA, 'Northern Cape Legislature Competition: Architectural Competition Entry, Stage 2, Document A', p 14.

56 Ibid. p 14.

57 Ibid. p 38.

58 Ibid. p 10.

59 'The New Legislature for the Province of the Northern Cape: Report by the Panel of Judges on the Adjudication of the Competition', p 9.

60 Ibid.

61 Some technical criticisms were raised with regards to unresolved planning, sectional and roof details, but this aside, comments are celebratory. See, Ibid. p 10.

62 Trees featured in the completed project, but unfortunately do not appear in the more recent photographs that illustrate this book.

63   LFS, 'Architectural Report: The New Legislature Buildings for the Northern Cape' (Johannesburg: LFS, 1998), p 3.

64   Tim Maggs, 'Dithakong', in David Morris and Peter Beaumont (eds), *Archaeology in the Northern Cape: Some Key Sites* (Kimberley: McGregor Museum, 2004), pp 37–43.

65   LFS, 'Architectural Report: The New Legislature Buildings for the Northern Cape', p 11.

66   Ibid. p 3.

67   Ibid.

68   Ibid. p 11.

69   Ibid. p 8.

70   Ibid.

71   Interviews, Johannesburg (August 2003, February 2005).

72   Urban Solutions, 'Urban Design Rationale: Northern Cape Legislature' (Johannesburg: Urban Solutions, 1997), p 7.

73   Interview with Da Cruz Almeida and Kevin Johnston, Johannesburg (August 2003).

74   LFS, 'Architectural Report: The New Legislature Buildings of the Northern Cape', p 6.

75   This was confirmed by: Papenfus, Joey ou Tim (Department of Public Works) who has managed logistics for public events at the Legislature, Patrick Moopelwa (senior manager for public education and communications at the Legislature) as well as Matome Mawasha (deputy secretary of parliamentary services). Interviews, Kimberley (February 2005).

76   Madiba is shorthand for Nelson Mandela.

77   LFS, 'Architectural Report: The New Legislature Buildings for the Northern Cape', p 8.

78   Ibid.

79   LFS, 'Northern Cape Legislature: Kimberley, South Africa', p 1.

80   Ibid.

81   Interview with Da Cruz Almeida and Johnston, Johannesburg (August 2003). Later with Johnston, Johannesburg (November 2004, February 2005).

82   IDT, 'The New Legislature Buildings for the Province of the Northern Cape: Architectural Competition Brief – Format, Rules and Information', p 18.

83   Interview, Johannesburg (November 2004).

84   Ibid.

85   Peter Beaumont, 'Wonderwerk Cave', in David Morris and Peter Beaumont (eds), *Archaeology in the Northern Cape: Some Key Sites* (Kimberley: McGregor Museum, 2004), pp 31–6.

86   Interview, Johannesburg (November 2004).

87   It is possible to climb the tower for a perspectival view, and the balcony is

intended as a platform for Presidential Address. However, the tower has not proved so useful in this regard and consequently, the towers' primary function is symbolic.

88 Indigenous cultures of Southern Africa believe in a spiritual realm of the ancestors. The ancestors look down on the affairs of men. It may be argued that the effect of their gaze maintains an ethical orientation, in that the living are obliged to acknowledge the wisdom of the dead.

89 Interviews, Johannesburg (February 2005).

90 LFS, 'Architectural Report: The New Legislature Buildings for the Northern Cape', p 5.

91 Icons were selected to be representative of different popular constituencies.

92 Stuart Hall, 'New Ethnicities', in Kobena Mercer (ed.) *Black Film, British Cinema* (London: Institute of Contemporary Art, 1988), pp 27–31; Stuart Hall, 'Cultural Identity and Diaspora', in Jonathan Rutherford (ed.) *Identity: Community, Culture, Difference* (London: Lawrence & Wishart, 1990), pp 222–37; Kobena Mercer, 'Diaspora Culture and the Dialogic Imagination: The Aesthetics of Black Independent Film in Britain', in Mbye B. Cham and Claire Andrade-Watkins (eds) *Blackframes: Critical Perspectives on Black Independent Cinema* (Cambridge, Mass: MIT Press, 1988), pp 50–61.

93 Hall, 'Cultural Identity and Diaspora', p 223.

94 Ibid.

95 Ibid. p 225.

96 Ibid.

97 Ibid. p 226.

98 Ibid. p 227.

99 Mercer, 'Diaspora Culture and the Dialogic Imagination: The Aesthetics of Black Independent Film in Britain', pp 58–9.

'We the People', Part 1: The Constitutional Court of South Africa at Constitution Hill, Johannesburg

A New Constitution

The new South African Constitution came into force on 4 February 1997, after being signed into law by President Nelson Mandela,[1] and in so doing brought 'to close a long and bitter struggle to establish constitutional democracy in South Africa'.[2] South Africa's move towards a constitutional democracy, with a bill of human rights, stands in marked contrast to the racist, authoritarian politics of the recent past.[3] At the dawn of the post-apartheid era, the ruling minority National Party realised that a future commitment to constitutional principles would be the best way to guard against retribution, while the majority African National Congress (ANC) wished to signal a change from the oppressive rule of the past, and to move in line with international constitutional trends. For this reason, politicians entering the multiparty negotiations at the Convention for a Democratic South Africa (CODESA, 20 December 1991) – where the future of South Africa's democratic turn was negotiated – broadly supported a move towards constitutional democracy. Yet the precise terms of this constitutional order were contentious. Negotiations at CODESA failed because agreement could not be found as to the political majority within the Constitutional Assembly, an elected body which was to be responsible for the drafting of the new Constitution. Circumstances had required the enactment of a constitutional order prior to the first democratic election, an order which would be required to clarify the very political terms upon which the election should be contested. The deep dilemma of such an enactment was the sense of an apparent, undemocratic process, where constitutional principles which speak in the name of 'the people' would be established behind the backs of a vote-less majority. The eventual solution involved a two-stage process, requiring the enactment of an interim constitution, which would come into effect on the date of the first democratic election and would be replaced soon after by a final constitution, drafted under democratic conditions. The Multiparty Negotiation Process, which replaced CODESA in September 1992, successfully produced an interim constitution.[4] Schedule 4 to the Interim Constitution contained 34 constitutional principles which were to constrain the content of the following democratic constitution. Since the final version could not be established, agreement had to be maintained in principle, and the Interim Constitution required that the final text be judged in accordance with these binding principles.[5]

The Constitutional Court of South Africa was established by the Interim Constitution as a new legal authority which had to ensure that the Final Constitution complied with the 34 principles, and would rule with supreme authority over all constitutional disputes. From an administrative point of view there was no reason why the existing Appellate Division – South Africa's highest court at that time, and which has since been renamed The Supreme Court of Appeal – could not have fulfilled the role of a constitutional watchdog. However, the judiciary of the Appellate Division was replete with elderly white apartheid-era judges. The expedient choice was to establish a further court of newly appointed judges, whose task was to preside over the constitution. By inference, this has meant that the Constitutional Court is the highest court in South Africa.

This institutional history demonstrates the humanistic and national–political significance of the Constitutional Court, and for which reason the questions of institutional identity that arise here register on a double surface – of private and public, of the intimate and the institutional. In prior chapters, we studied government buildings that were the markers of new political identities situated in newly defined geopolitical borders. The Mpumalanga and Northern Cape Legislatures were preoccupied with interpretive questions of local landscapes, climatic conditions and social custom, as well as formerly suppressed narratives. The particularities of geographic and social context were a leading concern. In this chapter, however, we move beyond expressions of the particular to include wider public and private narratives that pertain to histories of abuse and to the establishment of human rights.

The Johannesburg Fort

An insightful choice of site sparked the early success of this project. We shall return to consider factors that informed this choice, but to start with, we shall consider the wider implications for Constitution Hill positioned as it is on the site of the Old Johannesburg Fort. The history of the Old Fort begins with the establishment of an early prison, positioned on the crest of Hospital Hill immediately to the north of present-day Braamfontein.[6] The prison was built at the direction of Paul Kruger, president of the ZAR Government, and was opened in October 1893. The new high-security jail was intended to cater for the increasing criminal population of the time, as well as to 'intimidate and control dissident 'Uitlanders [or foreigners]'.[7] Strategically chosen, with its command of Johannesburg, the site allowed gun fire to be 'directed at anyone attempting to seize the city by force'.[8] The failed Jameson Raid of 1896 prompted the ZAR Government to build a series of fortifications with which to protect the city,

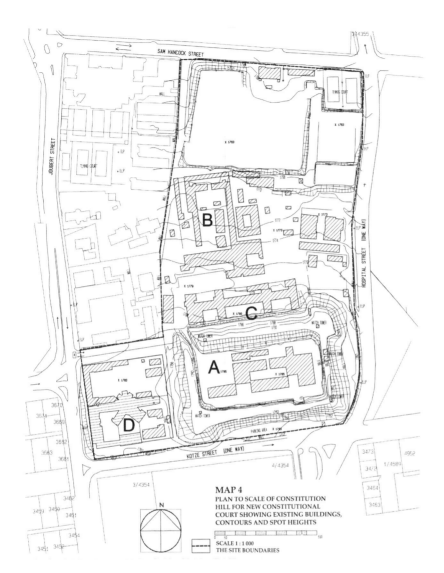

4.1   Prisons of the Johannesburg Fort: a) Old Fort, b) Number Four, c) Awaiting Trial Block, d) Women's Gaol. Courtesy of the Constitutional Court of South Africa.

one of which was built around the prison on Hospital Hill. The Old Fort was completed in 1899. Through time, this site grew to accommodate a large complex of prisons, including: a) the Old Fort, the original high-security prison which accommodated white prisoners, except for Nelson Mandela who was the only black prisoner to have been imprisoned here, b) the legendary sections Number Four and Five (jointly referred to as Number Four), which were renowned and feared for their harsh treatment of 'native' (black) prisoners who were held here (built 1902–1904), c) sections seven and eight (more commonly known as the Awaiting Trial Block, built in the 1920s), which accommodated black prisoners awaiting trial, as well as, d) the Women's Gaol (built 1907), which accommodated women, both black and white (see Figure 4.1). Together this complex became known as the Johannesburg Fort.

Generations of South African prisoners, spanning across the British colonial and apartheid era, have been incarcerated here. Prison populations were consistently diverse, including petty criminals, be they thieves or even pass book offenders, hardened criminals, and importantly, many political prisoners from the period of anti-apartheid resistance were imprisoned here.[9] Famous prison inmates include Mahatma Ghandi and the Treason Trial activists such as Nelson Mandela, Oliver Tambo, Walter Sisulu, Joe Slovo, Ruth First and Lilian Ngoyi. Records of prison inmates literally follow the contested political history of the region, from the South African War (1899–1902) to the various miners strikes of 1907, 1913, 1922; the Defiance Campaign of 1952; the Treason Trial of 1956; and on to various key points of anti-apartheid resistance: the Sharpeville shootings of 1961, the uprising of 1976, as well as the numerous states of emergency that were declared during the 1980s.

A Discourse on Human Rights

At the awards ceremony for the architectural competition of the new Constitutional Court, then President Nelson Mandela emphasised that Constitution Hill will stand '"as a beacon of light, hope and celebration. Its physical foundations will rise above the horrid memories of torture and suffering which once were perpetrated in the dark corners, cells and corridors of the Old Fort prison."'[10] It may be noted, here, how Mandela's words establish a set of parallel relations: the prison is to the court as injustice is to freedom, as the past will be to a brighter future. And it was not long before the provocative proximity of court to prison would be readily translated into a pervasive discourse on the nature of fundamental freedoms and the establishment of human rights.

The South African media was quick to pick up on the message of Constitution Hill, with numerous newspaper articles that put out news on the formation of the new court and from which we may observe some significant themes. To begin with, human rights are commonly linked to the memory of struggle, a politics of memory, that we should not forget the pains of the past: '[i]t is a site rich with memories of how the people of South Africa stood up for their rights, and of the oppressive response by the law and the legal system to their efforts.'[11] And yet this memory is also one that needs to be uncovered, because '[t]he site's history of injustice and brutality remains largely untold.'[12] And so, ironically, the fort contains a memory which persists without our knowing: '[n]umber four has always been a part of black life in Johannesburg. As children, many of us knew a brother, an uncle or even a father who had been inside … Like most people I know, I was terrified by the place, but I did not have first hand experience'.[13] For this reason, it is a place that needs to be discovered. Indeed, much like our formal concepts of right, this place nurtures principles of freedom which must be affirmed, and demonstrated to all: '[t]he Constitutional Court is emerging from its ruins as a symbol that affirms our dignity, regardless of our race or station in life.'[14]

Emphasis, in media reports, is also placed on the pain of the victim. This pain can either be mediated, that is to say it can be represented to 'us' as an experience that was endured by 'those' who suffered, their pain as proof of our freedom: '[a] place that once resounded with the smack of sjamboks and the cries of prisoners is to become a place of serenity and beauty that will give us all hope for the future.'[15] Or else we are presented with the unmediated pain of the actual victim who testifies: '[w]e were beaten and thrown around like rugby balls. We were tortured, killed and thrown out of windows. I lost many friends in this place.'[16] Some newspaper reports further the sense of personal violation by emphasising the personal aspects of the prisoner's experience, as is the case with the story about L'Solo Gama who was imprisoned at the Fort between 1940 and 1946. '"Jaaha," he sighs. "We had a difficult time in there ... hey ... very difficult ... You stopped being a human the moment you walked into that prison ... You were treated like a dog ... you were just an animal. So you had to try to be like an animal to survive."'[17] In this case, the personalisation of the victim places him in direct relation to the reader. We begin to imagine ourselves in the position of the solitary individual who was imprisoned – it could have been me. The possibility of a personalised identification is sometimes also facilitated by an appeal to the 'ordinary': '[s]ome were political prisoners. But the vast majority were "ordinary" folk who found themselves on the wrong side of the white man's law.'[18]

The voice of the victim, be it direct and personal or mediated and abstract, plays a decisive role in these presentations because the victim speaks to us from the other side of our freedom. Their stories delineate the threshold of our sense of human worth. And for this reason, the victim's eventual role must surely be to affirm the hope of a possible freedom. In the example of L'Solo Gama, the news report concludes with his words; '"[i]t's good they are building a court there now. People have rights these days and those who are arrested are arrested for a good reason, unlike in our days."'[19] And it will be seen that the architecture of Constitution Hill has built upon the substance of these public narratives.

Preparations for a New Court

The eleven judges of the Constitutional Court were intimately involved with steering developmental processes. Crucial insight into the early history of this project was provided by no less than four generous interviews at Judge Sachs' chambers.[20] I was particularly struck by the way in which Sachs crafted his detailed narrative, starting as he did with a discussion of the new insignia of the court (see Figure 4.2). Establishing a new insignia, and with it a new public identity, was the first artistic challenge to have confronted the judges and in many ways, this exercise prefigured key aesthetic questions that are pertinent to the architecture of the court. Sachs explained that the judges were eager to abandon the old apartheid era coat of arms because '[i]t was a symbol of the old racist authoritarian authority.'[21] And this introduced a fundamental question: '[t]he logo was a little Rubicon in a way, what should the symbol of the Court be? Did we go for the variance of Roman columns, blindfolded women, scales of justice, so common … or should we try establish something that we could feel was ours'?[22] The judges were mindful of the fact that the Constitutional Court was a new institution, and realised the freedom this allowed, choosing to invent themselves in accordance with the spirit of the new Constitution. Designer Caroline Parton was contacted and asked to submit a few designs. Parton's early sketches explored various themes, especially human figures and a tree. The symbolic significance of the tree, as spatial type for an African court, was previously elaborated in the chapters on Mpumalanga and the Northern Cape Legislatures. Eventually, the idea emerged to combine the two themes by placing the people under the tree. Initially, the logo was held within an enclosing circle, but a later suggestion was to let the leaves of the tree jot in and out of the circle, to free up this enclosing geometry to allow for 'growth and structure'.[23] Sachs emphasised that some 20 or 30 people gave input into the final design: '[i]t was a mixture of design by committee with a lot of chance and accident thrown in.'[24] Later we shall see how this insignia influenced the architecture for the court – indeed it raised some contentious positions regarding artistic expression.

Initially, the Constitutional Court was accommodated in Braampark, a somewhat generic office park development on the Braamfontein Ridge not far from the Old Fort. From the beginning, this was only ever intended as a temporary home, with a view to establishing more suitable accommodation at a later time. In 1996, the judges began their search for an appropriate site for the new court. Early discussions with the Department of Public Works identified a range of potential sites. The Old Post Office, a beautiful yet abandoned colonial building in the Johannesburg CBD was one possibility, but its tight urban context was not ideal.[25] Another interesting site near Crown Mines was also considered, with the symbolic advantage of being located half way between the CBD and Soweto, thus linking formerly white and black sides of Johannesburg in a manner reminiscent of the Northern Cape Legislature. But this site was somewhat disconnected and would have been 'subordinated to a commercial venture'.[26] A further option of interest was a site in Midrand – situated half way between Johannesburg and Pretoria. Yet symbolically, this choice seemed wrong because 'it would have made the court appear to be too cosy to the corporate world … That identification in a place without history, we felt, was inappropriate.'[27]

The Old Fort was also identified, and Judge Johann Kriegler informed me that he was excited by this option.[28] He was convinced that the advantage of this site spoke for itself. This was state-owned land and could be acquired without expense: the site seemed well located to the city; the historic nature of the site possessed symbolic richness; and since the prisons had moved from here some years back, the site was largely unoccupied.[29] In fact, the site was somewhat dilapidated and in need of redevelopment. Kriegler explains that he had an early discussion with Sachs to try and persuade him of this choice, while Sachs confirmed that Kriegler and he together began to rally around this choice, and it was not long before all eleven judges supported this site.

Establishing the Competition

A competition steering committee (CSC), with representatives from 'the Constitutional Court, the Department of Justice, the Department of Arts, Culture, Science and Technology, the Greater Johannesburg Metropolitan Council and independent professional members' was established by the Department of Public Works (DPW, as promoter of the competition).[30] The CSC, which was initially referred to as the New Constitutional Court Forum, convened their first meeting on 22 January 1997 and began planning the competition process.[31] From the start, the design competition was conceived in two stages, with an early 'ideas' stage, from which three to five finalists were to be selected by the jury and invited to submit detailed designs in a final round.[32] The primary shift in the development of the brief is from a national to an international competition. Sachs mentioned that this point was debated, and that initially he preferred the national option.[33] Ultimately, however, agreement was in favour of a more inclusive process as it was felt that should South African designers have something unique to offer, this would survive the rigour of anonymous adjudication. Inclusivity was also extended to the entry requirements, with rules stating that absolutely anyone may enter the first round of the competition.[34]

The brief opens with a vision statement by Jeff Radebe, then Member of Parliament and Minister of the DPW. He tells of the need to understand the past 'to identify the network of threads that speak of our pain and triumph … to weave a common consciousness that harmonises the conflicts and hurt of the past with the justice and reconciliation so necessary for the construction of a new society'.[35] This elegant brief addresses all important areas, including an introduction to the migrant and cosmopolitan character of Johannesburg (as surrounding context), a brief social history of the site, an extensive discussion on questions of architectural character, as well as technical details pertaining to spatial requirements, material and climatic concerns. A larger, long-term vision for the site is also communicated: '"Constitution Hill" … will become a major public space for Johannesburg and symbolic place for the nation, where the Constitutional Court and various national human rights institutions … will be accommodated together with … museums of national importance'.[36]

When discussing questions of architectural character, Sachs emphasised the court's fundamental commitment to engage with what he terms an 'African imagination'.[37] And he made reference to the insignia of the court, where justice is administered beneath a tree in accordance with African tradition (see Figure 4.2). Yet when it came to writing the brief, complex questions emerged in terms of how to translate this image into a statement

4.2   Insignia of the Constitutional Court of South Africa.
Courtesy of the Republic of South Africa.

of architectural character. For Sachs, the clarity of the tree icon became somewhat 'elusive' in this context, and did not seem to provide an artistic 'prototype'.[38] For this reason, discussion moved away from metaphors of justice and refocused around a statement of aesthetic qualities. Yet it may be seen that these qualities are not divorced from a preoccupation with the tree. Rather, they interrogate the meaning of the tree in a mediated way. The tree, after all, is intended as a counter-symbol, one which dethrones more conventional iconography of power, be it imposing classical façades, judges raised several feet above contradiction, or aloof, blindfolded women balancing scales. The tree envisages a more emotively humane and approachable space of adjudication.[39] Sachs explains that the judges wanted a court which would be inviting, warm, accommodating and transparent. Never imposing, and certainly not a representation of sovereign power. It should be noted that the brief makes no reference to the symbolic tree, except via the graphic layout for the cover which is derived from the new insignia of the court.

The brief's first statement of architectural character maintains that the new court:

should have a distinctive presence, as befits its unique role, and should convey an atmosphere of balance, rationality, security, tranquillity and humanity. It should be dignified and serious, but should have a welcoming, open and attractive character and make everyone feel free to enter and feel safe and protected once inside.[40]

In this passage, we can see how institutional requirements of pre-eminence are balanced with forms of social inclusivity. A building with distinctive presence, yet one which is also welcoming, making everyone feel free to enter. A rational, dignified and serious space, yet also one that is attractive, open and humane. Pre-eminence is required but without a sense of imposition – a symbolic duplicity which combines public/institutional with more personal/

intimate aspects. The brief also states that 'the building should be rooted in the South African landscape, both physically and culturally'.[41] These words appeal to some unique form of African imagination. Yet the limits of this locale are precisely not provided. Instead, the term 'African landscape' is both evocative and expansive, denoting a wide, distributed field of 'rooted' association. Importantly, the roots in question are plural in nature, and should not be understood to privilege any one particular social group, or any historical identification over another. Furthermore, identification should not be made in an overly literal way, nor be reduced to mere mannerisms. These requirements imply a form of African–cosmopolitan representation, an idea that was theorised in the previous chapter.

Adjudicating the Competition

The closing date for the competition was 6 November 1997.[42] The jurors met in mid-November 1997 for a full five days to adjudicate first-round submissions. They formed a mixed panel comprising the Mayor of Johannesburg (Issac Mogase), representatives from the Constitutional Court (Arthur Chaskalson, who was represented by Sachs), the DPW (Gerald Damstra), the National Monuments Council (NMC) and the South African Gender Commission (Thenjiwe Mtintso), a South African architect as nominated by local professional bodies (Willie Meyer), as well as two International architects (Charles Correa, Geoffrey Bawa), and Peter Davey, the then editor of *The Architectural Review*.[43] I was unfortunately unable to interview some of the prominent jurors: Bawa passed away shortly after his involvement on this jury; Correa initially agreed to an email-based interview but later declined my request; and Meyer, a well-known South African architect, is elderly and suffers ill health, and on the few times I contacted him was unable to speak. Nevertheless, I did interview some of the remaining jurors, and was able to find written jurors' reports for both rounds, as well as minutes to important post-adjudication meetings, where some of Correa's thoughts are recorded.

Prins, representing the NMC, explained that the jurors were looking for something new, something 'uniquely South African'.[44] Damstra, from DPW, remembered rigorous debate, yet noted that arguments were never 'deadlocked' in disagreement.[45] He felt that the well-structured brief was important in this respect, for it defined the parameters of the discussion. And he remembers the jurors' attempt to grapple with questions of what an African architecture should be like in the context of a modern court. Should African identity in design be 'linked' to style, to certain types of form, to climate or materials, and so on?[46] From this we have the important idea that architectural identity is not so much a self-defining property, something that belongs to the building object as such, but rather involves a relation to something external, something material, cultural, or historic. In other words, architectural identity involves a chain of signifiers. In the end, the winning approach was one that linked a 'wide range' of elements, evocative of local experience.[47] Regarding the winning scheme, Damstra mentioned the reference to a tree (in fact all jurors interviewed referred to the tree), bundled reed-like columns, sculptural features which included popular iconography, and rich naturalistic materials. As he explained: '[t]here was an organic quality that came into this design.'[48] It possessed an array of complex reference, rather than the dominance of a single symbol.

Davey explained that all jurors were patently aware of the symbolic aspects of this project.[49] 'Accessibility' was the key issue, both 'physically' and 'symbolically,' he said.[50] The court had to be approachable, requiring clarity, inclusivity and popular appeal. He recalled discussions about questions of legitimate African expression in the context of this contemporary court. The question seemed open-ended and unsure, yet the jurors were mindful of certain pitfalls. The jurors were afraid that African expression might land up as 'kitsch', and this possibility had to be avoided, Davey explained.[51] The winning scheme was successful because it was African via 'analogy'.[52] He spoke, in this respect, of symbolic resonances, such as the towers, derived from African craft. And he pointed to the extensive use of inside/outside relations, as well as the sculptural, accumulative nature of the building. Like South African society, the winning design is composed of a diversity of different forms: it is a disaggregated mass, a point to which we shall return. Lastly, some comments by Correa were minuted at a post-adjudication meeting, where he is reputed to have said that '[t]he chances were good that the winning entry would become a watershed in the history of South African architecture and that it would make a contribution to the development of a new style in architecture.'[53] Correa 'referred to a new "voice of African Architecture"'.[54]

It is remarkable that four of the five finalists were South African architects, while the fifth was entered from Zimbabwe – this, the reward of anonymous adjudications. And, one can only imagine that local architects benefited from proximity to the site and an intuitive feel for the challenge at hand. No hierarchy of place was given to the four second-place designs, although three schemes were commended for their energetic and imaginative development: namely the projects by OMM Design Workshop and Urban Solutions (OMMUS), Planning and Design Consultants (PDC) and Justin Snell.[55] Taken together, the five schemes demonstrate a diversity of design approach, and the discussion that follows will arrange the four unsuccessful schemes into pairs to highlight contrasting themes.

Design Submissions

Pearce Partnership (PP), an architectural practice based in neighbouring Zimbabwe, submitted their scheme in collaboration with a local firm, GAPP Architects and Urban Designers. The design comprises three cylindrical forms which kiss at their circumference (see Figures 4.3–4.4). This north–

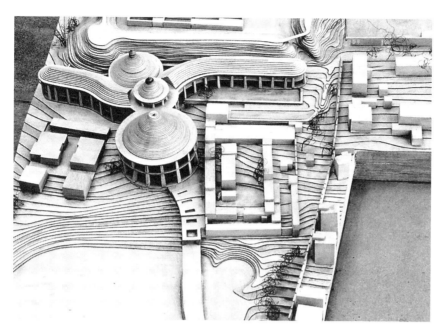

4.3 Design submission by PP, model (1998). Courtesy of the Republic of South Africa. Photograph by the author.

south orientation is contraposed by a long east–west wing of accommodation. Starting from the west, this long wing can be seem to snake along the ramparts of the Old Fort before curving towards the centre of the three circular forms, then back again as it moves beyond onto the eastern side of the site. This arrangement opens space where the Awaiting Trial Block once used to stand, and the footprint of this demolished structure is commemorated by a pool. Here, 'the walls of the original building (using original bricks) are rebuilt in the pool so that they just break the water's surface'.[56] The organic fluidity suggested by the plan stands in stark contrast to the fragmented, rectilinear order of the various prison complexes that inform this site. The largest of the three cylinders, which pushes out towards the north, can be seen to dominate the skyline when viewed from the north. Yet oddly, this prominent form accommodates parking in a spiral-like fashion on the lower levels, with a library above. The court chamber, by contrast, is positioned more discreetly to the south, where it appears to hide beside the ramparts of the Old Fort. Public/private relations are neatly resolved in the section where the ground and first floors are given over to public use, while judges are accommodated on the second floor. And although extensive views are granted to the north, the raised public galleries might also suggest aloof detachment.

Discussion with jurors pointed to the contentious nature of this design. Without doubt, this scheme profits from bold reference to traditional African forms, derived from cone-on-cylinder-style huts common throughout rural areas of South Africa. As the architects explain: 'traditional rural forms were consciously chosen in preference to rectilinear axial forms of usually western urban origins'.[57] The jurors acknowledge this contribution, maintaining that '[t]his is a design which, more than any other … attempts to imbue the building

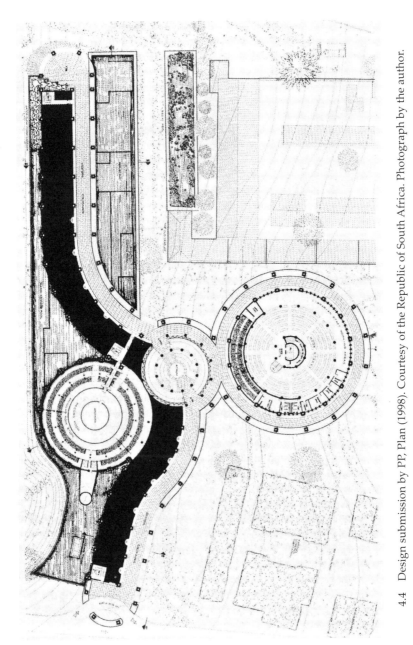

4.4 Design submission by PP, Plan (1998). Courtesy of the Republic of South Africa. Photograph by the author.

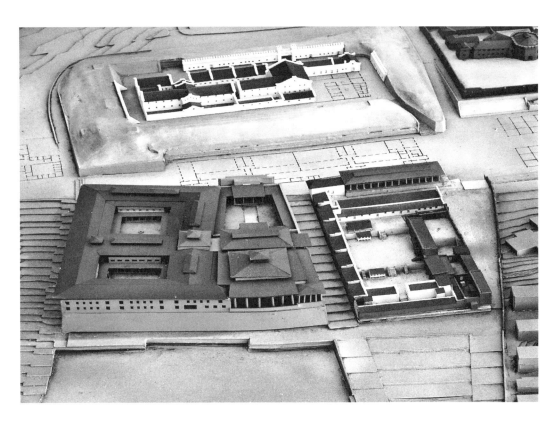

with a sense of African-ness'. But do these rural forms survive the massive jump in scale that is required when transposing a small residential hut into a large public structure required by the court? It's an interesting question, and Damstra, for instance, stated his belief that a transposition of this kind is legitimate, that indeed African architectural themes may be developed in this way. Yet for him, the deeper complexity of the project concerned whether this strategy is one that also resonates with the modern, urban and legal context of the court. After extended discussion, the jurors did not think this the case, expressing their concern that 'for all the welcome attempt to make the building symbolic of South Africa by taking as model essentially traditional rural forms, the design may express no more than the pseudo-authenticity of a game lodge'.[58]

4.5 Design submission by Justin Snell, model (1998). Courtesy of the Republic of South Africa. Photograph by the author.

The design submitted by Snell stands in marked contrast to the previous submission. For where PP insert 'foreign' forms associated with a rural vernacular, Snell seeks to order implied geometries and spatial types that exist on the site. The scheme evolves from a typology of low-lying brick buildings with simple pitched roofs formed around outdoor courts, as evidenced by the prison buildings on this site (see Figure 4.5). Quoting the *Shorter Oxford Dictionary*, the architect defines a Citadel as '[t]he fortress commanding a city which it serves to dominate or protect.'[59] The duplicity implied by this definition, to *dominate* or *protect*, inspires the leading analogy of this project

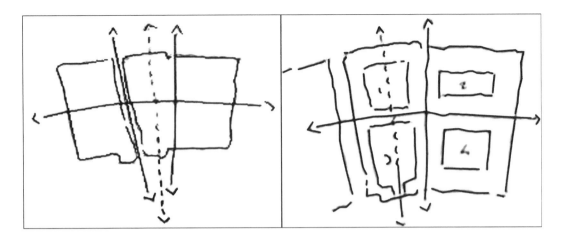

4.6   Design
submission by
Justin Snell,
conceptual sketch
(1998). Courtesy
of the Republic
of South Africa.
Photograph
by Henia
Czekanowska
and the author.

which seeks to mirror the prison as a court. A design sketch shows how the
new building, positioned to the east of Number Four, reinforces a symmetrical
order that is implied by the site (see Figure 4.6). This symmetry attempts to
establish a symbolic mirror transforming old into new, from *dominate* to *protect*.
'The "Native Goal" as the mirror of the Constitutional Court will become a
museum and commemoration of Constitution Hill's carcereal history.'[60] A
mirrored displacement from prison to court is additionally rendered through
a play on the words 'number' and 'four.' Hence: '[t]he memory of no. 4 is
simultaneously commemorated and transformed in the creation of a building
which revolves around four Courts, the fourth of which is the Constitutional
Court itself.'[61] Open-air courts for public entry, the judges and the library
as well as the indoor court chamber, make up the four, and together they
structure the bold rectilinear symmetries of this plan.

The strict order of the plan is projected into the surrounding site, and to the
city beyond, positioning Constitution Hill at the centre of an urban, Beaux-Arts-
like cross axis. A grand public space, 'Constitution Square', made possible by
the demolished Awaiting Trial Block, is established in front of the prison and
court.[62] This space establishes the grand east-to-west pedestrian axis, which
runs across the entire site. While a north-to-south cross-axis moves down the
'Great Steps', sandwiched between the court and Number Four, leading onto
terraced steps and gardens which graciously treat the north-most side of the
site.[63] A statue of Nelson Mandela stands at the intersection of these axes, and
it is at this point in the architectural narrative that one has the unfortunate
sense that we are standing on a piazza flown in from classical Rome.

The symbolic duplicity of court and prison that is written into the symmetry
of the plan also informs choice of building materials, which combine existing
with new material, '[i]n this way the new buildings can rise phoenix-like
out of the old having a new identity.'[64] Yet the new identity of our phoenix
is questionable. For despite the interesting word play – of domination or
protection, prison or court, and the symbolism of symmetrical mirrors, which
remembers what is inverted – this project nevertheless does not provide an

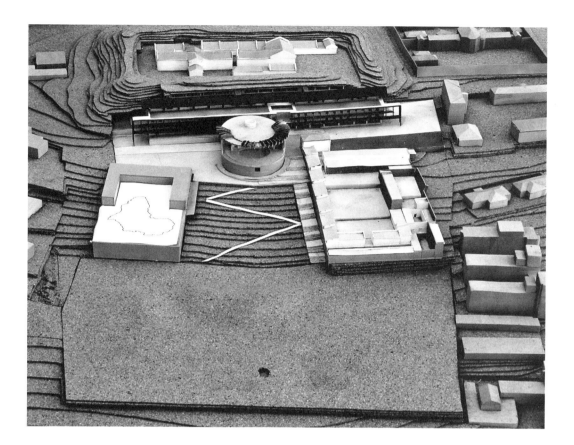

imaginary break. Indeed, the symbolic mirror envisaged by this design risks a reinstatement of past symbols and types. The jury applauded the generous and welcoming use of public spaces and gardens, the well-considered east–west passage across the site, the use of courtyard typology, as well as the poetic commemoration of the Awaiting Trial Block. But not surprisingly, they state their concern that 'the court chamber is dreary and authoritarian, more like a magistrates' court than a chamber in which the Constitution itself can be appropriately deliberated upon'.[65] They add: '[d]eveloped in the wrong way, this design could topple into a parody of Colonial classicism.'[66] And it is worth noting that issues raised by this scheme will resurface in the following chapter on Kliptown.

The design entered by Planning and Design Consultants (PDC) develops a bold yet simple plan which dialogues with the existing ramparts of the Old Fort (see Figures 4.7–4.8). Two long bars of two-storey accommodation are formed in an east-to-west orientation, one submerged beneath the ramparts, the other running parallel on the northern side, with a long pool of water between. The buried portion houses the library, whereby past fortifications are transformed into a space of future knowledge and learning, which, as the architects note, 'is a wonderful reversal'.[67] The other bar, running parallel to the buried library, accommodates judges' chambers on upper levels with

4.7   Design submission by PDC, model (1998). Courtesy of the Republic of South Africa. Photograph by the author.

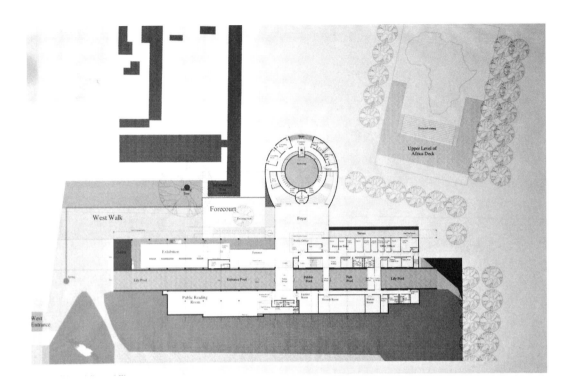

4.8 Design submission by PDC, Plan (1998). Courtesy of the Republic of South Africa. Photograph by the author.

public areas and administration on the ground floor. The space between is stepped in the sectional plan, where light filters through to the reflective pool at the lower level. This tight formation maximises open space to the north, and provides a quiet, rectilinear frame from which the court chamber makes its dramatic projection into space. The curved surface of the court chamber is double glazed with electro-chromic glass and timber filigree screens that alter the transparency of the glass, such that '[t]he chamber in session is instantly an internal world focused on the speaker: in recess, the sweep of the skyline and the passing thundershowers are brought into the chamber.'[68] The chamber has a powerful presence on the hill, where it looks down over the 'court lawns' and 'constitution field' on the northern side.[69]

The architects' written report emphasises the synthetic unity and iconic nature of their design. This approach hopes to produce an 'icon' that has 'transcended its symbolic parts and become a great social artefact that resides in the collective and individual memories of the citizens as the "Court"'.[70] Yet the transcendent icon that is offered is one steeped in the language of architectural modernism. The jurors' report at the first round commended this scheme for its clarity and careful site relations, but bemoans the fact that this design 'could in a sense be anywhere and we believe that it should respond more clearly to its role as a symbol of justice in South Africa'.[71] Unfortunately, however, the second submission did not address these concerns. Instead, the final written report appears to argue around the point. The report speaks of a 'tapestry' of influences, but fails to specify where these influences come from

4.9 Design submission by HJH, model (1998). Courtesy of the Republic of South Africa. Photograph by the author.

– no actual reference is made to historical particularities in this regard.[72] This skilful scheme ultimately collapses into a serene, yet false, universality, one that fails to address the symbolic questions that are raised by the brief.

Holm Jordaan and Holm's (HJH) submission contrasts with the previous, replacing PDC's iconic abstraction with a more figurative approach (see Figure 4.9). The written report opens with their primary iconic motif: 'HOLD HANDS … The constitution is about people. People from different backgrounds willingly come together. They stand in a circle holding hands.'[73] Accompanying sketches demonstrate how this idea is translated into architectural form (see Figure 4.10). Three human figures turn into towers, and are used to 'accentuate the three stakeholders: public entrance, judges' domain, library', which respectively represent 'the peoples' interest, the judiciary's judgement [and] the accumulated record and international wisdom on human rights'.[74] The towers also act as light scoops, filtering natural light into the interior of the building. The compact mass floats above ground, with a public entrance via the exhibition space, which is the only indoor space on the ground floor. A public foyer, the court chamber, library and administration are housed on the first floor, with the second floor given over to judges' accommodation. A

4.10   Design submission by HJH, conceptual sketch (1998). Courtesy of the Republic of South Africa.

spherical court chamber floats at the centre of the composition symbolising that '[t]he constitution is the centre point, precious, intangible, the discussion point between people, the fire warming us all.'[75] The architects also appeal to a tree as a metaphor for the new complex: 'TO GROW LIKE A TREE ... It grows out of the existing buildings ... the Constitutional Court bridges past differences and extracts from the environment a striving to orderly unification and co-existence.'[76]

Despite some technical criticism, the jurors' report from the first round welcomes the figurative symbolism of this design. Yet it also adds a cautionary note that 'the clarity with which these forms are expressed leaves room for improvement'.[77] And one does get the sense that building accommodation is inelegantly squeezed into a restricted formal envelope. The final plans make some improvement in this regard, yet the jurors 'did not think that the new [i.e. final] submission showed the full development which it was hoped for'.[78] The critical comments remain on a technical level, but I would suggest the failing of this design comes from its overly bold, foreign character: a spaceship that has landed to monitor proceedings at Constitution Hill.

The Winning Scheme

The four entries considered above show a wide range of building types informed by different conceptions of historical context and differing approaches to iconic symbolisation. The winning scheme, submitted by a consortium of two firms OMM Design Workshop and Urban Solutions (OMMUS), was the richest of the final submissions because it combines important aspects of the other four, with its feeling for multiple contexts supported by differing forms of iconic expression (see Figures 4.11–4.12).[79] It is a subtle and sophisticated scheme

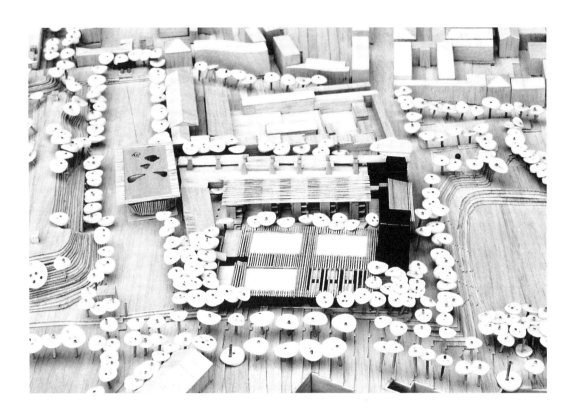

which resists simple description. The design reveals a unique, fragmented character, one which is carefully tuned to the particularities of the site and symbolises the cosmopolitan requirements of the brief. A serious manner is successfully synthesised with layers of free and inviting transparency. The design report, submitted at the second round, presents a dazzling elaboration of urban and architectural design concepts that helps to unpack the incredible density of this winning design. The text opens with a discussion of democratic urban space: '[t]he way cities are designed either invites normal human interaction or restricts it.'[80] One's freedom to sit, stand, chat, linger or move on, are fundamental supports for the democratic use of public urban space. The architects explain:

4.11 Winning submission by OMMUS, model (1998). Courtesy of the Republic of South Africa. Photograph by Henia Czekanowska and the author.

[g]rand dominant monuments are only needed to represent victories of war, exclusivity in the face of threat to an unpopular social system, economic or elite social power, or the unattainable – places of God or the gods. The Constitution, and therefore its houses and precinct, have nothing in common with any of these situations.[81]

These words demonstrate the authors' commitment to an overthrowing of the conventional symbols of public power, to the dethroning of the monument, itself a colonial type, in favour of more transparent and welcoming spaces of inclusivity. The design achieves this ambitious goal through various spatial and tectonic strategies. To start with, we may consider the way the court

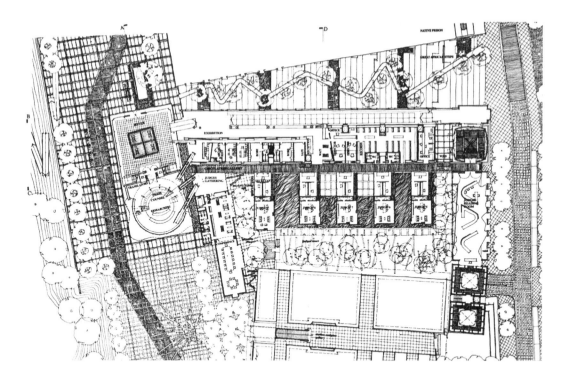

4.12   Winning submission by OMMUS, Plan (1998). Courtesy of the Republic of South Africa. Photograph by Henia Czekanowska and the author.

chamber is positioned on the site. This point was raised in interviews with designers Andrew Makin and Janina Masojade, of OMM Design Workshop, who emphasised the unique approach adopted by their design.[82] Submissions from the other four finalists either screen the chamber from the site, protecting it behind imposing walls (Snell), hide it beside the Ramparts (PP), or otherwise expose it to full public view while removing it from the public spaces of the urban ground plane (HJH and PDC). The winning scheme, by contrast, positions the court firmly on the ground. Faced in transparent and translucent glass, the public foyer and courtroom appear in full open view and with direct access from Constitution Square, which serves as the primary public space at the centre of this scheme. Entrance into the court chamber is via the public foyer, which in turn is accessed directly from Constitution Square. And together, court and foyer are unified in the building mass with a large parasol roof which projects into Constitution Square, where it provides outdoor shade.

The written report highlights spatial continuities with the surrounding environment, '[p]ublic space in the building is continuous with the urban public context', as well as the embedded nature of the plan, 'contours from the ground merge with the contours of the building … Landscaped places are "built" as rooms in a building'.[83] This concern with spatial continuity also influences the choice of materials, for example those normally applied to external surfaces 'are used internally to dissolve internal and external barriers'.[84] A dialogue is thereby established between the internal realm of the court and the open space of Constitution Square, which itself is linked back

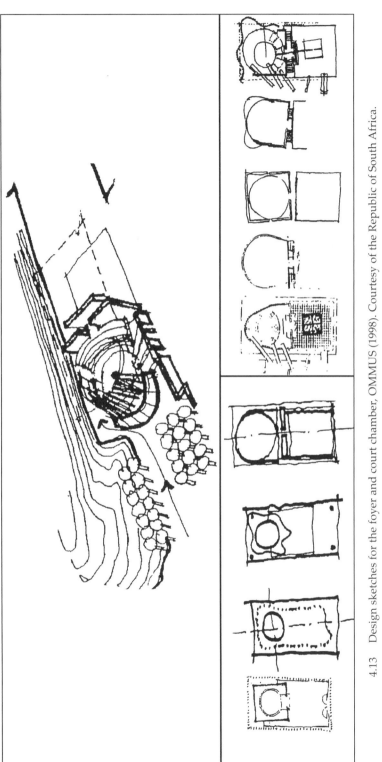

4.13 Design sketches for the foyer and court chamber, OMMUS (1998). Courtesy of the Republic of South Africa.

4.14   The Great African Steps, Constitutional Court of South Africa, OMMUS. Photograph by the author.

into the surrounding city via a carefully planned network of cross-axial routes which traverse the site. 'An African grandeur, a sense of dignity and great scale result from the building of great voids, not Eurocentric grand solids, not grand form [i.e. monumental form] but grand space, a grandeur to be physically experienced, not seen from a distance.'[85] These words articulate the democratic, participatory intentions of this design.

The architects' report also expands on the 'logic' of building form, maintaining that their design combines two distinct kinds of form: '[s]ingular, processional object buildings – to achieve the gravitas, the pre-eminence, grandeur and solitude' and 'buildings continuous with landscape, access and context – to achieve accessibility, integration, and democratic form.'[86] These twin strategies, which may be termed *object focus* and *embedded form*, inform the spatial design of the public foyer and court chamber. On the one hand, the public foyer and chamber are given a unified roof and distinct mass, which addresses the space of Constitution Square. In addition, a raised podium provides a base which gently lifts the building mass above Constitution Square.[87] The building is slightly removed in order to express its pre-eminent status and to add grandeur to the frontal character of the main western entrance façade. On the other hand, curvilinear geometries are employed to pull visitors around the southern side of the chamber. Entering from

4.15   The art gallery wing, Constitutional Court of South Africa, OMMUS. Photograph by the author.

the east, which is intended as the primary pedestrian entry to the site, one approaches the chamber from the rear, circulating around the southern side, then doubling back before experiencing the frontal formality of the western façade. This somewhat odd spiralling approach from the rear is intended as a countermotion to the object-like focus of the entrance façade.

The architects informed me that their design process involved repeated attempts to refine these complex and contradictory relations, as is evident from various early sketches for the court that embellish the written report (see Figure 4.13). Court, foyer and Constitution Square are positioned at the centre of the urban composition, while the remainder of the building is allowed to fall gently down the contours which descend toward the north, with the library wing on the southern side. The building mass lies parallel to Number Four in a similar manner to the scheme proposed by Snell: the Constitutional Court is a mirrored inversion of the prison. But unlike Snell's design, OMMUS' architecture also signals a new imaginary, a visionary break from the past.

The Great African Steps (see Figure 4.14), which lie parallel between Number Four and the art gallery wing (see Figure 4.15), connect across the site in a north–south direction. This long western façade of the art gallery wing is formed from transparent glass with adjustable screens that modulate the light. The use of glass allows a visual and spatial dialogue between the

4.16 Elevations
from OMMUS's
design
submission,
Constitutional
Court of South
Africa (1998).
Courtesy of
the Republic of
South Africa.
Photograph
by Henia
Czekanowska
and the author.

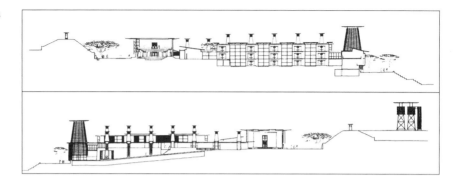

double, paralleled terraces of these indoor (art gallery) and outdoor (Great African Steps) spaces. And in the built design, successive door openings allow the gallery to spill out onto the African Steps, where terraces are widened to accommodate outdoor seating areas. A transparent, spatial continuity is so formed between these different public realms. Again, in the built design, this continuity is repeated subtly by the wall that separates the indoor gallery from the private spaces of the judges and offices of administration on the long eastern side of the gallery. This wall marks a clear boundary and security line to the private spaces of the complex, yet slotted gaps and openings are cut into this wall, thus allowing space to flow through to the other side and one gets an imaginary feeling for the full extent of this paralleled private world beyond. Glimpses of human movement can be seen on the other side, and this heightens the sense of continuity between public and private realms. This careful privacy gradient is without doubt one of the most successful aspects of the design. It provides a double spatialisation as thematic for the interrelated public and private significance of the South African Constitution.

The modernistic aspects of the design, such as a fascination with transparency and spatial continuity, are counterposed by other themes, especially the use of a fragmented, disaggregated building mass and multiple, symbolic resonances derived from iconic forms and tectonic references. Composed from fragments, the plan possesses an incremental character that adjusts itself to the particularities of site conditions and programmatic needs. This inclusive complexity also operates as a symbolic trope, a political theme of unity in diversity. 'Our built environments should continue life's multiplicity, expressing the same levels of diversity and range of experience as in our natural, cultural and social environments. The richness of our world arises from multiplicity.'[88]

The buildings' disaggregated mass is supplemented by the inclusion of sculptural, iconic forms which enliven façades, such as the library tower, which both acts as a beacon to be seen from afar and facilitates vertical circulation (see Figure 4.16). These sculpted elements resonate with tectonic themes derived from African craft traditions. The elegantly curved wire frame-like construction of the library tower is derived from traditional African basket weave, and similar resonances are repeated at the tops of air-duct chimneys,

which are reminiscent of baskets or hats. The report also speaks of material references to Africa, such as light-filtering screens derived, once again, from traditional basket weave, Sotho huts where storage spaces are modelled into thickened walls, memories of mud construction and battered earth walls, and polished screen floors which are reminiscent of traditional dung floors: '[w]e are a part of this African identity.'[89] These rural references are combined with modernistic, high-tech materials, such as floating curtain-glass construction, as well as material associations derived from the surrounding prisons. 'The cage of the library entrance and reading room recalls cages of confinement. Movable rectagrid [i.e. steel grid] sunscreens remind of permanent metal prison bars.'[90] The architects promote this choice of hybrid materiality: 'the current South African context gives opportunity to elevate the status of informal and alternative building technologies and materials ... the integration of urban and rural building practice – craft and hi-technology'.[91]

And finally, a further element in the hybrid make-up of this composition concerns the tree as a symbol for an African court. A tree was chosen for the insignia of the court, and previously we saw how this influenced the brief. Significantly, the front page of OMMUS' written report uses a similar image, only here it is a woodcut by artist Sandile Goje. In addition, their report compares shady trees to the columns and roof canopy of the foyer and court chamber: '[t]he shading branches of trees are a recurring analogy ... Beneath the canopy [to foyer and chamber], people meet, the roof is a parasol, a "collecting" form'.[92] Mention is also made of 'the shading canopy of trees seen in the filter of sky above and the shadowed ground at our feet. The association continues to the analogy of people gathering under trees, the tree under which the respected elder advises and listens to his extended family.'[93]

4.17   Rendered perspective from OMMUS's design submission, Constitutional Court of South Africa (1998). Courtesy of the Republic of South Africa Photograph by Henia Czekanowska and the author.

It will be remembered that this same symbol featured in previous chapters. The Legislature at Mpumalanga involved a hybridity of two juxtaposed, incommensurable symbols: *dome* and *tree* (see Figure 2.16). At Mpumalanga, you cannot be under the tree when you are inside the domed Assembly, and vice versa. The two symbols stand side by side, bearing witness to the divided histories and subjectivities of South Africa's past. At the Northern Cape Legislature, however, the symbolic trees stand in a stylised landscape (see Figure 3.18).[94] The People's Square mixes urban and naturalistic expression, providing a more mediated setting for the symbolic tree. Yet the tree still remains distinct from the internal space of the Assembly. Finally, at the Constitutional Court, our imaginary tree is translated into the space of the entrance foyer itself. In the built design, the foyer has slanting, branch-like columns, richly adorned with ceramic tiles with leaf and seed-like motifs supporting a fly-over concrete roof (see Figure 4.22). Dappled light filters down from slits in the ceiling, as though beneath a tree. This design combines the two symbolic types, *court* and *tree*, such that it is now possible to have the metaphoric sense of being under a tree while standing in the foyer of the court. The overriding sense is one of layering, of addition and complex inclusion, rather than of resolved synthesis. We have a hybrid narrative of court and tree, the one superimposed upon the other to include both in a singular space. Yet despite this singularity, traces of irresolvable difference remain.

This layering of court and tree is the stuff of popular legend. Not surprisingly, tour guides of the Constitutional Court elaborate on this very point, and Sachs has put out the message of 'justice under a tree' via news media.[95] Sachs also spoke fondly of the tree metaphor during interviews, and told how prominently this featured in his assessment during adjudication.[96] The tree also inspired artists and their handicrafts which embellish the court, especially Jane du Rand's ceramic embellishment of columns to the foyer. A carpet in the court chamber, designed by Andrew Verster, is based upon the streaked shadow effects cast on the ground by trees. Yet during an interview with the architects, I was fascinated to hear how they downplayed the importance of the tree.[97] They explained that the tree was not a starting point for their design, that the space of the foyer is what it is, an architectural creation, and that their reference to a tree made its way into their text as a literary device, as a way of communicating the uplifting, light-filled interior of their foyer design. The space would have been designed this way regardless of this reference to a tree, they said.

These differences of interpretation point to the over-determined nature of architectural symbols. The architects' understanding of architecture is often not that of non-architects, people who work, visit and enjoy this space, which includes you and me. In truth, the tree as architectural type is 'difficult' for architectural imagination, an imagination framed within a long history of theory and practice, discourses of architecture that have declared the self-evident nature of the object, an object transparent to the architects' gaze. But the complexity of the case cannot be tamed by these closures because architecture, this incommensurable object, also belongs to other imaginations. And, in my view, the architects should be commended for their good intuitions, which indeed are complexly translated into the space of this design, despite the difficulty that this poses for certain dominant discourses of design.

Gravitas

The jurors' reports noted a few reservations with regard to the winning scheme, the most significant of which concerned questions of *pre-eminence* and *gravitas*. The first report refers to the 'coloured image', which, although 'powerful, does not imply appropriate gravitas'.[98] In addition, '[t]he chamber should be carefully considered to ensure that the deliberations of the court are not disturbed by onlookers.'[99] This comment was presumably made with reference to perspective drawings, which were found among a collection of unsorted submission drawings in the Constitutional Court archive. The second jurors' report repeats similar concerns, stating that 'giving greater emphasis to the powerful image which this building provides requires further attention'.[100] Sachs referred to the competition entry's problematic 'bioscope-like' image, while Davey remembers the incredible lightness of the original design, and felt that more weight would be required (see Figure 4.17).[101] During my interviews, Maiken and Masojade explained that the issue of gravitas was discussed at the early project steering committee meetings (PSC).[102] One suggestion was to swap the relative positions of the library and court chamber. The idea was to create a processional route to the chamber. Entering off Constitution Hill, visitors would move past the library and through the long gallery before approaching the court. The architects resisted this move to swap the library with the chamber because the accessible nature of the chamber had been the first principle in their democratic imagination. Indeed, the experience of the built design is uncommon for one enters from Constitution Square directly into the public foyer with the court chamber ahead. The uplifting space of the foyer is captivating (see Figure 4.22), and it takes some time before one realises the presence of a gallery wing which descends off to the left. One has already arrived at one's destination, and the terraced decline of the gallery leads nowhere. The gallery space provides the sensation of an enclosed urban streetscape, or possibly a stylised landscape (see Figure 4.15). In either case, this linear space may be enjoyed on its own terms, and one is free to wander up and down without need of arrival. The effect is unusual, but not unpleasant.

The architects informed me that the foyer and the chamber were reworked many times, and the glass curtain walls of the foyer and court were ultimately replaced by a more solid, box-like construction (see Figure 4.18). Transparency is evoked in more subtle ways, for example via a long strip window on the south side of the chamber, which enables eye contact with Constitution Square. Floor-to-ceiling glass on the main west façade is retained, but only here the flat

4.18   Front
entrance (west)
to foyer of the
Constitutional
Court of South
Africa, OMMUS.
Photograph by
the author.

concrete roof projects beyond the glass envelope then hangs down vertically from above, forming a semi-enclosed outdoor space above the raised podium. We get a veranda-like effect at the point of entry, which filters light into the interior. The final design captures pre-eminence without monumentality, as was required by the brief.

The built design also loses the large parasol roof, and there is a general move away from iconic, sculptural form in favour of a tough, rectilinear exterior. A further change concerns the commemoration of the Awaiting Trial Block. Three vertical circulation cores from the original Awaiting Trial Block are retained, and given vertical emphasis via glass towers that extend their presence into the sky. The towers light up at night, and resonate with the residential towers of Hillbrow that appear on the skyline of Constitution Square. The footprint of the Awaiting Trial Block is also commemorated by brick pavers, and bricks taken from the Awaiting Trial Block are used to build the walls of the court chamber where they feature as a textured, unadorned surface. Despite these changes, the built design largely resembles the competition design – certainly all key architectural ideas were maintained. In this regard, the architects informed me that the working relationship with the client, and PSC alike, was exemplary.

4.19   Clay marquette studies for the front door of the Constitutional
Court of South Africa, Andrew Verster. Courtesy of Andrew Verster.

Integrating Handcrafted Elements

The building exterior has a somewhat stark, robust character, which responds to the austerity of the prison complex, as well as the tough urban environments of Braamfontein and Hillbrow that surround it. Interior spaces, by contrast, take on a popular, colourful and inviting manner. Moving through the building, one begins to appreciate the rich adornment through built-in handcrafted elements, such as doors, windows and carpets, each individually designed by artists and craftsmen/women.[103] Makin and Masojade refer to these as 'integrated components' rather than decorations per se.[104] These works provide a rich palette of public and personal narratives, and make a primary contribution to the democratic identity of the court. Guided tours of the court expand upon the narrative content of these works which, in most cases, deal with the Constitution, human rights, and fundamental questions of freedom.

The procurement process was managed by the architects in collaboration with an artworks committee, and all selections were made via transparent and accountable procedures, assisted by a mixed panel of assessors.[105] Some 30 craft-worthy sites were identified and put out on open tender so that anyone could submit proposals, while five prestigious sites were reserved for well-known artists. Special effort was also made to ensure that disadvantaged artists and craftsmen/women would have a fair chance of inclusion. The quality and diversity of handcrafted elements at the Constitutional Court is simply astonishing, and we shall now consider a few key sites.

My research took me to Durban where I met with Jane du Rand and Andrew Verster, both highly respected members of the arts and crafts community in South Africa. Verster won the limited competition for the front door to the Constitutional Court complex.[106] He also contributed other successful designs, including security gates to the judges' chambers, carpets, and a chandelier sculpture of the nine provinces of South Africa. The architects required a frame of 8.7 m high by 2.1 m wide, with the front door divided into a grid of four by seven panels, thus comprising 28 panels in total. Verster explained that 28 panels seemed to marry with the 27 provisions of the South African Bill of Rights, and from this came his idea to represent the 27 rights on individual panels. The 28th panel was used for mounting the door handle, where an explanation of the design is inscribed in Braille.

Each panel is illustrated with a human hand, or pair of hands, with descriptive text and a large number representing the relevant article from the Bill of Rights. The competition was won on the basis of a written report and some clay marquettes providing examples of the intended door panels, which were to be hand carved from solid wood. Vertair's original marquettes used hands as illustrative symbols for the articles of the Constitution, but Andries Botha – a sculptor who collaborated on this project – suggested the use of sign language. Verster was taken with this idea, and was quick to rework his design once more, exchanging illustrative symbols for drawings of hands which speak though sign language – the marginal language of the deaf (see Figure 4.19). All drawing and design for the final work were prepared by Verster, while Botha supervised the carving process, which in turn was executed by a team of seven carvers – an eighth carver joined toward the end. The carvers are all artists in their own right, Verster insists, and were free to carve in their preferred style. Each carver was allocated a horizontal row of four panels, and improvised upon Verster's drawn designs. For this reason, the door captures a wide range of textures, and a sense of organic freedom associated with African craft traditions. The door is, quite literally, the work of many hands, and speaks through many tongues (Figure 4.20). It embodies the Bill of Rights, not as autonomous legal precepts but through an imaginative ensemble that is both poetic and inclusive in its reference, participatory in its process, and intimate in its choice of representation.

Du Rand won the open tender for 'embellishment' of the columns in the public foyer of the court. The competition brief refers to the 'idea of Justice being administered by the wise elders of the community, under a tree', and explains how the columns have been purposefully arranged in clusters of two or three: '[t]hey stand like tree trunks in a forest'.[107] Du Rand's design

4.20   Front door of the Constitutional Court of South Africa,
Andrew Verster. Photograph by the author.

submission is composed of four coloured drawings and a written description of the foyer.[108] The first drawing begins by identifying seven clusters of columns, proposing that each be linked to an 'indigenous South African tree/tree-type from which we will draw inspiration for the decoration' (see Figure 4.21).[109] The columns consist of round and square sections, and the relative position of these sections alternates from column to column such that the square and round portions appear to jump up and down in a playful manner across the foyer. Du Rand's submission proposes to cover the square portion only, meaning 'that sometimes the decoration is at the "base", eye level, touch level, and will need much texture and detail taken from bark patterns and seed pods'.[110] In addition, '[s]ometimes the decoration will be in the sky – seen from below from a distance, with patterns based on leaf shapes, thorn shapes and hanging seed pods.'[111]

In interview, Du Rand explained about refinements that occurred subsequent to her tender.[112] Her original intention was to cover the whole square portion of the columns. But the architects wanted to see a continuity of concrete, along each column from floor to ceiling to maintain a sense of structural integrity. In response to this, Du Rand made photographic studies of light conditions in

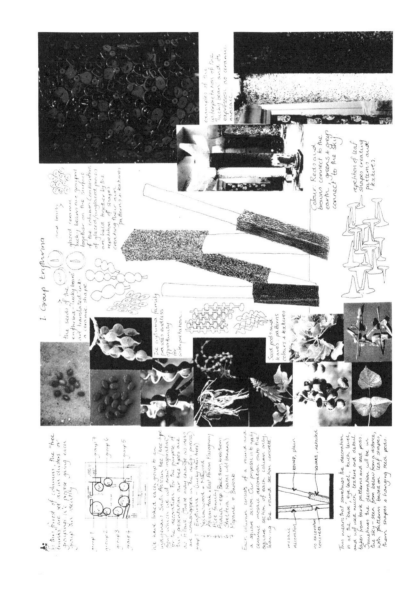

4.21   Mosaic designs for columns to the foyer, the Constitutional Court of South Africa, Jane du Rand. Courtesy of Jane du Rand. Photograph by Henia Czekanowska.

the foyer throughout the day. Inspired by the way strips of light fell from the roof to form shafts of light on the columns, she developed the idea of dividing column surfaces into equal thirds. This provided a regulating geometry, and she explored the possibilities of wrapping mosaics around the columns into these divisions of three. 'I wanted to capture this sense of shafts of light', she said.[113] The final design demonstrates a complex layering of coloured strips which relate to column width in various portions of three. This successful strategy allows for a continuity of concrete, from floor to ceiling, while creating an orderly relation between column and mosaic (see Figure 4.22).

In this example, as with others, we see how the architects of the Constitutional Court attempt to integrate crafts and decorative elements with the spatial and material order of their design. In the chapter on Mpumalanga, we considered a theoretical discussion on the inclusion of *foreign elements* – formal fragments, details, surface treatments, signs and tropes derived from African experience – and we may now add personal and public narratives as well, elements that are brought into post-apartheid designs as though from outside dominant practice. At Mpumalanga, African elements were added to the surface of a somewhat conventional building structure, such that the building's apparent African authenticity was often in denial of its typological and structural form. For this reason, I commented that the Mpumalanga Legislature is wearing a mask. And in Kimberley, we saw how the fragmentation of building elements was celebrated across a range of different registers: spatial, structural, material, narrative, and so forth. Complex relations between *skin* and *mask* were achieved through a compositional logic of proximity and disruption. The Constitutional Court, however, highlights a different strategy through artful integration of various foreign elements. In this, the architecture of the Constitutional Court narrows the tension between mask and skin. Yet even so, complex duplicities remain. The integrity of structure, of spatial continuity and transparency – all modernist themes – are maintained behind and around the other elements that bring further layers of tectonic and imaginative resonance, as well as the inclusion of diverse, personal and public narratives. The Constitutional Court attempts a synthesis of these many parts, yet this apparent unity has not resulted in a closed totality. Rather, a series of sympathetic inclusions openly engage with a discursive theme on human rights. In this, the Constitutional Court showcases a remarkable density of formal and narrative elements, where differences superimpose on each other. We may speak of a synthesising of *mask* and *skin*, but it's a unity of sympathy, rather than totality, for the many representations remain open and are ultimately unresolved.

Another remarkable craft element is the row of sunscreens that line the long western façade. Fixed to the exterior of the building, these screens act as security bars and filter light through windows into the gallery interior. They exist at the visual threshold between the gallery interior and the Great African Steps outside. The design was put out on open tender and won by architect Lewis Levin and artist Patrick Rorke. Their respective contribution was based upon a neat division where Levin designed the screens and Rorke

4.22   Tree columns of the foyer, with mosaics and dappled light, Constitutional Court of South Africa, OMMUS and Jane de Rand. Photograph by the author.

executed engravings which narrativise the surface. The submission consisted of a written description, drawings and photographs of a marquette.[114]

Levin speaks enthusiastically about his design, citing various influences, one of which came from ethno-mathematics.[115] Ethno-mathematical studies, for instance, examine fractal geometries in traditional African beadwork.[116] Levin also refers to pentatonic scales and Ghanian Kuba cloth. But more importantly, a major influence on his design came via recent experimentation with kinetic sculptures and GIF computer animations. He explained his fascination with an animation he had experienced, which consisted of a grid of squares that move in response to user response: motion of the computer mouse would cause individual squares to tip and swivel. Levin took this concept of an interactive, swivelling motion, and combined it with his fascination for ethno-maths and African beadwork traditions, where random effects of different beads are ordered by their serial position along a string. These ideas were translated into what Levin calls a 'bead-plate', which is the basic sub-assembly block of his design.[117] Each bead-plate is 360 mm square with a pair of triangular side wings. Bead-plates pivot from their triangular sides where they are attached to a framework grid, or abacus, which in turn is fastened to the building façade (see Figure 4.23).

Steel rods are attached in varying positions, running horizontally across the surface of the bead plates, allowing each to fall at a different angle of rotation, but it is also possible for visitors to play with the rotation of plates. And in this way, a repetitive sub-assembly is used to generate a complex pattern that is varied throughout. Random variations also affect colour and texture. The bead-plates are made from 3CR12, a low-grade stainless steel. Levin has been exploring this material in previous projects, and has developed a series of chemical processes which result in various surface patinas that vary in texture and colour. The patinas are like a 'bird's feather', Levin explains, because depending upon the incidence – the angle of light hitting the plate – reflected colour will appear to change, meaning there is a relation between rotation angle and effectual surface colour.[118] The plates are identical but are randomly treated in different ways to achieve a variety of finishes. His design allowed the manufacturers to influence the process, and their choices are registered in the final product. 'I wanted everyone to be an artist', he said.[119] The overall effect is of a vibrant surface, one which reveals, obscures and reflects light in a multitude of different ways, and successfully breaks up the long western façade while retaining moments of visual contact with the other side.

4.23 Sunscreen to the gallery wing, the Constitutional Court of South Africa, Lewis Levin and Patrick Rorke. Photograph by the author.

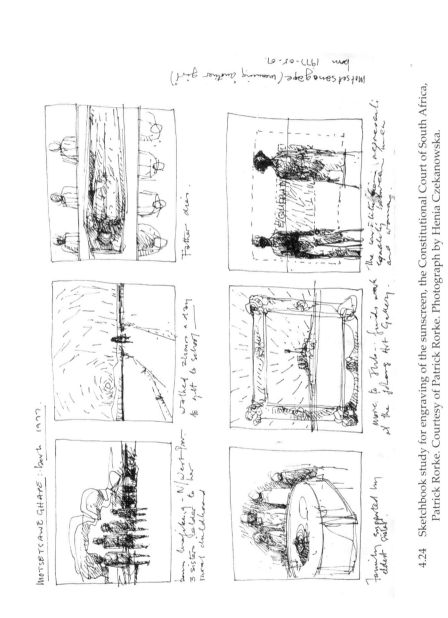

4.24   Sketchbook study for engraving of the sunscreen, the Constitutional Court of South Africa, Patrick Rorke. Courtesy of Patrick Rorke. Photograph by Henia Czekanowska.

On their own terms, however, the screens are somewhat formalistic, which is where Rorke's input introduced a further significance. Rorke explained that Levin had developed the basic ideas for his bead-plates before they met.[120] Rorke made the suggestion that the surfaces of the plates be engraved with images and narratives. The idea seemed good and they agreed to collaborate. Initially, Rorke was looking at written histories of the site which he wanted to illustrate on the screens, but later he decided to expand his reference by collecting oral histories from people in the surrounding areas. The Constitutional Court is a 'remarkable building', one that has achieved a 'certain innocence' he says, because it has a connection to society.[121] For this reason, the decision to represent personal stories of ordinary people has profound resonances. During his time with people on the street, Rorke would ask personal questions, as well as perceptions of the court. And, he would draw images in his sketchbook while the interviewee was speaking, supplementing these with short written captions (see Figure 4.24). Then he would show the drawings to his participants, asking them whether he had captured their stories. Some people were favourable, others indifferent, and still others seemed openly hostile. People interviewed were selected from a wide mix: different ages, genders and stations in life. Yet Rorke admitted his preference for listening to the voice of marginalised people. The marginalised give us a more 'compelling' reflection upon our society.[122] Their stories are represented more so than the views of 'fat cats and politicians', he said.[123] I was interested by the interpretive freedom that is afforded when stories are depicted through graphic means alone. I put this question to Rorke, and he explained that he did not want to 'fix the meaning' of these images because to fix the human narrative of life would be 'problematic'.[124] Rorke's engravings are especially cogent because they work with incomplete narratives – or open signifiers – that engage contemporary society while refusing simplistic closure. The sunscreens add further import to the interrelated public and private significance of the court.

The call for craft-related tenders was a success, yet client and architect alike were aware that formal tender procedures can be exclusionary. For this reason, the architects attempted to secure work from black South Africans, artists and crafters who did not submit, and would not have submitted, via the formal protocols of a public tender. Anthea Martin of the African Art Centre, a non-governmental organisation working with local black artists in Durban, collaborated with Masojade and helped to find suitable candidates for various designs.[125] The work submitted was used for carpets, light fittings, door handles, as well as a stair-nosing detail. But in some cases, work submitted had to be modified before it could be used for its intended purpose. Carpet designs, for instance, were made from the work of two painters, Sifiso ka-Mkame and Zamani Makhanya. The painters submitted examples of their paintings, and while Masojade loved these, they were too complex for carpet designs. Martin suggested that detailed photos be taken from selected areas of these paintings, and that these be worked into carpet designs. Masojade

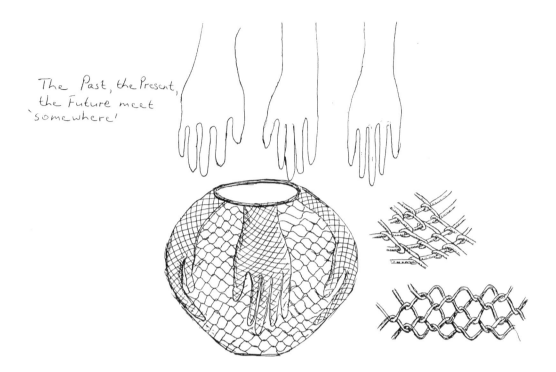

The Past, the Present, the Future meet 'somewhere'

4.25 Sketch design for light fitting for the Constitutional Court of South Africa, Lindelani Ngwenya. Courtesy of Lindelani Ngwenya.

agreed to this approach, and she informed me that the zoomed-in images were transformed by her office with graphics software to produce the final designs.[126] Initially, the judges were not so sure owing to the bold patterns and colours of these designs, but were persuaded, and most love the final result.

While in Durban, I had the pleasure of meeting with ka-Mkame and Makhanya at their painting studio.[127] They showed me their works and spoke fondly of their involvement in this project. I also had the pleasure of meeting with Lindelani Ngwenya who was invited to submit a design for some light fittings. Ngwenya is a fine arts graduate from Durban University of Technology who makes woven sculptures. He explained to me about his love for copper wire, which is soft and flexible, with colours which are 'very African'.[128] Ngwenya also explained how African culture, traditionally at least, has not distinguished between art and craft, and for this reason he enjoys creating works that sit in between these two categories, such as a bowl with figurative or sculptural features. He also speaks of the spiritual dimension of things, and explained that working with copper weave allows his sculptures to take on a mysterious, other-worldly quality. Ngwenya's early drawings for the light fittings included figurative aspects, but the architects were looking for something more geometric, for pragmatic reasons (see Figure 4.25). Later, he reworked his design in the form of a long pipe with an organic, meandering profile, 'like a winding route through the veld', he said.[129] The shape is also reminiscent of Zulu beer strainers, or *ivovo*, yet this reference, as Ngwenya explains, was not intentional. His new approach found approval,

and Ngwenya was commissioned to make a series of these light fittings. He worked together with two helpers, and all light fittings were handmade, and each is unique. It was a 'labour of love', he said.[130] The structure is made from a series of wire loops which form the circumference, with rods running along the length which is some 4–5 m long (see Figure 4.26 left). Ngwenya explains the technique involved is similar to that used for traditional basket weave, only using copper and aluminium wire instead of grass. The light fittings can be seen along the length of the gallery, where they hang with grace and charm (see Figure 4.26 right).

4.26   Weaving the light fittings (left), that hang above the gallery wing (right). Courtesy of Anthea Martin (left), photograph by the author (right).

Concluding Remarks

The French political philosopher, Claude Lefort, argues that a defence of human rights does not require a commitment to an essentialist notion of man, be it moral or natural. Rather, Lefort points to the fact that the various declarations of the freedom of man – and by this we may include general commitment to notions of human rights, as well as more formal, historical declarations, and legal bills of rights – are primarily political statements of demand. The concept of human right is not the child of philosophical speculation, but rather the legal conclusion to a history of struggle, a social motion which has pressed toward the realisation of civic freedoms for all. The principle of freedom, then, is less a positive term than a referential relation to, and inversion of, a history of oppression. Lefort writes: '[w]hat we refer to in positive terms as "political freedom" can of course be called "resistance to oppression".'[131] Significantly in this regard, Lefort notices that the French Declaration of the Rights of Man involves a conversation of man with his fellow men. The preamble to the South African Constitution follows this pattern: '[w]e, the people of South Africa, Recognise the injustices of our past; Honour those who suffered for justice and freedom in our land; Respect those who have worked to build and develop our country; and Believe that South Africa belongs to all who live in it, united in our diversity.'[132] The declaration of right, therefore, is in fact a self-declaration. It is

a declaration by which human beings, speaking through their representatives, revealed themselves to be both the subject and the object of the utterance in which they named the human elements in one another, "spoke to" one another, appeared before one another, and therefore erected themselves into their own judges, their own witnesses.[133]

In philosophical terms, emancipated man and woman now become both the subject and the object of his and her own politico-moral consciousness. And from this assertion, it becomes necessary to grant humanity to the other in order that this same humanity be received by the self in return.

Lefort also observes that the formation of social rights is twinned with the emergence of a public political space, a space of public discussion and debate. Indeed, the conversational nature of right – a conversation which is enacted between subjects, subjects who have 'erected themselves into their own judges, their own witnesses' – *is* discursively constituted by this public space. Lefort explains: 'individuals are both the products and the instigators of that space' and in fact, the terrain of this discursive publicity delineates democratic culture.[134] Which is also to say that an *outsid*e – or an-*other* – condition exists, or potentially exists, beyond the confines of this democratic space. What is the nature of this frontier? We may answer from historical experience: terror, subjugation and violence mark the boundary between those who are included in the space of humane reciprocity and those who are silenced. Therefore, a conversation about the rights of man will necessarily involve a reflection upon histories of oppression and subjugation because these narratives, quite literally, mark the historical limits of a transition toward democracy. For this reason, a social discourse of right needs to be informed by the voices of those who suffered: suffered because their rights were denied. Significantly, the South African Constitution, like many other declarations of right, mobilises a recognition of 'the injustices of our past', and honours 'those who suffered for justice and freedom in our land'. Lefort's concept of right highlights questions of exclusion, marginality, and of ethical reciprocity that, I believe, Fanon would embrace.

Media reports, considered at the start of this chapter, demonstrate all the salient features of Lefort's elaboration. This reporting shows a discourse on the rights of man. It is a discourse built upon the symbolic proximity of *court* and *prison*, a relation which points to the limits of human freedom, of rights and abuse, and which simultaneously opens an imaginary space for democratic inclusion. These observations introduce the profound duplicity of the site, and it is this same duplicity that animates the architecture of the Constitutional Court. The physical proximity of these two building types, court and prison, are transposed by the architecture of this project which seeks a public expression of complex inclusion, unresolved synthesis, openness, transparency, a layering of public and private realms and imagining, as well as a dethroning of the conventional symbols of power. The design initiates a conversational, participatory kind of architecture where, paraphrasing Lefort, we as subjects can imaginatively appear before one another to consider the fundamental constitution of our freedom. These formations are built in direct contrast to the material presence and historical memory of the prison complex that surrounds to promote a positive hope for the future of South African polity.

Yet our *leitmotif* of prison and court conceals a silent third, an unspoken figure, represented by the *contemporary prisons in South Africa*. Upon entry to the museum at Number Four, visitors are led to read a quotation from Nelson Mandela, written overhead in prominent letters: '[i]t is said that no one truly knows a nation until one has been inside its jails. A nation should not be judged by how it treats its highest citizens, but its lowest ones – and South Africa treated its African citizens like animals.'[135]

Unfortunately, little has changed as contemporary prison conditions in South Africa continue to be plagued by systemic patterns of unacceptable overcrowding, rape, abuse and terminal disease, especially HIV/Aids.[136] These well-documented facts certainly do concern the judges of the Constitutional Court who are openly committed to prison reform, and one must hope that in time this legacy will be overturned. Importantly, this disturbing continuation of abuse shows the glaring limit of this narrative. The symbolisations at the Constitutional Court register in the imaginary. They are a positive sign that a worthy motion has begun, *but the sign alone does not represent the fulfilment of freedom*.

Notes

1 On 10 December 1996, the 1996 Constitution (the Constitution of the Republic of South Africa Act 108 of 1996) followed the so-called 'Interim Constitution' (Constitution of the Republic of South Africa Act 200 of 1993) which was enacted to provide a transition from the previous non-democratic era to one of constitutional democracy.

2 Iain Currie and Johan de Waal, *The Bill of Rights Handbook* (Landsdowne: Juta, 2005), p 7.

3 South African constitutions prior to the Interim Constitution did not contain a Bill of Rights and therefore did not provide a normative framework for reviewing legislation, namely: the Union Constitution (South Africa Act 1909 (9 Edw VII, c 9).), the Republic Constitution (Constitution of the Republic of South

Africa Act 32 of 1961.) and the Tricameral Constitution (Constitution of the Republic of South Africa Act 110 of 1983).

4   Constitution of the Republic of South Africa Act 200 of 1993.

5   Socio-legal history of the South African Constitution is provided by: Mathew Chaskalson et al., *Constitutional Law of South Africa* (Kenwyn: Juta, 1999); Currie and Waal, *The Bill of Rights Handbook*; Constitutional Court 'The Constitutional Court of South Africa: The First Ten Years,' (Johannesburg: Constitutional Court, 2004).

6   A history of the Old Fort is provided by research reports prepared for this project: Elsabe Brink, 'Our History in the Making: The Johannesburg Fort 1893–1983' (Johannesburg: South African Heritage Resource Agency, 2000); University of the Witwatersrand History Workshop, 'History Workshop Report: Buildings, Hospital Hill' (Johannesburg: University of the Witwatersrand History Workshop, 2004).

7   Brink, 'Our History in the Making: The Johannesburg Fort 1893–1983', part 2, p 22.

8   Ibid. part 2, p 23.

9   Apartheid law restricted the number of black South Africans who were allowed to live in white, urban areas, and these restrictions were regulated by pass books. Black South Africans were required to carry a pass book at all times, and failure to comply would commonly result in imprisonment. Natives (Abolition of Passes and Coordination of Documents) Act 67 of 1952.

10   'A Beacon of Light Hope and Celebration,' *Worx News* 3, no. 4 (1998): p 3. Also see: Lee-Ann Alfreds, 'Total Transformation for Jo'burg's Old Fort', *The Star*, 9 April 1998, p 3; Taryn Lamberti, 'Mandela Names Winning Architects', *Business Day*, 9 April 1998, p 3.

11   Carmel Rickard, 'Gates to Open on a New Era of Democracy', *Sunday Times*, 26 October 1997, p 16.

12   Lee Rondganger, 'Symbol of Oppression Becomes Tool of Freedom', *The Star*, 24 June 2003, p 9.

13   Steve Kwena Mokwena, 'Inside Number Four', *Mail and Guardian*, 12–18 March 2004, p 6.

14   Ibid.

15   'Strong Constitution', *Sowetan*, 19 June 2002, p 21.

16   This testimony is by Yvonne Mhlauli in Anna Cox, 'Old Fort – a Place of Pain and Tears', *The Star*, 25 November 2003, p 12.

17   Lucas Ledwaba, 'Fortress of Past Pains', *Thisday*, 15 March 2004, p 8.

18   Mokwena, 'Inside Number Four', p 6. Also in a similar vein: Lucy Kaplan, 'Past in Present Tense', *Mail and Guardian*, 8–15 April 2004, p 17, p 19.

19   Ledwaba, 'Fortress of Past Pains'. The voice of prisoners such as Gama and others gains expression in the museums at Constitution Hill, see: Lauren Segal, Karen Martin and Sharon Cort (eds), *Number Four: The Making of Constitution Hill* (London: Penguin Books, 2006).

20   Interviews, Johannesburg (November 2004).

21 Ibid.

22 Ibid.

23 Ibid.

24 Ibid.

25 Ibid.

26 Ibid.

27 Ibid.

28 Interview, Johannesburg (November 2004).

29 Inmates were moved from the Old Fort to Diepkloof Prison in 1983, see: Brink, 'Our History in the Making: The Johannesburg Fort 1893–1983', part 2, p 122.

30 DPW, 'Brief and Conditions: Competition for the New Constitutional Court of South Africa' (Cape Town: DPW, 1997), p 26.

31 DPW, 'New Constitutional Court: Minutes of the Meeting Held on 5 January 1997' (Johannesburg: SAHRA, 1997).

32 Derek Japha and Vivienne Japha, 'Preliminary Notes on the Proposed Competition for the Constitutional Court' (Johannesburg: Albie Sachs, 1996); Derek Japha, 'Constitutional Court: Draft Brief' (Johannesburg: SAHRA, 1997); Derek Japha, 'Draft Competition Brief for the New Constitutional Court Building of South Africa' (Johannesburg: SAHRA, 1997).

33 Interviews, Johannesburg (November 2004).

34 The competition rules stated that candidates invited to submit in the second round had either to be registered as South African architects or, if not an architect or an architect registered in a foreign country, then candidates would need to enter into a satisfactory agreement with a local Gauteng-based firm of architects for the purposes of completing the design, see: DPW, 'Brief and Conditions: Competition for the New Constitutional Court of South Africa', pp 25–8.

35 Ibid. p 7.

36 Ibid. p 14.

37 Interviews, Johannesburg (November 2004).

38 Ibid.

39 From a different perspective, however, this post-apartheid romance of the tree is perhaps somewhat sobered when we consider that the precolonial tree was, in its day, a functional space of justice, of discipline, of the enactment of power – and in which respect, the tree hardly differs from that of a conventional (i.e. Western) court of law.

40 DPW, 'Brief and Conditions: Competition for the New Constitutional Court of South Africa', p 17.

41 Ibid.

42 A registrar's report notes that a total of 171 design submissions were received, 30 of which were from abroad. 'Registrar's Summary and Comments on the Proceedings of the Panel of Assessors 10–17 November 1997' (Johannesburg:

SAHRA, 1997); Jacques Liebenberg, 'General Notification to Participants' (Pretoria: DPW, 1998).

43   DPW, 'Brief and Conditions: Competition for the New Constitutional Court of South Africa', p 26.

44   Interview, Johannesburg (November, 2005).

45   Interview, Pretoria (November, 2005).

46   Ibid.

47   Ibid.

48   Ibid.

49   Interview, London (May, 2006).

50   Ibid.

51   Ibid.

52   Ibid.

53   CSC, 'Minutes of the Special Meeting of the Competition Steering Committee Meeting, Held on 13 March 1998' (Johannesburg: SAHRA, 1998), p 2.

54   Ibid.

55   'Architectural Competition for the Constitutional Court: Report by the Jury on the Conclusion of the Judging of the Constitutional Court Building' (Pretoria: DPW, 1998).

56   PP found a portion of their second-round report which, fortunately, covered the most important points, see: PP, 'The Constitutional Court of South Africa: Second Report' (Zimbabwe: PP, 1998), p 8.

57   Ibid. p 11.

58   'Constitutional Court: Report by the Competition Jury on the First Stage of the Competition' (Pretoria: DPW, 1997), p 12.

59   Justin Snell, First Round Submission Drawings (Johannesburg: Constitution Hill, 1997).

60   Justin Snell, Second Round Submission Drawings (Johannesburg: Constitution Hill, 1998).

61   Ibid.

62   Ibid.

63   Ibid.

64   Justin Snell, First Round Submission Drawings

65   'Constitutional Court: Report by the Competition Jury on the First Stage of the Competition', p 13.

66   Ibid. pp 13–14.

67   Jeff Stacey, previously with PDC, gave me two design reports, one of which would appear to be an early report, and the other, a portion of the final report for the second round, see: PDC, 'Report' (Johannesburg: PDC, 1997); PDC, 'Report: Second Round' (Johannesburg: PDC, 1998).

68 PDC, 'Report', p 3.

69 PDC, Second Round Submission Drawings (Johannesburg: Constitution Hill, 1998).

70 PDC, 'Report', p 6.

71 'Constitutional Court: Report by the Competition Jury on the First Stage of the Competition', p 13.

72 PDC, 'Report: Second Round'.

73 HJH, 'Report' (Pretoria: HJH, 1997), p 4.

74 Ibid. p 4.

75 Ibid. p 6.

76 Ibid. p 4.

77 'Constitutional Court: Report by the Competition Jury on the First Stage of the Competition', p 14.

78 'Architectural Competition for the Constitutional Court: Report by the Jury on the Conclusion of the Judging of the Constitutional Court Building'.

79 The design was a joint effort, with OMM Design Workshop taking a lead with regard to architectural design, while Urban Solutions was more involved with urban design aspects of the submission, a pattern that continued throughout the project.

80 OMMUS, 'The New Constitutional Building of South Africa' (Durban: OMMUS, 1998), p 1.

81 Ibid. p 1.

82 Interviews, Durban (January 2005, December 2005). The design team also consisted of Paul Wygers and Eric Ortis-Hansen of Urban Solutions.

83 OMMUS, 'The New Constitutional Building of South Africa', p 5, p 7.

84 Ibid. p 14.

85 Ibid. p 10.

86 Ibid. p 9.

87 The base is emphasised in the final design.

88 OMMUS, 'The New Constitutional Building of South Africa', p 1.

89 Ibid. p 15.

90 Ibid. p 14.

91 Ibid. p 15.

92 Ibid. p 16.

93 Ibid. p 14.

94 See p 110, endnote 62.

95 Sean O'Toole, 'Hanging Judge', *Sunday Times Lifestyle*, 22 February 2004, p 6; Albie Sachs, 'Every Picture Tells a Story', *Mail and Guardian*, 27 February–4 March 2004, p 2.

96   Interviews, Johannesburg (November 2004).

97   Interview, Durban (January 2005).

98   'Constitutional Court: Report by the Competition Jury on the First Stage of the Competition', p 15.

99   Ibid.

100   'Architectural Competition for the Constitutional Court: Report by the Jury on the Conclusion of the Judging of the Constitutional Court Building'.

101   Interviews, Johannesburg (November 2004). Interview, London (May 2006).

102   Interviews, Durban (January 2005, December 2005). The project steering committee was formed (post-competition) to help guide the realisation of the design.

103   Inclusion of handcrafted elements was proposed in the competition submission report: OMMUS, 'The New Constitutional Building of South Africa,' p 15.

104   Interviews, Durban (January 2005, December 2005).

105   JDA, 'National Artwork Competitions for the New Constitutional Court Building' (Johannesburg: JDA), section 1, p 17.

106   Interview, Durban (December 2005).

107   JDA, 'National Artwork Competitions for the New Constitutional Court Building', section 2, p 7.

108   Jane du Rand, 'Description of the Foyer Experience' (Durban: Jane du Rand).

109   Jane du Rand, Submission Drawings (Durban: Jane du Rand), dwg. 1.

110   Ibid.

111   Ibid.

112   Interview, Durban (December 2005).

113   Ibid.

114   Lewis Levin and Patrick Rorke, 'Constitution Hill National Artworks Competition: A Proposal for the Sunscreens' (Johannesburg: Lewis Levin).

115   Interview, Johannesburg (October 2005).

116   Paulus Gerdes (ed.), *Geometry from Africa. Mathematical and Educational Explorations* (Washington DC: Mathematical Association of America, 1999).

117   Interview, Johannesburg (October 2005).

118   Ibid.

119   Ibid.

120   Interview, Johannesburg (October 2005).

121   Ibid.

122   Ibid.

123   Ibid.

124   Ibid.

125   Interview, Durban (December 2005).

126   Interview, Durban (December 2005).

127   Interviews, Durban (December 2005). On this occasion I also met Siphiswe Zulu, who submitted paintings for use as carpet designs, only his work was submitted via the NSA gallery.

128   Interviews, Durban (December 2005).

129   Ibid.

130   Ibid.

131   Claude Lefort, *Democracy and Political Theory* (Cambridge: Polity Press, 1988), p 31.

132   Preamble to the Constitution of the Republic of South Africa, Act 108 of 1996.

133   Lefort, *Democracy and Political Theory*, p 38.

134   Ibid. p 30.

135   This quotation is gleaned from: Nelson Mandela, *Long Walk to Freedom: The Autobiography of Nelson Mandela* (London: Abacus, 1995), p 233.

136   Mfanelo Patrick Ntsobi, 'Privatisation of Prisons and Prison Services in South Africa' (Masters Thesis, University of the Western Cape, 2005).

'We the People', Part 2: The Walter Sisulu Square of Dedication, Kliptown

5.1 Delegates at the Congress of the People, Kliptown (1955). Permission to reprint extracts from *Thirty Years of the Freedom Charter*, by Raymond Suttner and Jeremy Cronin, was granted by Ravan Press (Macmillan SA).

The Congress of the People

'God, I tell you. By the time we were ready at three o'clock it was just a sea of heads. You know, we couldn't understand where these people were coming from. Bus loads. Lorry loads. Motor cars. People walking by foot. They were coming from everywhere', Chetty remembers.[1] According to official figures, 2,884 delegates were present at the Congress of the People, as well as some 7,000 spectators (see Figure 5.1).[2] The event took place over two days on 25 and 26 June 1955, on an abandoned patch of land in Kliptown and was planned to allow representative delegates from across the country to vote on the final form of the Freedom Charter, a declaration of fundamental freedoms and human rights. The Freedom Charter, which was ratified by the African National Congress (ANC) a year later (March 1956), reads:

We, the people of South Africa, declare for all our country and the world to know:
That South Africa belongs to all who live in it, black and white, and that no government can justly claim authority unless it is based on the will of all the people ...
The people shall govern! ...
All national groups shall have equal rights! ...
The people shall share in the country's wealth! ...
The land shall be shared among those who work it! ...
All shall be equal before the law! ...
All shall enjoy equal human rights! ...
There shall be work and security! ...
The doors of learning and of culture shall be opened! ...
There shall be houses, security and comfort! ...
There shall be peace and friendship! ...
These freedoms we will fight for, side by side, throughout our lives, until we have won our liberty.[3]

Albert Luthuli, the then president of the ANC, stated that '[n]othing in the history of the libratory movement in South Africa quite caught the popular imagination as this did'.[4] Commentators have observed that the Congress marked a turning point in South African politics. For the first time, liberation movements in SA had transcended a politics of resistance, and a coalition was formed around a positive intent. Suttner and Cronin have described the event as 'the most representative gathering' in South African history.[5] The Freedom Charter is 'a people's document ... created through a democratic process, unprecedented in this country and probably in most other countries of the world'.[6] Historically speaking, the charter was formulated at a crucial point: following the 1948 election which marked the birth of grand apartheid and the Defiance Campaign of 1952, as well as prior to the Treason Trial of 1956– 61, where documents confiscated at the Congress were used as key evidence against the accused.[7] And ultimately, the legacy of the Freedom Charter found fulfilment in the 1996 Constitution of South Africa, the two documents being similar in many ways, especially with regard to the wide-scoped inclusion of political, cultural and socio-economic rights.

Kliptown

Situated some 20 km south-west of Johannesburg, Kliptown is one of the earliest urban settlements within the greater Johannesburg region, pre-dating nearby Soweto by approximately 60 years.[8] Farming activity in this area used to supply milk and fresh produce to the mining camp town of early Johannesburg, although few traces of these agricultural beginnings remain.[9] In 1903, the Johannesburg City Council purchased Klipspruit farm with a view to establishing a gravitational sewage works,[10] and by 1904, an influx of black

5.2   Aerial photograph of the design competition site, Kliptown. Courtesy of the Johannesburg Development Agency.

and Indian people arrived here due to an outbreak of bubonic plague at the Indian Location in central Johannesburg. The new inhabitants were initially accommodated in emergency camps, settlements which were to evolve into the housing stock of Kliptown.[11]

Kliptown did not fit the apartheid segregationalist plan, but instead grew into a cosmopolitan town. Situated on the periphery of Johannesburg, it was an area where apartheid laws were often not enforced. Officially speaking, the Transvaal Provincial Administration had control of Kliptown, 'but since its office was based in Pretoria they rarely visited the area'.[12] Like other infamous 'grey areas' in South Africa, such as Sophiatown and District Six, Kliptown was a place where different cultural and racial groups lived together: African,

Indian, Malay, Chinese and European. Interracial marriage, later banned by the Apartheid Prohibition of Mixed Marriages Act of 1949, was not uncommon. As one resident of Kliptown confirms: 'the government ... didn't allow mixed marriages in the Transvaal ... People would get married in the Cape or in Kimberley or Lourenco Marques or even overseas ... Then they will come back and live here. They were never harassed.'[13] Kliptown's multicultural past was, without doubt, one of the reasons why this area was selected for the Congress. According to Douglas Rodd, the nearby railway station – in close proximity to Soweto – the spacious nature of the site, and the fact that political activists were familiar with this area, also would have featured in that decision.[14]

Despite its historical significance, the site of the Congress has remained something of an enigma. One of the greatest public events in the history of South African politics occurred here, on a largely desolate stretch of land etched by the paths of pedestrians who used to criss-cross as they journeyed from home to work, in an highly impoverished area on the margins of greater Johannesburg (see Figure 5.2). In 2003, a national architectural competition was held for the design of Freedom Square, a project which was later renamed 'The Walter Sisulu Square of Dedication'. Freedom Square was conceived in recognition of 'the spirit of human hope that animated ... the ideals of the Charter'.[15]

It may be noted that all previous competitions were motivated by programmatic need, and building sites were selected with well-defined criteria in mind. In Kliptown, however, things would occur the other way round. The site was well known but the nature of the required development proved difficult to define. Developmental options were worsened by what was perceived to be the indistinct character of the site. At this early stage, the precise location of the Congress had not been verified. And significantly, the site lacked distinct boundaries: the open space seemed to bleed into the dense, low-lying residential fabric of the surrounding township, and this embedded character raised equally indistinct questions of ownership. This project frames crucial issues of economic empowerment, of participation and ownership. The Walter Sisulu Square's primary ambition has been to commemorate an event, the historic traces of which have all but vanished, yet neither the programme nor the site – indeed not even 'the client', for initially at least, there was none – could be called upon to provide clear direction.

Urban context has been a recurring theme of this book. In previous chapters, contextual questions arose as to the hegemonic character of existing urban environments, which were largely derived from Western spaces and types. In responding to this circumstance, post-apartheid public design has sought to expand the field of contextual reference, to signify a symbolic break with the past, and to establish imaginative dialogues with silenced and excluded histories. In most cases, the new architecture has not merely rejected the old, but rather has combined different elements to form hybrid appropriations that resonate on multiple levels. Kliptown shows a unique situation in this regard as in this case, we are dealing with one of South Africa's infamous 'grey areas', an urban space where apartheid segregation failed to take hold, where

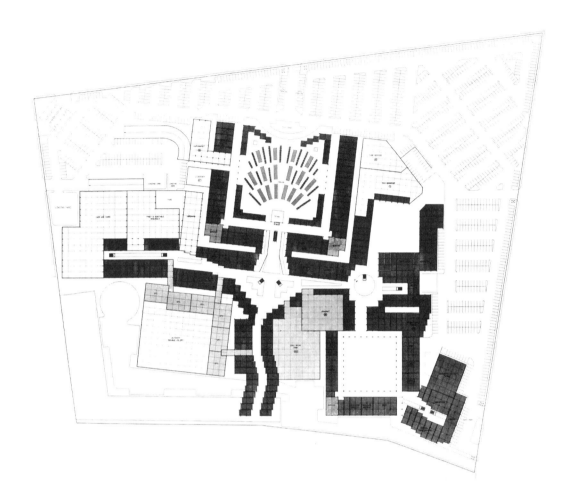

diverse histories coincide. The complex spatialities and hybrid traditions of historic Kliptown provide us with the first instance of what may be termed an 'authentic' context. The word 'authentic' is chosen here in a self-consciously political sense because historic Kliptown offers a de-racialised glimpse of how things might have been – a rich source for design. Yet, despite this remarkable fact, the seemingly indistinct character of the site would plague successive imaginations for the Freedom Square.

5.3   Proposed mixed-use development for Kliptown, Plan (1991). Courtesy of Meyer Pienaar Smith Architects, (MPS).

A False Start

Sometime in the early 1990s, a firm of commercial property developers, Nkosana Investment (Pty) Ltd, acquired developmental rights for an abandoned patch of land behind Union Street in Kliptown. Nkosana Investment struck a deal with Stocks and Stocks Properties to develop this site, the precise details of which remain obscure.[16] However, the first architectural drawings for the

5.4 Proposed mixed-use development for Kliptown, Perspective (1991). Courtesy of Meyer Pienaar Smith Architects (MPS).

development of the area, prepared by Meyer Pienaar Smith Architects (MPS, which also worked on the Mpumalanga Legislature), are dated November 1991 (see Figures 5.3–5.4). The design is conceived as a number of open-air courts connected by internalised streets.[17] This unique, hybrid programme was envisaged as a commercial development grafted onto existing patterns of trade and movement that are prevalent in Kliptown. But as Ellis explained, this proposal proved untenable because financial institutions were nervous to commit funds. Raising finance for development in a marginalised 'black' area such as Kliptown, at this time, was almost impossible. Nevertheless, a second scheme was formed not long after, this time by Louis Peens Architects, and designed as a more conventional shopping centre in an attempt to secure finance. Finally, a third shopping centre-type design was prepared by MPS, a design which was eventually resubmitted as MPS's entry to the architectural competition for Freedom Square.

In 1994, the intended shopping centre development was noted by the regional branch of the National Monuments Council (NMC). A conciliatory letter of the same year, authored by the NMC and addressed to Stocks and Stocks, states that '[a]lthough the Committee was not opposed to the development of the square, the square should be commemorated in some way ... A suitably worded NMC plaque could be erected at the new development.'[18] A newspaper report of June 1995, however, would raise the alarm: '[f]orty years ago today it was the site of history; soon it will be a shopping mall.'[19] Despite this protest, a site development plan for the intended centre was submitted to council authorities, and was considered by a sitting of the NMC on 7 March 1996.[20] Moves were eventually made to establish a forum for discussing the intended scheme.[21] By July, NMC resistance had begun to mount, with minutes noting that '[t]he adoption of the Freedom Charter was too important an idea to be relegated into a small and insignificant open space in the midst of a modern shopping mall.'[22] In November 1996, it was decided that the site should be 'provisionally' declared a 'national monument', and the idea of an international architectural competition was promoted by the NMC.[23]

A Participatory Vision

At this time, the Greater Johannesburg Metropolitan Chamber (GJMC) began to strategise development for the Kliptown area, and by May 1997, the 'Greater Kliptown Development Framework Plan' (GKDFP) was established.[24] Promoted as a '"must-see" site for domestic, national and international tourists', Kliptown is to be 'put on the map'.[25] A Freedom Square Project Implementation Team (FSPIT) was established within the GJMC to mastermind the future of Freedom Square, and to establish a brief for the intended competition. The committee was mixed, with representatives from the GJMC; NMC; the Department of Arts, Culture, Science and Technology; and two Wits

University academics, namely Professor Caroline Hamilton (Graduate School for the Humanities and Social Sciences) and Professor Lindsey Bremner (Department of Architecture), as well as various representatives associated with Kliptown. The work done by this team was crystallised in their business plan of November 1997.[26] This document incorporates the recommendations of the NMC as well as the GKDFP and, crucially, it introduces a new visionary focus which emphasises the international significance of the Freedom Charter and joins this to performative forms of commemoration. The stated purpose of the project is 'to achieve the proper celebration of this site's international, national and local historical significance'.[27] In this, it is hoped that Freedom Square will transcend the constraints of a nationalist narrative to inspire 'an international commitment to the support of the struggles for freedom and human rights'.[28] Hamilton explained that for many years, Kliptown had been marginalised and that she was hoping to focus resources and interest into the area.[29] 'We were trying to think big, to think International', she said. This orientation was also premised on the hopes of foreign investment into the project, as confirmed by the GKDFP.[30]

This broad vision was coupled with an equally diverse programme, 'a place in which a multiplicity of uses will occur, co-existing and complimenting each other'.[31] The report lays down a conceptual plan for a two-stage, international design competition. The first stage would be 'open to all', and would 'call for conceptual designs for the area against a comprehensive brief' to be identified in terms of 'community needs'.[32] During this first stage, a parallel process was to be established to allow 'other disciplines' and, importantly, 'communities who live and work in the area' to participate in the project and to 'give expression to, the unique history of the site'.[33] A series of performative events were to be staged in Kliptown to create 'art works and performance pieces that convey their interpretation of the site'.[34] Local artists and community groups were to be involved in this process, and local histories were to be recorded. A multidisciplinary involvement was also intended to include research input from anthropologists, sociologists, political scientists and historians, as well as performing and visual artists. These participatory events and research inputs were to be orchestrated by the Graduate School for the Humanities and Social Sciences as an 'innovative' form of 'public culture', the results of which were to be included in the brief for the second stage of the design competition.[35] Like the Congress itself, the commemorative architecture of Freedom Square was set to evolve from forms of interpretive participation. Regrettably, these participatory intentions were never realised.

Defining Conservation Guidelines

The involvement of academics Professors Hamilton and Bremner – both members of the FSPIT – had contributed to what I shall call a *socio-discursive*

5.5 Informal trade on Union Street, Kliptown. Photographs by the author.

vision for Kliptown, one in which international prestige is linked to grass roots participation. This intention had the potential to spark a public awareness of the legacy of the Freedom Charter, and a public discourse on the theme of human rights. Unfortunately, this vision was abandoned. In the meantime, however, a somewhat different although not incompatible agenda was put forward by the NMC. The NMC's contribution was formed around what I shall call a more *scientific–historical* emphasis on heritage concerns that was initiated by Rodd et al.'s survey of the site.[36] This survey sought to establish the facts of the case: where the Congress took place, what Kliptown would have looked like at that time and, by inference, which aspects of the site constituted 'authentic' heritage. The survey comments on the status of buildings in Kliptown, especially along Union Street, which in many cases were rebuilt through time, so that the surrounding urban tissue would have been somewhat different at the time of the Congress. It stated that 'no old buildings of intrinsic architectural merit have been identified', yet the desirability of preserving the 'vibrant social and economic character of the area' was noted.[37] This vibrant character can be experienced on Union Street, which is probably the oldest surviving 'black' retail strip in greater Johannesburg (see Figure 5.5). Running in an east–west direction, Union Street borders the southern side of the open landscape associated with the Congress. This retail strip is remarkable for the symbiotic relations that used to exist between formal and informal trade, where mostly black street traders would hug the pavements selling their wares in front of street-level shops, most of which were occupied by Indian shopkeepers.

The survey's contextual considerations initiated discussions among NMC representatives, whose primary concern was to establish conservation guidelines for the area. Minutes to regional NMC meetings held over the period June 1998 to February 1999 demonstrate the contested and uncertain nature of this undertaking.[38] '[T]he big issue is what are we trying to conserve', and indeed how to create a 'tangible memory of an event which was not very tangible in the first place'.[39] Union Street is identified as the only 'sign of place' that is linked to Freedom Square, and it must be noted that written accounts of the Congress have commonly identified the site as being the open ground behind the shops on Union Street.[40] Union Street is thus considered to be the concrete trace of the Congress.[41] Debate then ensued as to whether the NMC should be concerned with a 'restoration … of certain buildings so as to conserve the street' whether the 'street-scape' should be conserved, or whether it is the general 'ambience' of the area that must be preserved, rather than 'actual buildings'.[42] At a later meeting, these deliberations were complicated by the realisation that preserving Union Street might be construed as 'celebrating poverty', and the possible involvement of the local community in addressing this issue was debated.[43] By October 1999, these deliberations had produced a set of conservation guidelines and principles, which were later included as an annexure to the final competition brief, to which we shall return.

Finalisation of the Competition Brief

The following stage of the project is associated with the Johannesburg Development Agency (JDA) which came on board to manage the wider developmental initiatives of greater Kliptown. The JDA also managed the architectural competition and, in the final design brief of 2002, the JDA is listed as the 'client' and 'promoter' of Freedom Square.[44] Unlike competition briefs encountered in previous chapters – and, for that matter, the 1997 GKDFP and 1997 business plan – we now have a national competition to be adjudicated in one stage. The key element in this shift away from the previous commitment to a two-stage, international competition was a project deadline that was established by the JDA and Blue IQ – an investment arm of the Gauteng Provincial Government. Graeme Reid, who was previously a member of the FSPIT and then later chief executive of the JDA, explained that 2005 was set as the public celebration for the opening of Freedom Square, a showcase for the achievements of Blue IQ and a date which was established for commemoration of the 50th anniversary of the 1955 Congress.[45] This deadline, it would seem, allowed little time for the complex administration of an international competition. As Prins and Callinicos confirmed, the tight programme did not allow sufficient time for a thorough two-stage process of adjudication, which is highly regrettable.[46]

Section A of the competition brief explains that '[t]he brief for Freedom Square is as open-ended and as non-prescriptive as possible. Such an approach is in keeping with the participatory nature of the writing of the Freedom Charter'.[47] Therefore, competitors are invited to 'write their own brief', and are asked to do so in the context of a one-stage competition, which privileges conceptual design without any clear programmatic or aesthetic criteria.[48] In so doing, the commitment to social participation that was fought for in the early stages of this project is translated into an open-ended abstraction, which merely exists to affirm the arbitrary imaginings of the designer/architect, who is invited to draw on paper without any involvement or guidance drawn from social players. The client, after all, has been redefined as the JDA, which in this context appears to act as a development agency with a bag of money, but without clear ideas for their own initiative. This observation, however, is not the full story because the JDA's objectives are clarified elsewhere in 'Joburg 2030', which sets out a 30-year vision for greater Johannesburg, placing economic objectives ahead of social-service delivery.[49] A similar emphasis is also apparent in the updated Kliptown Development Business Plan (KDBP) of 2004, which speaks the language of international tourism and sustainable business investment, but where 'social development' gets marginalised.[50]

Certain aspects of the FSPIT's vision are maintained, especially in section B where parts of the text are derived from previous drafts. This section highlights 'the site's international, national and local historic significance and conservation value'.[51] Yet crucially, the FSPIT grafted international interest onto participatory processes to harmonise global and local concerns. The final brief, however, pays scarce attention to actual needs. Admittedly, this omission is remedied somewhat by section C, where possible functions are discussed. But the text is exceptionally vague, stating for example the need for 'community development', and 'more housing'.[52] These 'needs', which were inadequately researched and inadequately specified, 'serve only to inspire an informed response from competitors'.[53] Ultimately, the structure of the text invites competitors to read these needs under the cavalier injunction to 'write you own brief'.[54] Conservational requirements, by contrast, are better specified, hence Freedom Square 'needs to be developed in relation to the adjacent shops in Union Street, nearby points of transportation ... houses to the south ... [and] informal sports and meetings activities'.[55] In particular, '[t]he role of Union Street needs to be acknowledged ... [and] ... [c]ognizance should be taken of the lively culture of informal trading which characterises the area adjoining the Square.'[56]

The brief supports a contextual approach to design, hence 'what this competition seeks to do, using sensitive, conservative and creative means is to make something that is uniquely suited to the South African context, appeals to local sentiment, and by virtue of its excellence would enjoy international recognition'.[57] But the terms of this commitment remain vague. Indeed, the arbitrariness and state of indecision that is communicated by this brief contrasts with competition documents that were encountered in previous chapters, all of which endeavoured to give substance to questions of programme, material context and, in some cases, architectural character. Failure to clarify these issues meant that the competition jury was being asked to adjudicate without clear assessment criteria, and was to do so in the context of a single stage, ideas-based competition, which was to commemorate an intangible event on an equally indistinct site. It is therefore not surprising that debate as to appropriate character and questions of design resolution was largely overlooked by the jury.

Adjudicating the Competition

The jury was a mixed panel, comprising a representative from the JDA (Graeme Reid), the mayor of Johannesburg (Amos Masondo), as well as the Gauteng MEC for finance (Jabu Moleketi), a historian (Luli Callinicos), three local architects (Zola Kgaka, Mira Fassler Kamstra and Khotso Moleko), as well as an internationally renowned architect from the USA (Professor Stanley Saitowitz, who also served as chairperson of the jury). A total of 34 design entries were received, which were examined over two days in June 2002.[58] I was able to secure interviews with the local architects concerned, as well as Reid, Callinicos and Prins, who was present in his capacity as administrator.[59]

Kgaka, an architect from Johannesburg, explained that most of the submissions failed to capture the 'spirit' of the Freedom Charter, and did not achieve an appropriate vision for the area.[60] The winning scheme seemed unique in this regard because it was like a 'seed' which, when planted, would allow the wider Kliptown area to grow through time.[61] Kgaka emphasised the fact that Kliptown had not developed under apartheid and, for this reason, the bold urban intentions of the winning scheme were appropriate. Nevertheless, she recalls intensive debate about the winning scheme because, although the intentions were good, the design seemed insensitive to its context: the building scale was overbearing and this was clearly wrong in the context of old Kliptown. The jury voted in favour of the winning scheme because of its urban strategy and not because of the details of its architectural design per se, she said. It was believed that the problems of scale and of relations to urban context could be resolved without losing the better intentions of the winning design. Fassler Kamstra – who was a juror for the Northern Cape Legislature – made similar observations, emphasising that failings of character, scale and context, as identified in the jurors' written report, were issues that could be solved through design resolution, and these problems did not jeopardise the quality of the winning submission.[62] She emphasises the fact that the winning scheme was the only real contender: it was one of the few schemes that did not 'sentimentalise' the context of poverty in Kliptown.[63]

Callinicos felt a strong feature of the winning submission was the way it addressed tensions of heritage and development, an issue that had been discussed by the NMC, debates to which she had previously been party.[64] The winning scheme seemed to promote a positive transformation of the Kliptown area, while commemorating the past. Yet, Callinicos also expressed dissatisfaction with the completed project, which is not evocative of the past and seems largely insensitive to the surrounding buildings of old Kliptown. Khotso Moleko – who was a juror for the Legislature at Mpumalanga – was even more critical, maintaining that most entries failed to address the conceptual nature of the brief, and did not demonstrate an adequate 'feeling' for the Freedom Charter.[65] The winning scheme was a 'compromised choice' – the architecture and symbolism failed to convince.[66] The chosen scheme was selected by the jury because it had established clear 'developmental strategies' for the area, from which it was possible to 'calculate jobs and houses', he said.[67] Reid, then chief executive of the JDA, strongly supports the design, arguing that the project is intended for the future context of Kliptown.[68] If anything, the scale of the development may be 'too small' because the area is soon to be a thriving economic centre, he said.[69] He noted that the other designs were unsatisfactory and that in many cases, there was a 'patronising approach to poverty'.[70] In my view, however, Reid's thought implies a false duplicity – of poverty versus development – while a more sophisticated approach to this locale would surely wish to confuse the simplicity of this binary to allow for mixed and inclusive alternatives, both old and new. It is necessary, therefore, to ask whether any of the rejected schemes provide valid alternatives to the shortcomings of the winning scheme.

All jurors emphasised that the winning selection was unanimous, yet clearly there are substantial differences as to the success of the final scheme

5.6 Design
submission
by PCWG,
Plan (2002).
Courtesy of the
Johannesburg
Development
Agency.

– which was not the case with previous competitions. Jurors' comments also demonstrate that the winning scheme was chosen for its concepts and developmental intentions, while questions of architectural resolution were suspended because it was anticipated that the project would be modified through a process of detailed design. This expectation was in keeping with requirements of the competition documents, which reserved the right for the competition administrator – in consultation with the JDA project board – to modify the terms of the winning brief.[71] This provision suggests that design details would be clarified at a later stage, with input from the client, and therefore the jury felt content to register their misgivings in writing. The jurors' written report sets out a list of 'reservations' and 'recommendations' with respect to the winning scheme, some details of which will be discussed in due course. No protocol was, however, established to ensure that these problems would be addressed.[72] Key architectural considerations regarding programmatic requirement, urban context, architectural character and design resolution were left to the discretion of the client who, it would seem, was ill

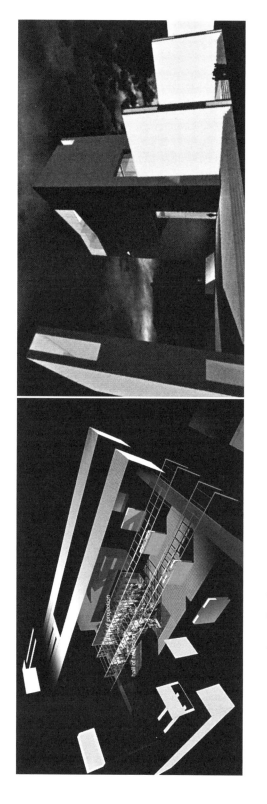

5.7a: The Halls of Projection and Reflection, PCWG's design submission (2002) (left to right) b: Ten monumental walls, PCWG's design submission (2002). Courtesy of the Johannesburg Development Agency.

equipped to deal with these complex matters, especially given the fast-track deadlines that were chosen for this scheme.

Design Submissions

Officials at the JDA informed me that competition submission reports – in other words, written reports – had been given to the project architects, StudioMAS (SM), for safe keeping, but the whereabouts of the submission drawings was unknown. Fortunately, I managed to locate the original competition submission drawings, which have been preserved thanks to the efforts of Gene Duiker of the Kliptown Our Town Trust (KOTT).[73] I found the drawings in a large wooden chest at the rear end of the Kliptown Our Town Museum, where rain from a leaky roof dribbled down an adjacent wall, threatening to damage the fragile contents of the locked container.[74] Duiker, who delights in the political implications of counter-histories, was pleased to allow me to study the drawings and to take photographs of all 34 submissions.[75]

We shall now move on to consider the winning scheme, as well as the three that were selected by the jury for being worthy of an 'honourable mention', a title which was awarded without hierarchy of distinction.[76] The submission by Paragon Architects, Comrie Wilkinson and Green (PCWG) is of distinguished quality, consisting as it does of nine large colour panels, with sketches, drawings and detailed computer-rendered perspectives (see Figures 5.6–5.7). A set of seven sequential sketch plans demonstrates the evolution of the design concept. The first sketch, entitled '[t]he place as found and remembered' represents the spatial containment of the site as it would have been during the Congress.[77] The meeting space is delimited by a split-pole fence on its northern and southern boundaries by the railway tracks to the west and Old Kliptown Street to the east. Rows of bluegum trees also line the northern and eastern sides. PCWG's first move was to find the lost traces of these historic edges and to invent new ways for reinstating them on the site via a series of boundary walls, a tower and an edge building which holds the north-west side of the site. A long 'timeline' wall cuts across the entire site, in a north–south direction, to reinstate the edge of Old Kliptown Street.[78]

This scheme promotes a somewhat institutional, museum-centred imagination, which is nevertheless remedied by the interactive nature of the architecture. Situated between the two long wings of this 'H'-shaped plan sits the 'Hall of Projection' and the 'Hall of Reflection' where visitors can interact with images that are projected onto glass screens.[79] A flyover roof structure extends beyond the Hall of Freedom to embrace public space at the centre of the site (see Figure 5.7a). A dynamic spatial interaction is here formed at the intersection of the timeline, the line of wall monuments and the shaded outdoor spaces defined by the flyover roof structure. The architectural orchestration relies on a sense of spatial continuity which flows around exploded building elements in a manner reminiscent of Brasilia-style modernism. Outdoor spaces

are activated by a variety of architectural events, allowing visitors to interact with the history of the Congress and the Freedom Charter – a positive aspect of this design. For example, ten wall monuments, which commemorate the ten clauses of the Freedom Charter, may be entered via a door situated at one of the narrow ends of each wall (see Figure 5.7 b). Words and projected images are used to animate the significance of each of the ten clauses of the Freedom Charter. The jury admired the 'inventiveness and energy' of this design, but also felt that 'the number of elements and amount of buildings overwhelm the presence of the square which although powerfully illustrated, lacks the scale and generosity of a place of gathering of this significance'.[80] No comments are made with regard to the architectural character of this scheme, yet one may assume that had this design been entered into the other competitions, the jurors could have questioned the institutional modernism of this design which, in a sense, could be built anywhere.

The other designs awarded with 'honourable mention' place a stronger emphasis on the historic site of the Congress which, in either case, features in its entirety as an open public domain – space rather than built form, commemorating the memory of the event. A submission by Kruger Roos Architects and Urban Designers (KRA) provides a poetic reading of the existing landscape (see Figures 5.8–5.9). Seen from the air, the site bears the traces of multiple uses through time: 'pedestrians criss-crossed through this place on their way to work, transport and shops.'[81] These are the flowing, immediate and impermanent traces of everyday life in Kliptown (see Figure 5.2). The architects explain: '[t]he freedom square is seen as part of a local

5.8   Design submission by KRA, model (2002). Courtesy of the Johannesburg Development Agency.

5.9 Design submission by KRA, Plan (2002). Courtesy of the Johannesburg Development Agency.

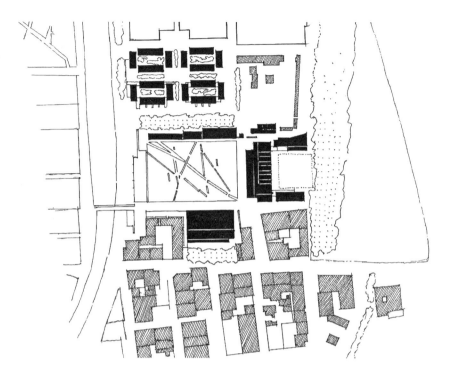

community where people engage with the place as they go about their daily lives.' Their design therefore seeks to create a 'living monument' to the 'action' and 'achievement' of daily life, rather than 'immortalising the past'.[82] This commitment is also in keeping with their reading of the Freedom Charter, the spirit of which 'is not static and should not be encapsulated in a massive, permanent commemorative structure'.[83]

The design contains and frames the historic space of the Congress, which is served by new building structures that surround it: a market and commercial facilities to the north and south, entertainment and cultural facilities to the west, and a multifunctioning hall on the western edge of the square. The intended programme also includes a resource centre, advice centre, education centre, garden of remembrance, civic square, parking facilities, belfry and housing. At the centre of this configuration is the new Freedom Square, the surface of which has been incised by a splatter of diagonal paths which cut across the formalised geometry of the square. Paths 'most visible' on the existing site have been etched into the landscape, and '[w]ithin these incisions are laid objects that will serve as virtuous momentos of human spirit in the form of poetry, art and sculpture. Glazed over, the visitor can walk over these objects tracing the path taken by others … in their struggle for freedom'.[84] The design entry, which consisted of a single page, comprises a descriptive text, sketches and drawings, as well as photographs of a model which shows how the glazed incisions light up at night to form a 'theatre of life'.[85]

The jury praised this design for its 'rich variety of celebration', its 'sensitivity' and 'economy', yet also notes that '[t]he scheme focuses on a very

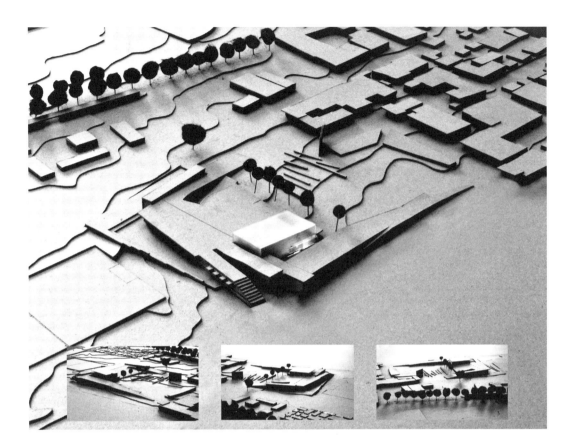

circumscribed area of transformation. This is felt to be a limitation. Unlike the winning scheme the square seems isolated, insular and limited in its celebration of the scale of significance.'[86] The historic setting for the Congress acquires a new significance when viewed through the lens of KRA's poetic design, which transcends previous troubled imaginations that struggle with this 'problematic' site. Instead, this design celebrates a new aesthetic vision, premised on vibrant patterns of adaptation and use that characterise the daily life of Kliptown. The translation of these patterns is, however, realised through the autonomous expression of an aesthetic form. Neat urban edges of Freedom Square frame the space as though it were a work of art, a form of aesthetic closure, which arguably removes it from the actual life of the township.

5.10 Design submission by MRAB, model (2002). Courtesy of the Johannesburg Development Agency.

The design by Mashabane Rose Associates, entered in association with Lindsey Bremner (MRAB), works with a similar imagination, with built interventions responding to local patterns of everyday life. However, in this case, poetic translation is unconstrained by spatial closure (see Figures 5.10–5.11). MRAB's submission consists of five carefully composed sheets, one of which represents the primary metaphoric intention of their design. A historic photograph depicts crumpled papers, bearing the many demands that were concretised in the Freedom Charter, and an accompanying caption states

5.11   Design submission by MRAB, Plan (2002). Courtesy of the Johannesburg Development Agency.

that '[p]inned in countless pieces of paper to the podium of the congress of the people, freedom was not conceived of as a utopian blueprint prepared by leaders or technocrats, but as something rooted in peoples' everyday life experience and its transformations.'[87] Below this image exists another which depicts informal garment traders who typically lay their wares on the ground in a loose tapestry of colour – an arresting display that attracts the attention of pedestrians who buy as they pass. The appropriation of nameless, discarded space, as illustrated by this scene, provides a metaphor for Kliptown's creative urban traditions. The metaphoric relation suggested by the conjunction of these images is one which links a narrative of freedom, rooted in the imperfect contestations of history, to resilient forms of everyday life. The supporting text continues: '[o]ur narrative for freedom square couples the commemoration of an historic event, with the valorization of local economies, modes of associational life and ways of being in the city.'[88] These poetic intentions are spatialised by a subtle plan which appropriates the existing wasteland, folding architecture, urban space and landscape – natural and cultural – upon each other.[89]

Museum and community facilities delineate the northern edge of 'Freedom Charter Square', redefining the historic space of the Congress.[90] Careful attention to natural contours of the site allows the building mass to bury itself. The ground-plane, the leading motif, flows seamlessly over the buried mass, across the Freedom Charter Square which doubles as a football pitch

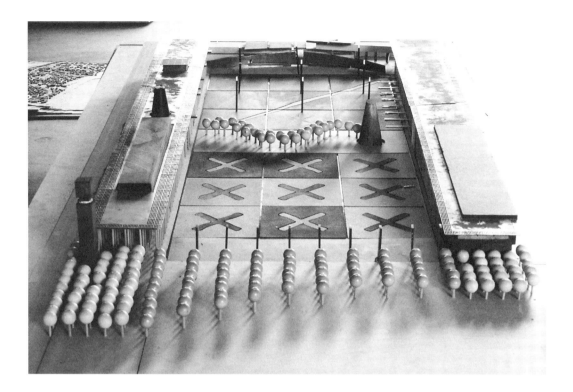

and back into the life of the township. A conceptual sketch explains how '[t]he surface of the earth is lifted, folded, modulated and etched to frame a tapestry of narratives, historical, social and cultural.'[91] Approaching from the north, visitors gain access to the submerged roof of the complex via 'landscaped steps', beyond which it is possible to follow a 'rooftop promenade' with 'views over Charter Square football field, [and] Freedom Charter Precinct'.[92] At this point, the visitor is walking over the landscaped roof of the museum housed below, where the buried 'interpretive space' contains 'oral history recording booths' positioned to record stories of contemporary Kliptown residents. There is also a 'witness testimony cinema' that allows for 'special viewing of selected footage'.[93] To the west, a translucent glass box projects above the rooftop promenade, where it glows at night above the auditorium/community hall within. Moving forward, the landscaped roof ramps down towards a line of trees replanted to mark the historic northern boundary of Freedom Charter Square. The abandoned space, associated with the Freedom Charter, is returned to the community, while the memory of the event is layered into the landscape.

Visitors approaching from the east, along Old Kliptown Street, follow the natural contours that lead towards the square, and slip into the central space between a fan of ten splayed concrete benches, etched with the ten clauses of the Freedom Charter. On the other side of Freedom Charter Square – to the west – a concrete stage, with embedded light bulbs, allows public events to address the square, and serves as a memory of the historic podium that

5.12   Winning submission by SM, model (2002). Courtesy of the Johannesburg Development Agency. Photograph by the author.

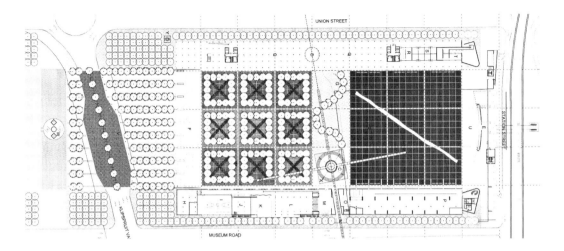

5.13 Winning submission by SM, Plan (2002). Courtesy of the Johannesburg Development Agency.

was constructed for the Congress. Overhead lights are strung from hanging wires in a makeshift fashion that recalls the improvised spirit of the event. The southern boundary of the square is served by a low-key retail strip which lines the back of existing shops fronting onto Union Street. This sensitive integration of discrete architectural elements into the complex structure of the existing landscape successfully redefines the limits of the historic site through a series of porous boundaries that allow space to feed back into the daily life of Kliptown. The architects explain this aspect as follows: '[i]n Kliptown private space is small and cramped. Things spill out, edges are socialised, becoming places where public life is consolidated.'[94] The breadth and sophistication of this design provides a valid alternative to the winning submission, and it is regretful that the jury was unwilling to support this scheme. Nevertheless, the jury maintains that '[a]lthough geometry appears ambiguous, it is prescriptive in the paths it establishes, and in the specific programmatic elements, such as a museum and a shabeen.'[95]

The Winning Scheme

The winning design by SM was a presentation of distinctive quality (see Figures 5.12–5.13). Ten large A0 panels – comprising written text, sketches, photographic images and rendered drawings – detail a project that was unique in that it joined large-scale urban strategies with symbolic interventions.[96] This project represents a countermotion to the previous scheme as where MRAB took inspiration from what may be termed the 'authenticity' of the site – in particular its complex, fragmented and hybrid character – SM, by contrast, seeks to impose a totalising order as remedy for deprived Kliptown. A key feature of this submission is the grand vision that is proposed for the area. It is argued that towns positioned at the centre of Gauteng will eventually merge into a large metropolis, an urban area which the architects wish to name 'Madiba City'.[97] Madiba City is to include a series of public precincts that will give 'identity to the city as a whole'.[98] Freedom Square is presented as one of these precincts, a development which 'would not only give Soweto a new identity, but would become one of the most important sites in the city itself'.[99] This vision is translated into a grand Beaux Arts axis, which runs in an east–west direction along the Kliptown golf course, linking informal settlements on the west side of the railway tracks through to the N1 motorway in the east. This east–west axis is terminated by a relocated railway station in the west, and a proposed new South African Parliament complex to the east.[100] It is unlikely, however, that either of these intended relocations will come to fruition. The golf course, which formerly used to double as an apartheid-style buffer strip between white and black urban areas, is to be redesigned as urban parkland, and provide formal gardens in front of the Parliament. Three- and four-storey perimeter housing blocks line the northern side of the park, complementing existing housing stock situated to the south. This geometry projects into the Freedom Square precinct, formed from two long blocks of accommodation and defining the north and south borders of the site, the so-called North and South Structures. The South Structure, a colonnaded arcade, provides a covered market for informal traders and replaces the old urban fabric on the northern side of Union Street. The less permeable North Structure is positioned to the other side of the square, accommodating formal commercial and community functions. These two arms, with the intended train station positioned at its head, establish firm boundaries to the historical site. The open space so formed is sub-divided into two open public squares situated to the east and west of a cross-axis derived from the position of Old Kliptown Street. The competition jury was impressed by the visionary nature of this design, praising the scheme for 'its bold scale and … its exemplary potential to change Soweto into a city'.[101] The scale of this vision would ultimately translate into the Kliptown Urban Design Framework – prepared by SM – a document which details infrastructural, environmental, housing and commercial development of greater Kliptown.[102] Our enquiry, however, will only focus on Freedom Square, which sits at the centre of this development.

The formalism of this design is infused with symbolism derived from the geometry of public spaces, the orientation of monuments and the positioning of functional programme. Architectural elements combine to tell a narrative of past oppression and freedom from apartheid. The 'Old Square', situated to the east on the spot where the historic Congress is thought to have occurred, symbolises South Africa's past, while the 'New Square', which is of identical shape and size positioned to the west, symbolises the future (see Figure 5.13). Both spaces are laid out on a three-by-three square grid. The resulting squares represent the nine provinces of South Africa, and each is paved with natural stone taken from the region it represents.[103] At the Old Square, the presence of the grid is symbolically drawn with white over black stone: 'its rigidity symbolises the inflexibility of the old regime.'[104] The trace of an old footpath, which may be seen in aerial photographs of the site, is etched diagonally

5.14   Section through the Freedom Charter Monument from SM's design submission (2002). Courtesy of the Johannesburg Development Agency.

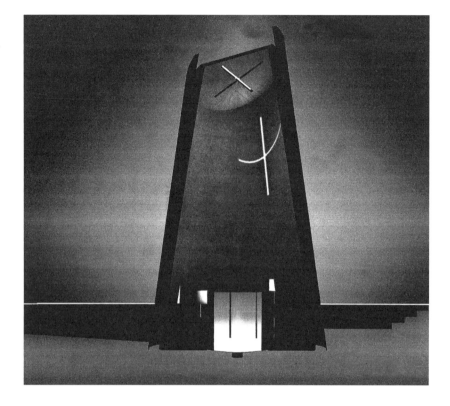

across the Old Square as a 'symbol for crossing out' the presence of the old regime.[105] The New Square, by contrast, represents democratic freedom, and is treated with 'softer and more tangible materials'.[106] Nine 'X'-shaped crosses formed from railway sleepers are laid into the squares: these are intended as a memory of the democratic ballot, where South Africans drew their first voters' cross.

Co-authored by architects Pierre Swanepoel and Justin Snell, the winning submission is reminiscent of Snell's earlier design for the Constitutional Court (see Figures 4.5–4.6). The competition drawings, for instance, explain that the grid is suggestive of a complex symbolism which, on the one hand, refers to 'architectural and philosophical ordering principles' associated with ancient Greece.[107] In this sense, the grid evokes 'the central principle of Greek democracy, isonomea, meaning equality, equal distribution, equilibrium, balance, equality of political rights'.[108] On the other hand, the grid also refers to town- planning principles, as well as forms of social control associated with colonial administration and apartheid. The repetition of this motif across the two squares informs a public narrative to declare that the oppressive urban order of the past must be reoriented towards a more inclusive and equitable future. Yet as was the case with Snell's design for the Constitutional Court, the use of inverted doubles – in this case the grid – is fundamentally ambiguous, and unfortunately fails to signify a clear symbolic change. We may also note a familiar use of symmetrical geometries, grand cross-axial planning, and the

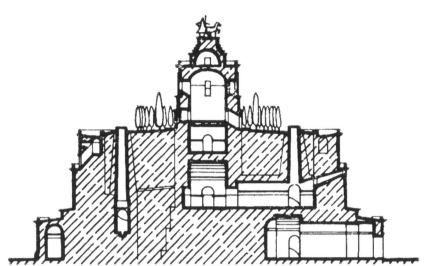

5.15 Section through Hadrian's Mausoleum (ca AD130). Courtesy of Athlone Press.

symbolic use of numbers.[109] Indeed, as was the case with the Constitutional Court submission, numerical symbolism permeates the design for Kliptown, hence a symmetrical relation between the symbolic spaces of the past and the future, nine squares for nine provinces, the nine architectural principles of a 'design charter' which are said to inform the architecture of this scheme (namely identity, legibility, history, symbolism, equality, programme, analogy, accessibility, robustness), a Freedom Charter museum of nine rooms with the Freedom Charter Monument as tenth in commemoration of the ten freedoms of the Freedom Charter, and a line of ten symbolic columns which celebrate entry to the square from Klipspruit Road.[110] A Mandela Fountain is proposed as 'a landmark … [with] eight fountains [four main/four subsidiary] on the points of the compass surrounding a statue of Mandela – i.e. Nelson's column'.[111] Neoclassical themes also inform the Freedom Charter Monument, with its dark interior lit by a cross-shaped hole at the top of the cone, and a monumental flame as centrepiece surrounded by a circular table of ten stones engraved with the ten clauses of the Freedom Charter (see Figure 5.14). The sombre quality of this space is reminiscent of a colonial memorial, and I was dismayed to learn from Snell that his design for the Freedom Charter Monument was inspired by the architectural type of an imperial Roman mausoleum (see Figure 5.15).[112]

In marked contrast to Snell's earlier design for the Constitutional Court, however, the written discourse of this scheme also explores African histories and traditions and, to that extent, exceeds other competition entries. Yet oddly enough, the jurors' report fails to comment on this significant aspect. The conical form of the Freedom Charter Monument (see Figure 5.16) is said to embody a range of references, 'from Great Zimbabwe to the megalithic tombs of Europe, from the tepees of America to mausolea of the east'.[113] The Kwashisanyama (see Figure 5.17), a food preparation area that punctures through the middle of the colonnaded market, is cogent for its reinterpretation

5.16   The Freedom Charter Monument, Walter Sisulu Square, SM.
Photograph by the author.

5.17   Kwashisanyama at the South Structure, Walter Sisulu Square, SM.
Photograph by the author.

5.18
Colonnaded
market area
of the South
Structure, Walter
Sisulu Square,
SM. Photograph
by the author.

of a uniquely modern, African way of eating, where food is prepared in an informal manner in front of the customer on an open fire. The architects explain that this way of eating was 'originally given to cafes in industrial areas, which became popular lunch spots for workers in factories and within mining camps … The conical form of Kwashisanyama has been borrowed from the chimney of the self-made punctured drum stove', the latter being associated with this manner of food preparation.[114] Finally, the colonnaded market of the South Structure (see Figure 5.18), which runs parallel to the retail strip along Union Street, is described in the submission as a 'forest of columns':[115]

The idea has a number of origins varying from columns inspired by a forest of tree trunks or borrowing from the market in Venice. The idea is also a direct analogy … of the many wooden poles supporting the temporary trading stalls of Union Road as well as David Goldblatt's photograph of the African meeting space in the forest.[116]

Yet despite this evocative description, the arcade is unrelenting. The architectural resolution, in both elevation and section, is diagrammatic and overbearing. This scheme feels out of place with the intricate and fragmentary character of historical Kliptown. And the reference to African histories is inadequately translated into the architecture of this design. Instead, the stiff, repetitive geometry is more suggestive of rationalist neoclassicism – an association that has proven contentious. The completed project, however, does attempt to remedy this problem through the use of surface textures – which will be discussed shortly – and projecting elements, such as balconies, which break up the monotony of the long façades. The South Structure in its completed form, for example, introduces slanted columns, which spring from tall square bases – a detail which attempts to denote the sense of a 'forest', as described in the earlier competition submission, and undoubtedly also derived from the slanting tree-columns of the Constitutional Court.

Problems of scale and architectural character were noted by the jury: 'if not handled with greater sensitivity than is evident, the buildings may be out of scale, formalistic and inappropriate in the context of what Kliptown should aspire to become'.[117] Nevertheless, support for this design would follow from the conceptual requirements of the brief, and hence the jury maintains that 'the strength of the scheme … lies in its ideas rather than its architectural language which needs further consideration'.[118] The jury thus recommended that 'the scale of the buildings around the square should be reduced … serious consideration [should] be given to the design of these buildings and in particular to their height'.[119]

Contestations

The winning scheme was unveiled at a formal ceremony held in Kliptown on 26 June 2002, a date chosen to coincide with the 47th anniversary of the Congress.[120] By this stage, Freedom Square had been officially renamed the Walter Sisulu Square of Dedication in honour of the late ANC leader. Construction commenced a year later, with a sod-turning ceremony held in June 2003.[121] Despite the recommendations of the jurors' report, the ideational and diagrammatic nature of this design was frozen from the start, and the project as built suffers from inadequate design development, as well as some inattention to issues of scale and programme.

The post-competition period was marked by a series of conflicts that emerged between the differing interests of various parties, which in most cases would only result in small, incremental adjustments to the overriding order of the scheme. Perhaps the most significant contestation was with respect to the destruction of Union Street. In SM's competition drawing, it may be seen that the long South Structure replaces the existing shops that line the northern side of Union Street. It may be argued that the erasure of Union Street was in direct contravention of conservation guidelines as drawn up the NMC – guidelines which were included as an annexure to the competition brief.[122] The NMC's intention to preserve the historic fabric of Union Street is without question and yet, oddly, the competition jury did not include formal representation from the NMC. Callinicos, who at the time was a member of the NMC, was appointed to the jury in her capacity as a historian rather than as a representative of the NMC – her criticisms as to the insensitive nature of the

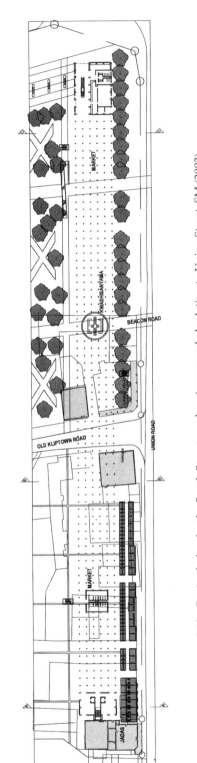

5.19   Revised plan for the South Structure showing amended relation to Union Street, SM (2003).
Courtesy of the Johannesburg Development Agency.

completed project were noted earlier. Yet despite this oversight, the winning scheme had to be approved by the South African Heritage Resource Agency (SAHRA, formerly the NMC) Advisory Committee before construction could begin because as previously noted, the site had been declared a national monument. The architects submitted their design presentation to the SAHRA Advisory Committee on 1 August 2002.[123] The SAHRA archive contains a series of alarmed submissions from members of the Advisory Committee, who were deeply opposed to the heritage implications of the design. Individual submissions were collated into a formal written response.[124] Positive aspects are noted – such as the idea of 'Madiba City', the 'X' symbolism of democracy and the design for the North Structure – whereas larger symbolic and urban shortcomings are heavily criticised, as is the intended destruction of historical structures on Union Street, in particular shops belonging to Jada and Tacoliah. On the question of political and architectural identity, the report states that '[i]nternational traditions seem to take precedence over indigenous concepts … In particular, the use of the ancient Greek symbolism for the concept of democracy in the design is not considered relevant to the national identity of South Africans.'[125] A key recommendation was that '[t]he overall scale of the proposal should be revisited to be more in keeping with the understated nature of the surrounding area.'[126] Regrettably, this suggestion was not followed.

The architects prepared a response to SAHRA's criticism in the form of a 46-page report, which describes important changes to the original competition design.[127] The resulting redesign for the South Structure is detailed in the relevant section of this report where revised plans and sections show how the South Structure has been set back from Union Street, with the inclusion of trees to line the eastern part of Union Street (see Figure 5.19).[128] Historic retail shops of Jada, Takolia and Epstein are preserved, together with newly created urban infill which is built to accommodate informal trade in the area between Jada and Tokolia. The South Structure also flies, uninterrupted, above these low-lying structures in a late attempt to include a memory of old Kliptown (see Figure 5.20). Jada, Takolia and Epstein are respectively reused as a museum, food market and opportunity for informal trade. The built project follows these amendments.

Further perspectives on the redevelopment of Union Street were provided by 'Indian' traders in the area. I interviewed Unice Jada, Rashid Jada, Abdul Samad Takolias – who prefers to be called Sam – and their councillor Mohamed Saeed Cachalia, as well as Indra Hansraj, the former owner of Epsteins. From them, I heard the distressing story of how the traders of Union Street were forced to vacate their shops. With the exception of Epstein, the shopkeepers along Union Street were renting their shops, a pattern from apartheid laws which had prohibited 'non-whites' from purchasing land. Without security of tenure, the traders found themselves in a vulnerable position, as their interests were not accommodated by the intended development. Jada and Takolia approached Cachalia, an attorney and councillor with the City of Johannesburg, to assist them in discussions

5.20 Sectional model showing amended relation between the South Structure and existing shops along Union Street, SM (2003). Courtesy of the Johannesburg Development Agency.

with the Joburg Property Company and the JDA. A series of meetings were held in an attempt to resolve the matter and, unfortunately, negotiators for the project 'tried to bully Sam and Jada … to victimise them … they were told to go', Cachalia said.[129] But the shopkeepers stood their ground, and eventually a deal was struck whereby new land was made available along Klipspruit Valley Road at an attractive price, and new premises were built at the traders expense.[130]

Sam was outspoken and emotional, explaining that he and the others had been trading in the area for some 75 years, only to face the irony of forced eviction in the post-apartheid era:

I was 12 years old when the Congress of the People took place. The cops raided our shop. Nelson Mandela hid in our house, and my father protected him. Walter Sisulu hid in Jada's house … At the end of the day I will give my keys to Nelson Mandela, and walk away … we were treated badly.[131]

I asked Sam for his views on the destruction of Union Street, to which he replied: '[i]t was a disaster. The road should never have been destroyed. We were never taken into consideration.'[132] Unice and Rashid Jada, on the other hand, seemed pragmatic, explaining that they were initially upset and did not wish to move, but after three years of negotiation 'we got what we wanted'.[133] 'You know you can't fight the giants, you have to work with them', Unice said.[134] Hansraj's story is a little different as he claims to have been the only true land owner among the traders of Union Street.[135] And it was with great pride that he showed me old photographs of his family and their shop. Yet he too was forced to leave. 'We were unhappy to go, but there was no choice … in the end we got a good deal.'[136]

I was left to ponder the implications of this unnecessary conflict which, due to persistent and defiant negotiations, was eventually resolved in a manner that was beneficial to the traders. Yet the process was not without consequences. Barry Friedman, one of the project managers for this job, explained that the protracted negotiations between the client and the traders of Union Street caused awkward delays and unexpectedly added to the extent of the project because new shop premises had to be built.[137] In the case of Jada and Badat, the last shopkeepers to relocate, early construction operations were forced to manoeuvre around the obtrusive presence of these shops, which could not be demolished until the negotiations were resolved. The destruction of historic fabric along Union Street was unnecessary, especially given the large extent of unoccupied land available in the area. On a programmatic level, it makes little sense to erase existing shops only to replace them with a costly, new retail market. It is also alarming to note in this regard that this scheme was the only competition entry to have proposed a thorough destruction of Union Street.

Programme, Scale and Need

The competition brief spoke of lofty ideals: '[t]he aim is to create a precinct that exists … to challenge oppression wherever it may occur, to assert … the nature of freedom'.[138] Yet this intention stands in contrast to the Kliptown Development Business Plan of 2004 (KDBP), where the stated purpose of the development is to '[c]reate business opportunities and employment in the retail, manufacturing, tourism, transport, services and construction industries'.[139] In keeping with this vision, the functional programme of the Walter Sisulu Square, as it has been realised in the final scheme, is governed by a tight financial logic which privileges sustainable, rental space. The JDA's strategic intention has been to inject a lump sum of developmental capital into Kliptown in the hopes that this investment will boost a sustainable, local economy. Bluntly put, the idea has been to kick-start and to bail out. Accordingly, the Walter Sisulu Square has to be self-sustaining, and there are good reasons why this should be the case. Yet this approach has also resulted in the marginalisation of social needs. This can be seen in the final programming of the Walter Sisulu Square, which is dominated, almost exclusively, by rentable space, and where social functions have been excluded. SM's competition design showed a balance of commercial, tourist and social elements intended for the local community. In the completed project, however, the only social element is the community hall, a space which may be hired out for various functions. Training spaces, sports facilities, a police station and community advice centre that were included in the original design have been removed. Instead, the completed

5.21   Rendered perspective of the Old Square from SM's design submission (2002). Courtesy of the Johannesburg Development Agency.

project accommodates a down-sized museum, various small shops at ground level, banking facilities, an enlarged tourist centre positioned as the primary gateway to Soweto, conference facilities, a restaurant and hotel. The 'flexible' nature of the building superstructure, and the dominance of generic leasable commercial space resembles the investment logic of a conventional shopping centre. In what way does this development improve upon the commercial logic that inspired the earlier shopping centres that, scandalously, were envisaged for this site?[140] It should also be remembered that the first shopping centre design intended for this site, in fact, proposed a unique – or at least unique for a shopping centre-type development – mixed programme, which included commercial, tourist, as well as various social, functions. This early commercial design included more social programme than can be found in the completed project.

Wandering around the upper levels of the North Structure, one is amazed by the sheer scale of the interior spaces. This is architecture 'on the loose', unencumbered by the constraints of 'real' needs. One gets a similar feeling in the informal market of the South Structure, with its lofty, cathedral-like expanse of wasted space, and one cannot but wonder why the informal traders could not have been accommodated in a more modest fashion (see Figure 5.18). The barren quality of open space positioned at the centre of this scheme stands in contrast to the slick commercial image that was used to promote it (see Figure 5.21). The windswept terrain of the Old Square, with its seemingly

endless hard paved surface devoid of places to sit or opportunity for shade from the harsh sun, is quite uninhabitable, and one struggles to imagine how this space might be used by the residents of Kliptown on a daily basis (see Figure 5.22). We may compare the uninviting formality of this space to the more insightful intention of MRAB's design, where the public square doubled as a football pitch, where site boundaries are blurred, and where spaces and functions give back to the life of the township (see Figures 5.10–5.11). Instead, at the Walter Sisulu Square, the Old Square feels as though it is reserved for formal occasions, while the everyday is ignored. The New Square is a little better in this regard as here, the three-by-three grid of the plan is marked by trees and 'X'-shaped benches to accommodate informal clothes traders who had previously used this area for displaying their colourful wares. The vast size of this square, however, accommodates inadequate opportunities for trade, and once again spatial dimensions are ill-conceived. This project seems self-satisfied with the imposing scale of its rigid geometry, and functions are merely forced to fit.

5.22   The Old Square, Walter Sisulu Square, SM. Photograph by the author.

The excessive scale of the superstructure stands in marked contrast to the needy social life of surrounding Kliptown. A detailed 106-page survey of the Greater Kliptown area was conducted by Manto Management, aimed at identifying 'priority needs'.[141] Since this report was only commissioned late in April 2004, the public money that paid for this study had no influence upon the design for the Walter Sisulu Square. Yet this report details numerous practical programmes that could begin to address these problems, and it is a great shame that these recommendations were not considered in the design for the Walter Sisulu Square. For example, a health and wellness centre, a community advice centre and educational facilities of some kind could, indeed should have been included in the Walter Sisulu Square. Furthermore, these social facilities could easily have been afforded had the design been less extravagant in other areas. The running costs could have been cross-subsidised by the predominance of leasable space. Instead, the JDA's KDBF has effectively divorced economic and infrastructural development from social development: a policy where social development is marginalised under sub-project 6.1, which merely flags the need for 'a long-term social development strategy', together with sub-project 6.2 which identifies '[n]umereous interim programmes or quick wins'.[142]

It should be noted that SM's design approach was not derived from programmatic need, but rather took advantage of the indecisive character of the competition brief. Their competition entry was conceived as a robust superstructure, one that could be appropriated and reappropriated in various ways: 'the buildings at Freedom Square must be able to "stand the test of time" … The robust building framework allows for the ease of design interventions and the flexibility to accommodate change.'[143] In adopting this approach, the architecture for the Water Sisulu Square has introduced a fundamental duality drawn between an uncompromising architectural geometry on the one hand, and the uncertainty of the surrounding urban context on the other. It is a duality that justifies the need for a bold statement of developmental intent, yet without providing adequate substance to the complex social character of the site and the needs of its residents. Once again, we return to the perceived indistinct – indeed problematic – nature of the site that plagued the earlier history of Freedom Square.

Building Identity through Texture

During my time with architect Pierre Swanepoel, I enquired about SM's approach to issues of expressive language and identity. Swanepoel emphasised the conceptual nature of his original competition entry, which had sought to 'embody the ideals of freedom', and to do so by establishing urban principles and a 'value system' for the design.[144] The resolution of architectural language was addressed subsequently during the process of design development. 'We don't know what an urban [modern] African architecture should be', Swanepoel observed and consequently, the aesthetic for the scheme was allowed to evolve from 'available skills' and 'textures' of the surrounding site.[145] He kindly supplied me with copies of PowerPoint presentations that were shown to various stakeholders during the post-competition period – 2002–2004 – presentations which effectively document the architectural development of the scheme. A key image depicts a skeletal structure with backbone and

5.23 Grid and infill as used in concrete frame buildings and African handcrafts, PowerPoint presentation by StudioMAS (2003). Courtesy of StudioMAS.

rib cage.[146] This image was used to demonstrate how the building had been conceived as a flexible superstructure, or a 'carcass', and, as previously noted, it was suggested that this approach would allow for differing uses through time.[147] The incumbent duality of structure and programme that is suggested by this image was translated into a duality of structure and textured infill, which was to become the primary relation through which architectural identity was conceived. To communicate the sense of this duality, the presentation also depicts images of generic Johannesburg buildings made from concrete frame and brick infill, situated alongside further images derived from African craft and building traditions, sapling framework constructions, textile mats, beadwork and woven baskets (see Figure 5.23). In each case, a relation of grid to decorative infill is made explicit. A similar chain of references is also made in the 'Texture Presentation',[148] which Swanepoel explains was prepared as part of his own attempt to develop a 'visual language' for the scheme.[149] Notably, the competition entry had envisaged an intention of this kind, where it was stated that '[l]ike its surroundings, it [in other words, the building structure] will become a patchwork of cultures and materials; it will gain a rustic patina that allows it to sustain and be homogeneous with its adjacent feeding fabric.'[150] This idea of a contextually derived patchwork of textures is particularity expressive in the case of the Kwashisanyama (see Figure 5.17), the conic roof structure of which is covered by rusted corrugated iron sheets taken from the demolished shops of Union Street, while the Freedom Charter Monument (see Figure 5.16) is built from bricks that were salvaged from the same shops in order to preserve a memory of the textures of historic Union Street. It will be remembered that a similar approach was adopted at the Constitutional Court, where bricks from the ATB were symbolically reused in the chamber. This approach suggests a new permutation of what has previously been described as a play of 'mask' and 'skin', the implications of which will be discussed in the concluding remarks of this chapter.

Creating Texture through SMME Involvement

The relation of structure to infill also involved a strategy for dividing up the manufacturing process, allowing for the involvement of local, small business concerns (SMMEs). Black Economic Empowerment protocols were established for Kliptown, which required that local labour and small-business concerns would be included in the process of construction.[151]

An SMME presentation, by SM, depicts two photographs of a Basotho house.[152] One picture shows a wall under construction, made from a sapling frame with mud and brick infill, and adjacent to this, a second picture shows a Basotho woman in colourful attire, standing in front of her equally decorative house.[153] Swanepoel explained, with reference to these images, that his firm was looking for links to African traditions that could help to communicate their concept of a building carcass decorated with a textured patina. SM had

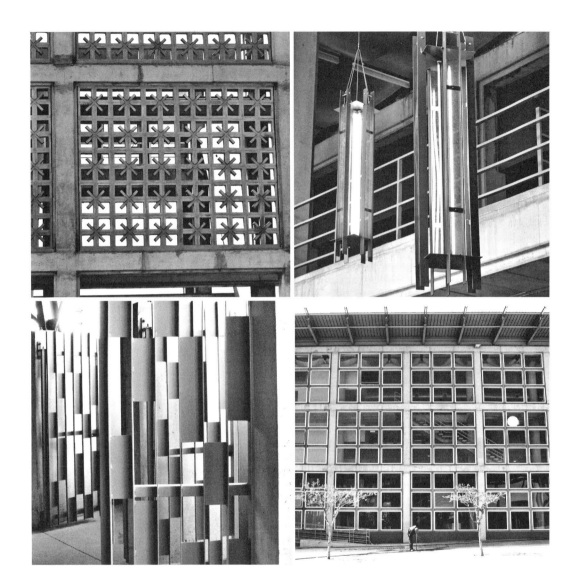

provided the structure, only now it was necessary to add 'life and culture'.[154] This same presentation moves on to identify key sites for SMME involvement. A hierarchy of structural frame and subsidiary elements, for example, allows security screens, glazed panels, sunscreens, acoustic panels and so on to be subcontracted to SMMEs. To some extent, this approach parallels that adopted at the Constitutional Court, where numerous competitions were held to ensure the involvement of artists and crafters who contributed to the rich narrative density of Constitution Hill. At Kliptown, however, tight building deadlines and budgetary constraints meant that the work done by SMMEs was strictly controlled. In most cases, SM designed the subsidiary elements, such as *brise-soleil* blocks with a voter's cross motif, lanterns, steel gates and window frames and so on (see consecutively, Figure 5.24). These

5.24 a–d: Subsidiary elements manufactured by SMMEs, Walter Sisulu Square, SM (left to right, top to bottom). Photographs by author.

5.25 Acoustic panels to the walls of the community hall, Walter Sisulu Square, SM. Photograph by the author.

elements were mostly built by SMMEs, and were conceived with respect to the availability of, or necessity to train, sustainable labour skills. Yet unlike the Constitutional Court, the participation of SMMEs did not democratise the imaginative content of the Walter Sisulu Square.

I took time to interview a number of SMME contributors to learn their stories and experiences on the job. In this regard, I spoke to Precious Makwe of SM who worked with SMMEs, as well as Nkosinathi Manzana who helped manage the project for the JDA.[155] Without a doubt, the most collaborative, and therefore noteworthy, example is the case of the woven acoustic panels, which treat and decorate the walls of the community hall (see Figure 5.25). SM's original concept for these panels was to explore colour and textures through the use of shade-netting embroidered with wool, and to work in collaboration with local weavers. Makwe ran an early workshop in Kliptown to identify and to guide suitable candidates for the job.[156] The weavers, most of whom were women, were given small pieces of A4-sized netting and coloured wool, and were asked to experiment with various techniques. 'We asked for a textured cloth with colour … but most made small patterns', Makwe said.[157] Pattern making is a primary feature of much African craft, and the weavers struggled to create the new, desired effect. Eventually, one of the weavers produced a panel with red against a black background, a

treatment which was informed by texture rather than pattern: 'this was the breakthrough', Makwe said.[158] The technique used here involved a form of knitting which, once studied, was transferred to the other weavers (see Figure 5.26). Janet Landey of Party Designs, who was contracted to help manage this collaborative process, explained that a series of trial panels were developed using the new technique. These were presented to the architects who made selections and finalised their design.[159]

5.26 Weaving the acoustic panels, Janet Landey and the team of weavers. Courtesy of Janet Landey.

Each acoustic panel is subdivided into a three-by-three grid of nine blocks. Individual blocks measure 1.2 x 1.5 m, and are treated with a different coloured texture of knit wool. Five panel designs were established, and these repeat across the long internal walls of the community hall. Once installed, the walls appear as a geometric patchwork of coloured textures. Makwe emphasised that the textured treatment of each block was contributed by the weavers, but the geometric distribution of coloured blocks was made in accordance with SM's design.[160] In fact, the layout was silk-screened onto the netting before coloured textures were individually applied to ensure that the final product would be in accordance with the intended design. One panel, however, was done in a more improvised way and in this particular case, the weavers were allowed to establish their own distribution of coloured blocks. The final result was 'really beautiful', Makwe said.[161]

The weavers I interviewed spoke fondly of their involvement, and mentioned that they had been well paid.[162] I took this opportunity to enquire about the urban and social influence of the Walter Sisulu Square. 'Kliptown was one of the most gloomy places when we came here … but now it is much better', one of the ladies said.[163] Pressing a little further, I also asked about the usefulness of the square and the choice of programme, to which I heard the following reply: 'I don't know if it will be used … the space is too big', and 'a clinic, really, that would have been much better!'[164] Yet despite these comments, I was pleased to learn that the ladies have subsequently had much success with making and selling embroidered handbags. The technique involved is influenced by that learned at the Walter Sisulu Square, only the support fabric is a hessian cloth which is much easier to work with than the fire-retardant netting that was required for the acoustic panels. I was also interested to learn that pattern making is central to the weaver's own designs, but 'at the square the architects did not want any patterns', they said.[165] This comment made me realise that an opportunity had been lost because the collaborative process had been curtailed. SM consistently controlled the imaginative content of their design, a fact which, no doubt, was partly due to the existence of tight building deadlines. Nevertheless, I feel that more open-ended forms of collaboration with SMMEs – such as the weavers and their preferred approach to design – would have been more appropriate. And unfortunately, the final design of the acoustic panels is somewhat sterile, with its sustained repetition of coloured squares. This stands in contrast to the process that was followed at the Constitutional Court, where craft input was allowed to speak with its own voice. It is precisely the richness of multiple imaginations that is lacking at the Walter Sisulu Square.

Concluding Remarks

The Walter Sisulu Square and the Constitutional Court are parallel projects in many ways, as both are formed on national heritage sites, tied to a social narrative on human rights. Both involved the making of public space, and worked with various forms of public participation for the creation of this space. Both projects were also developed under the auspices of Blue IQ and the JDA. Yet despite these similarities, the developmental histories that produced these projects proved rather different, and the nature of the respective sites is a key factor for appreciating the measure of this difference.

At Constitution Hill, the stature and autonomy of the court is mirrored by the equally distinct character of the site. Despite the good, inclusive intentions of the architecture at Constitution Hill, the Old Fort nevertheless provides a somewhat secluded space where the surrounding busy urban life is suitably buffered, being removed by the ramparts of the fort, the sloping topography, and the busy roads that border the site. The architecture at Constitution Hill may have overturned exclusionary symbols of power – through the creation of inviting public gestures and the use of embedded, transparent architectural forms – but this inversion, arguably, was only possible because the power, prestige and autonomy of the court was, from the start, firmly intact. Indeed, the judges of the Constitutional Court would appear to dethrone the locus of power, while simultaneously reasserting it. The secluded nature of Constitution Hill proved the perfect foil to a transparent architecture for, in truth, an open design of this kind would not have worked so well were it situated in the middle of neighbouring Hillbrow. The Constitutional Court, rightly, signals the hope of fundamental change, yet this narrative remains somewhat rarefied.

Constitution Hill has benefited from various forms of autonomy – be these institutional, geographical, contextual or symbolic. By contrast, the Walter Sisulu Square was to remain, throughout its developmental stage, a project without a clear institutional ground, without a well-defined programme, on an indistinct and relatively unbounded spread of land situated in an impoverished and neglected area. For these reasons, the project floundered in uncertainty. The Walter Sisulu Square wants to share in the privileged stature of the Constitutional Court. Yet unlike the court, the square had no clear boundary – be that institutional, geographical or symbolic – against the 'difficult' conditions of the life that surrounds it. This perceived lack of a clear context was addressed through the imposition of a pure geometry, an imposition which has shown scarce regard for the unique, historic character of the site. The historic fabric along Union Street, so rich in spatial clues, was treated as a tabula rasa. The Walter Sisulu Square wished to represent the participatory spirit of the Freedom Charter, but the terms of this commitment proved difficult to define. An impressive set of participatory protocols was established for the project, jobs were created and skills transferred. But the scheme failed to raise these important concerns beyond the bread-and-butter issues of the day. Unlike Constitution Hill, the Walter Sisulu Square does not disseminate a wider public discourse on the legacy of the Freedom Charter, nor were attempts made to democratise the symbolic content of the square. And ironically, the clean geometric closure that informs this design has nevertheless resulted in a project that is divided against itself.

A play of mask and skin has been a recurrent theme of this book and, significantly, the Walter Sisulu Square presents a new configuration in this regard. At Kliptown, a stark contrast has been drawn between a superstructural order which is imposed upon the site, distancing itself from the existing character of historic Kliptown, versus the hybrid identities and histories of the surrounding context, which are rendered as a surface-patina. The precise manner of this relation suggests that the geometry of the scheme is an order that belongs to 'Architecture' with a capital 'A', a trope which signifies the autonomous intentions of the architect. After all, geometric imposition was the key intuition; it was the aspect that the architects were most eager to defend and, as we have seen, only small, incremental changes were made to the original design. What may be termed the 'authentic' complexity of the site was repressed by the architecture of this scheme, only to return in the form of a patina as the trope of social identity. The architect's original notion of a circumstantial patina has the potential to create a richness of layering through time, a process which could greatly enrich the symbolic content of the Walter Sisulu Square. If emancipated, this patina-of-the-social might even begin to erode the Architecture of this scheme. In practice, however, SM sought to curtail the possibilities of this idea. Unlike the Constitutional Court, this project has failed to be inclusive of other voices and imaginations. The resulting duality of 'carcass' and 'patina' is one that fails to represent the participatory spirit of the Freedom Charter. At Kliptown, the relation of mask (or patina, as an inclusion of other narratives) to skin (or carcass, as a naturalised expression of modern architectural identity) appears to be trapped within a non-responsive, static and defiant duplicity.

Notes

1 Raymond Suttner and Jeremy Cronin, *Thirty Years of the Freedom Charter* (Johannesburg: Ravan Press, 1986), p 88.

2 A detailed account of the Congress is provided by ibid.

3 *The Freedom Charter of South Africa* (Helsinki: World Peace Council, 1975), pp 7–11.

4 Albert Luthuli, *Let My People Go: An Autobiography* (London: Collins, 1962), p 159.

5 Suttner and Cronin, *Thirty Years of the Freedom Charter*, p 86.

6 Ibid. p 128.

7 For the importance of the Freedom Charter with respect to the history of apartheid, see: Tom Lodge, *Black Politics in South Africa since 1945* (London: Longman, 1983); Brian Lapping, *Apartheid: A History* (London: Paladin, 1986).

8 The name 'Soweto' was officially adopted as late as 1963, yet the residential areas of present-day Soweto may be traced back to Orlando, which was laid out in 1935.

9 Original research on the history of Kliptown was coordinated by Gene Duiker of the Kliptown Our Town Trust (KOTT). This research informs the public displays at the Kliptown Our Town Museum in Kliptown.

10 Present-day Kliptown is built on two farms, Klipspruit No. 298 and Klipriviersoog No. 299.

11 Douglas Rodd et al., 'Freedom Square, Kliptown, Johannesburg: Survey of Historical Significance and Architectural Heritage' (Johannesburg: SAHRA, 1998), pp 5–6.

12 KOTT, Kliptown Our Town Museum (Kliptown: KOTT).

13 Ibid.

14 Rodd et al., 'Freedom Square, Kliptown, Johannesburg: Survey of Historical Significance and Architectural Heritage'.

15   JDA, 'Freedom Square Precinct: Architectural Competition Brief' (Johannesburg: JDA, 2002), p 11.

16   Graeme Reid, JDA chief executive and then member of the Johannesburg City Council, remembers that developmental rights were sold to the developer in question, which in turn sold these rights to Stocks and Stocks (interview with Reid, Johannesburg, September 2005). The architects who worked on this option confirmed their involvement with Stocks and Stocks and Irvine Khoza of Nkosana Investment (interviews with Patrick McInerney of Meyer Pienaar Architects, Johannesburg, November 2005 and December 2005; Interview with Louis Peens of Louis Peens Architects, Johannesburg, January 2006). George Ellis, then development and leasing director for Stocks and Stocks, recalls that Stocks and Stocks had acquired developmental rights for the site, and that some business arrangement had been established with Khoza, but was unclear as to exact dates or further details (interview with Ellis, Johannesburg, February 2006). I also tried to secure an interview with Irvine Khoza, but without success.

17   MPS, 'Kliptown Dust Bowl Project: Proposed Soweto Shopping Centre' (Johannesburg: MPS, 1991).

18   Birch, letter to the manager, Stocks Construction (Pty) Ltd (Johannesburg: SAHRA, 22 December 1994).

19   Gareth van Onselen, 'And the People *Did* Govern', *Sunday Times Metro*, 25 June 1995, p 3.

20   J. de Jager, letter to Stocks and Stocks (Johannesburg: SAHRA, 15 March 1996).

21   W. Martinson, letter to the chief executive officer, GJTMC (Johannesburg: SAHRA, 9 October 1995).

22   NMC, 'Discussion in Respect of Proposed Development of Shopping Centre at "Freedom Square", Kliptown' (Johannesburg: SAHRA, 1996).

23   NMC, 'Proposed Provincial Declaration as a National Monument: Freedom Square, Kliptown, Johannesburg' (Johannesburg: SAHRA, 1998).

24   Scott Wilson Kirkpatrik Urban and Regional Planners, 'Greater Kliptown Development Framework Plan: Final Report' (Johannesburg: Scott Wilson Kirkpatrik, 1997).

25   Ibid. p 12.

26   FSPIT, 'Freedom Square Project: Business Plan' (Johannesburg: Lindsey Bremner, 1997).

27   Ibid. p 1.

28   Ibid.

29   Interview, Johannesburg (November 2005).

30   SWK, 'Greater Kliptown Development Framework Plan: Final Report', p 12.

31   FSPIT, 'Freedom Square Project: Business Plan', p 1.

32   Ibid. p 6.

33   Ibid.

34   Ibid.

35   Ibid. p 9.

36 Rodd et al., 'Freedom Square, Kliptown, Johannesburg: Survey of Historical Significance and Architectural Heritage'.

37 Ibid. p 77.

38 NMC, 'Minutes of Meeting, Re. Freedom Square' (Johannesburg: SAHRA, 1998); NMC, 'Minutes of a Workshop of the Johannesburg Plans Committee: Northern Region on a Conservation Policy for Freedom Square, Kliptown, Soweto' (Johannesburg: SAHRA, 1999); NMC, 'Minutes of the Second Workshop on Developing a Conservation Policy for the Conservation and Development of the Freedom Square Precinct' (Johannesburg: SAHRA, 1999).

39 NMC, 'Minutes of a Workshop of the Johannesburg Plans Committee: Northern Region on a Conservation Policy for Freedom Square, Kliptown, Soweto'.

40 Ibid.

41 Ibid.

42 Ibid.

43 NMC, 'Minutes of the Second Workshop on Developing a Conservation Policy for the Conservation and Development of the Freedom Square Precinct'.

44 JDA, 'Freedom Square Precinct: Architectural Competition Brief', p 27.

45 Interview, Johannesburg (September 2005).

46 Herbert Prins served as competition administrator. Interview, Johannesburg (November 2005). Luli Callinicos is a well-known historian, and was a competition juror. Interview, Johannesburg (November 2005).

47 JDA, 'Freedom Square Precinct: Architectural Competition Brief', p 2.

48 Ibid.

49 City of Johannesburg, 'Joburg 2030: Full Report' (Johannesburg: City of Johannesburg, 2002).

50 JDA, 'Kliptown Development Business Plan' (Johannesburg: JDA, 2004), p 16.

51 JDA, 'Freedom Square Precinct: Architectural Competition Brief', p 11.

52 Ibid. pp 17–18.

53 Ibid. p 19.

54 Ibid. p 2.

55 Ibid. p 20.

56 Ibid. p 21.

57 Ibid. p 1.

58 'Freedom Square Architectural Competition: Report by the Judges' (Johannesburg: 2002), p 2.

59 Unfortunately, Saitowitz declined my request for an email-based response to specific questions.

60 Interview, Johannesburg (October 2005).

61 Ibid.

62 Interview, Johannesburg (September 2005).

63   Ibid.

64   Interview, Johannesburg (November 2005).

65   Interview, Johannesburg (December 2004).

66   Ibid.

67   Ibid.

68   Interview, Johannesburg (September 2005).

69   Ibid.

70   Ibid.

71   JDA, 'Freedom Square Precinct: Architectural Competition Brief', p 3.

72   'Freedom Square Architectural Competition: Report by the Judges', pp 7–9.

73   Professor Bremner alerted my attention to the whereabouts of the original drawings, about which she has published, see: Lindsay Bremner, 'Reframing Township Spaces: The Kliptown Project', *Public Culture: Society for Transnational Cultural Studies* 16, no. 3 (2004): pp 521–31.

74   On a later visit (during 2009), I was upset to hear that Duiker was unwell and equally distressed to discover that the contents of his Kliptown Our Town Museum had been cleared away. From enquiries made, it would appear that the competition entries have been destroyed – which represents a terrible loss.

75   Gene Duiker is the CEO of KOTT and sits on the Greater Kliptown Development Forum. Interviews with Gene Duiker, Kliptown (December 2004, October 2005, November 2005).

76   'Freedom Square Architectural Competition: Report by the Judges', p 9.

77   PCWG, submission drawings (Johannesburg: PCWG, 2002).

78   Ibid.

79   Ibid.

80   'Freedom Square Architectural Competition: Report by the Judge', p 11.

81   KRA, submission drawing (Cape Town: KRA, 2002).

82   Ibid.

83   Ibid.

84   Ibid.

85   Ibid.

86   'Freedom Square Architectural Competition: Report by the Judges', p 10.

87   MRAB, submission drawings (Kliptown: Kliptown Our Town Museum, 2002).

88   Ibid.

89   The design also defines a wider programmatic strategy for the surrounding area.

90   MRAB, submission drawings.

91   Ibid.

92   Ibid.

93   Ibid.

94   Ibid.

95   'Freedom Square Architectural Competition: Report by the Judges', p 10.

96   I was unable to locate the architect's written report, but this proved inconsequential as the written component is included on the drawing, and for which reason footnote references refer to the respective drawings.

97   Madiba is a popular and endearing nickname for Nelson Mandela. SM, submission drawings (Johannesburg: SM, 2002), dwg. 1.

98   Ibid.

99   Ibid.

100   Parliament is currently located in Cape Town, the legislative capital of South Africa, and there are no plans to move it.

101   'Freedom Square Architectural Competition: Report by the Judges', p 3.

102   SM, 'Kliptown Urban Design Framework' (Johannesburg: SM, 2003).

103   This intention has not been realised in the completed project, which uses regular paving blocks.

104   SM, submission drawings, dwg. 3.

105   Ibid.

106   Ibid.

107   Ibid.

108   Ibid.

109   This fact was emphasised by Snell. Interview, Johannesburg (December, 2004).

110   The competition drawings show an underground passage linking the ninth room of the museum to the Freedom Charter Monument, which is intended as the tenth space in the narrative sequence of the museum. However, this link was not realised in the built project, and access to the Freedom Charter Monument is possible only from the ground-plane of the square.

111   SM, submission drawings, dwg. 9.

112   Interview with Snell, Johannesburg (December 2004).

113   SM, submission drawings, dwg. 8.

114   Ibid.

115   Ibid, dwg. 5.

116   Ibid.

117   'Freedom Square Architectural Competition: Report by the Judges', p 7.

118   Ibid.

119   Ibid. p 8.

120   'News in Camera', *Sowetan*, 27 June 2002, p 2.

121   SAPA, 'Turning a Sod for Sisulu', *Sunday Times Metro*, 29 June 2003, p 2.

122   JDA, 'Freedom Square Precinct: Architectural Competition Brief', Annexure F.

123   SAHRA, 'Proposal for the Development of the Freedom Square (Walter Sisulu) Precinct, Kliptown, Soweto: Comments by the Sahra Advisory Committee' (Johannesburg: SAHRA, 2002).

124   Ibid.

125   Ibid.

126   Ibid.

127   SM, 'Report of the StudioMAS Presentation Made to SAHRA on the Walter Sisulu Square of Dedication Precinct, 14 August' (Johannesburg: Herbert Prins, 2003). An accompanying conservation policy was also prepared: Herbert Prins, 'Conservation Policy for the Core Area Kliptown, Soweto' (Johannesburg: Herbert Prins, 2003).

128   SM, 'Report of the StudioMAS Presentation Made to SAHRA on the Walter Sisulu Square of Dedication Precinct, 14 August', pp 26–7.

129   Interview with Cachalia, Johannesburg (November 2005).

130   The legal agreement states that should transfer of ownership prove problematic, then a 49-year lease for the property will come into effect. See: 'Heads of Agreement between City of Johannesburg Metropolitan Municipality Herein Represented by the City of Joburg Property Company (Proprietary) Limited (Council) and Jada's Economic Stores (Proprietary) Limited (Jada) Registration No. 61/00509/07' (Kliptown: Jada's Economic Stores).

131   Interview with 'Sam' Takolias, Kliptown (October 2005).

132   Ibid.

133   Interviews, Kliptown (October 2005).

134   Ibid.

135   Interview, Kliptown (October 2005). Hansraj informed me that the final settlement included 6,500 m^2 of land as compensation for the land owned along Union Street, and a new shop on Klipspruit Valley Road, which was subject to similar agreement as the others.

136   Ibid.

137   Interview, Johannesburg (October 2005).

138   JDA, 'Freedom Square Precinct: Architectural Competition Brief', p 11.

139   JDA, 'Kliptown Development Business Plan', p 2.

140   The project at Kliptown was developed in conjunction with an impressive set of consultative protocols, and a commitment to local economic empowerment. The consultative process, managed by Nomi Muthialu Associates, however, did not, and could not have altered the privilege status of rental-type space at the Walter Sisulu Square. As such, the architects original design and the JDA's programmatic intentions for the square were the 'given' parameter around which more particular, contentious 'bread-and-butter' issues were debated by the local people. Interviews with Strini Pillay of Nomi Muthialu Associates, who led community liaison: Johannesburg, October 2005, November 2005, January 2006. This difficult, yet crucial, process brought genuine legitimacy to the scheme. However, in contrast to earlier, participatory visions for Freedom

Square – visions that were inspired by the legacy of the Freedom Charter – local voices did not significantly inform key directives that distinguish the architectural and symbolic character of the square.

141 The report highlights many important aspects, for instance the predominance of youth (65 per cent within the age of 15–30 years), most of whom lack adequate education (84 per cent of respondents were not engaged in any form of education), as well as problems of unemployment (70 per cent), poor self-esteem (57 per cent), high levels of violence against women (rated as the highest risk by 73 per cent of female respondents), high levels of drug and alcohol abuse (rated as the main challenge facing men by 73 per cent of the male respondents), and the prevalence of HIV/Aids (57 per cent). Manto Management, 'Greater Kliptown Development Project: Social Development Needs Assessment Report' (Johannesburg: Manto Management, 2004), p 3.

142 JDA, 'Kliptown Development Business Plan', p 16. Nomi Muthialu Associates (NMA) was appointed by the JDA to take forward questions of social development. Tamara Parker (NMA) explained that 56 social projects were originally identified by the needs assessment, attention to which would have required a budget of some R32 million. However, of the total R280 million budget for Kliptown, only R2 million was allocated by the JDA for social programmes. Consequently, social development had to be restricted to five short- and six long-term projects. Yet none of these projects are included in the Walter Sisulu Square. Interview, Johannesburg (November 2004).

143 SM, submission drawings, dwg. 1.

144 Interviews, Johannesburg (August 2003, November 2004).

145 Interview, Johannesburg (November 2004).

146 SM, 'Presentation to Project Team July 2003' (Johannesburg: SM, 2003).

147 Interview, Johannesburg (November 2005).

148 SM, 'Texture Presentation' (Johannesburg: SM, 2003).

149 Interview, Johannesburg (November 2005).

150 SM, submission drawings, dwg. 1.

151 Interview with Strini Pillay (NMA), Johannesburg (October 2005). Interview with Molefe Liale (Asa-Liale), Johannesburg (February 2006).

152 SM, 'SMME Development Opportunity' (Johannesburg: SM, 2003).

153 African women – within the geographic area of present-day South Africa – have traditionally been the decorators of domestic architecture.

154 Interview, Johannesburg (November 2005).

155 Interview with Eric Chauke, who cast breezole blocks, did paving on the square as well as plumbing, Kliptown (January 2006); interview with Pastor Johannes Louw, who did brickwork for the Freedom Charter Monument, Kliptown (January 2006); interview Janet Landey, Janet Vilakazi and Michael Dlamini (Party Designs) who coordinated the acoustic panels, Kliptown (January 2006); interview with Ida Masemola, Sphiwe Ntimba and Josephine Ntohla, who did weaving for the acoustic panels, Kliptown (December 2005); interview with Precious Makwe, Johannesburg (November 2005); and interview with Nkosinathi Manzana, Johannesburg (February 2006).

156   Interview, Johannesburg (November 2005).

157   Ibid.

158   Ibid.

159   Interview, Kliptown (January 2006).

160   Interview, Johannesburg (November 2005).

161   Ibid.

162   Interview with Ida Masemola, Sphiwe Ntimba and Josephine Ntohla, Kliptown (December 2005).

163   Ibid.

164   Ibid. I repeatedly asked questions of this kind when interviewing local people who were involved, the substance of which does not feature in this chapter. In nearly every case, the response was ambivalent. I was left to conclude that the Walter Sisulu Square has brought a sense of hope but the insensitive scale, and lack of social programme, was usually questioned by those I interviewed.

165   Ibid.

Honouring Our Other 'We': Freedom Park, Pretoria

Of Reconciliation and Nation

Freedom Park is a monumental scheme, one that wishes to symbolise a reconciled nation. In the words of then President Thabo Mbeki, this 'Legacy Project'[1] 'is the most ambitious heritage project to be undertaken by the new democratic government ... an ambitious and noble task.'[2] The fulfilment of this ambition involved a convoluted path, with far-reaching and extended debate as to the unique properties of African indigenous knowledge and cultural practices, the recovery of traditions, and a search for 'authentic' forms of representation. It may be noted that in prior chapters, public designs evolved primarily in relation to programmatic needs – be they perceived or real. In most cases, pragmatics would lead the process, and the symbolisation of 'Africa' would be grafted onto the logistics of the scheme. At Freedom Park, however, things worked the other way round, with ideological concerns taking a much more *determinate* role and where the search for deeply authentic modes of symbolisation has wished to determine the very essence of this scheme. Spanning some ten years from 2000–2010, the development of this pre-eminent project charts the successive foci of the leaders that gave it shape, and the project can be read as palimpsest of this complex process.

According to the Freedom Park Trust's (FPT) 'Position Paper', an early policy document of 2000, the inception of the Park emerged in response to the call 'for the erection of monuments, museums and commemorations of great leaders and historic events' for which the President's Office had literally been 'inundated with requests from diverse sources'.[3] An important influence, in this respect, derives from South Africa's Truth and Reconciliation Commission (TRC). Following the 1994 election, the TRC 'took shape within the politics of negotiated compromise between the outgoing exponents of white minority rule and the incoming champions of constitutional democracy'.[4] The TRC, in effect, traded amnesty for truth through a process of 'full disclosure' of violent acts associated with 'political objective[s]' in the years 1960–1993 – in other words, from the period of the Sharpeville massacre until the negotiated settlement.[5] Some '22,000 victim testimonials' were considered by the commission and about 10% of these were 'aired in public hearings'.[6] The official report of the TRC notes that the legal basis for amnesty was derived from 'legal instruments that emerged from the political negotiations' these being 'recorded in postscript … to the Constitution of South Africa'.[7] The aforementioned postscript states that '[t]he Pursuit of national unity, the well-being of all South African citizens and peace require reconciliation between the people of South Africa and the reconstruction of society.'[8] From this sentence, we may note how the 'pursuit of national unity' is linked to 'well-being' – indeed, the need for healing – and the need for 'reconciliation', and it is precisely this twin thematic – of nation and of reconciliation – that underpins the primary intention of Freedom Park.[9]

Three Phases of the Park

Lindiwe Gadd, who had served as the first CEO of the FPT, disclosed in an interview her understanding that the conceptualisation of the Park had moved through three distinct stages, which may be characterised as an early conceptual stage where the project was largely in the hands of the Department of Arts, Culture, Science and Technology (DACST); followed by a second stage that led up to the Union Internationale des Architects (UIA) international design competition and at which time Mbeki began to be involved with the Park; and finally, a third stage which followed after the failed results of the UIA competition and at which time Dr Mongane Wally Serote, poet and CEO of Freedom Park, provided leadership.[10]

Three leading documents, gleaned from the Freedom Park archive, are supportive of Gadd's insightful comments, that is a 'Position Paper' of 2000, a 'Conceptual Framework' document, and a 'A Vision for the Design Brief' of 2004 authored by the Three-Persons Committee.[11] Beginning with the first, the 'Position Paper' intends for the Park to explore a 'panoramic, holistic, [and] non-racial commitment to Africa and South Africa … to represent, in a visible, experiential, and interactive manner, our developing national consciousness and identity'.[12] The paper suggests three 'interactive themes' that 'would embrace the vision of the Freedom Park' – the struggle for political liberation 'beginning with the earliest 17th-century Khoi and slave uprisings' until modern times, democracy and reconciliation to pronounce South Africa as 'a universal case study for many other multi-cultural societies' and finally, nation-building to inform 'our steps towards conceptualising a national consciousness'.[13] On this last point, the paper insightfully adds that a national consciousness 'is not "given", or handed down from above', and for which reason 'debates and contradictions' need to inform the process through which that consciousness is to be conceived.[14] The three themes – struggle, democracy, and nation-building – envisaged a narrative of national liberation that looked to be drawn from established historical sources.[15]

The Freedom Park Conceptual Framework builds on the humanistic and national political intentions of the early Position Paper, hence '[t]he story of South Africa is the story of the struggle of humanity to survive in his/her environment and to live harmoniously with fellow humankind ... and to use heritage ... in the development of a national consciousness and identity'.[16] The Conceptual Framework is, however, much more explicit as to the legacy of subjugated local histories and practices – '[f]or centuries, many myths and prejudices have concealed the true history of South Africa ... Freedom Park is to address the gaps, distortions and biases and provide new perspectives of South Africa's heritage'.[17] The envisaged narrative of the Park is one that starts at the beginning with '[t]he existence of early life forms and geological formations in South Africa [which] can be traced back to 3.6 billion years [ago,] in Barberton, which is regarded as one of the most ancient places on earth.'[18] The leading theme of the 'struggle of humanity' is here re-conceptualised across an expanded timescale which starts from the local development of 'single to multi-cellular life' onto paleontological sites in South Africa that are widely thought to represent the cradle of humankind, through the drift of the continents onto the Iron Age and the early emergence of 'indigenous knowledge systems' (IKS) in South Africa, the arrival of Europeans, the legacy of colonialism and slavery, and in modern times the story of the struggle against apartheid, the triumph of democracy and finally 'a vision of the future embedded in the African Renaissance'.[19]

This expanded narrative may be attributed to the influence of Mbeki who, at this time, developed a pervasive imagination for the role of heritage, and Freedom Park in particular. The evolution of Mbeki's thought may be gleaned from his political speeches over the years 1998–2002 where he makes frequent reference to ethical and political questions of subjective identity, belonging and questions of national heritage. In his 'African Renaissance Statement' of August 1998, for instance, Mbeki seeks to confront the legacy of colonial prejudice, and calls for a process of cultural rebirth and self-discovery.

They sought to oblige us to accept that as Africans we had contributed nothing to human civilization except as beasts of burden ... The beginning of our rebirth as a Continent must be our own rediscovery of our soul, captured and made permanently available in the great works of creativity represented by the pyramids and sphinxes of Egypt, the stone buildings of Axum and the ruins of Carthage and Zimbabwe.[20]

His inaugural speech of June 1999 would later inform that his office would 'work to rediscover and claim the African heritage, for the benefit especially of our young generations'.[21] And by 2001, Mbeki had fashioned the humanistic, Afrocentric ideals that would inform Freedom Park:

As the place of the origin of all humanity, Africa has an unequalled role to play as a valued place for the affirmation of the common humanity of all humanity, regardless of race, colour or nationality ... She has the possibility to be a place of celebration of the unique identity and sanctity of each human being, regardless of gender.[22]

Two years later, Mbeki was to introduce Freedom Park as a 'hallowed' and deeply authentic place, one that testifies to the origin of the humanity of humankind – 'South Africa is the common home of all humanity.'[23]

The introduction of an expanded narrative, beginning some 3.6 billion years ago, may be understood as an attempt to deal with tensions that arise between the Park's ethical orientations – namely to valorise formerly silenced forms of indigenous knowledge and practice – and a need to deal with issues of national identity and nation-building. In previous chapters, questions of subjective identity were largely raised in relation to quite specific circumstances, which in most cases allowed for a fair degree of imaginative, if not pragmatic freedom. At Freedom Park, however, questions of identity would be directly coupled to the institutional and somewhat more limiting protocols of nationalism. Mbeki's introduction of an expanded timescale helps to mitigate against the narrowed focus of a nationalistic narrative – it is one that allows for imaginative conversation with precolonial histories and subjectivities.[24] And not withstanding the good intentions of this approach, a crucial question of narrative function with respect to nationalism should be noted here. Benedict Anderson, for instance, has famously observed that:

[i]f nation-states are widely conceded to be "new" and "historical," the nations to which they give political expression always loom out of an immemorial past, and, still more important, glide into a limitless future. It is the magic of nationalism to turn chance into destiny. With Debray we might say, "Yes, it is quite accidental that I am born French; but after all, France is eternal."[25]

Nationalist mythology is, all too commonly, fixated with questions of origin and lineage because the modern nation state wishes to seal the authority of its 'authenticity' by appealing to an assumed continuity that stretches into the distant past – an ideological structure made possible by the seamless continuity and closure of narrative. Our fathers, the 'they' who lived 'back then', are enlisted into the fold of our present day 'imagined community'.[26] The problem with this narrative form is the potential for an unquestioned authority of the origin, and a blind obedience to people, to nation and the state. From a critical perspective, we are led to ask: to what extent does Freedom Park open a genuine dialogue with silenced voices and to what extent does this conversation enlist an obedience to power, a false unity fashioned from behind the pluralities of democratic dissent?

The last of the three documents that we shall consider – Vision for the Design Brief of 2004 – was tabled a year after the failed outcome of the UIA architectural design competition. This document bears the influence of Serote, a poet and traditional healer who succeeded Lindiwe as the second CEO of the FPT.[27] This text consolidates the intentions of the others we have considered above, yet moves to focus upon ideas of indigenous authenticity, coupling these to a binding form of nationalism. The brief 'seeks to show-case African history and heritage as bearers of our traditions and values … the organising principles are based on African philosophy, African Indigenous Knowledge, and African Renaissance'.[28] The challenge of African philosophy – or perhaps we should rather say an African approach to the formation of knowledge – is one that 'places the determination of knowledge … in the hands of indigenous people … to move away from the pervasive determination of indigenous knowledge through the gaze of non-indigenous people'.[29] And in so doing, the brief wisely cautions against an assumed 'return to some golden age … instead this undertaking must be transformative towards a new future of a different kind'.[30] It should be noted here that the significance of indigenous cultural traditions and indigenous knowledge systems (IKS) was on the Park's agenda from the start, hence the Position Paper of 2000 speaks of the role of 'Living Heritage',[31] which is deemed to include 'intangible aspects of our heritage, such as rich oral culture … praise poetry, music, dance, ritual, customs and languages'.[32] But it is under the leadership of Serote that these concerns move centre stage. Despite the Park's intended critical approach – 'nothing has been taken at face value … everything is to be critically analysed and theorised' – the new focus is one that places a moral emphasis upon traditional values, over the wider plurality of contemporary experience.[33] Notably, this emphasis upon indigenous forms as the source of authentic African identity was to initiate an extended period of cultural research and debate, significant aspects of which will be noted where relevant to the architecture of the Park.

Once more, we return to questions of cultural lineage and authority, and the point that must be made about traditions and so-called common values is the way that these produce a seamless continuity with the past, collapsing differences into similitude, which all too commonly involves a fabrication of obedience and thereby consent. Ironically, the sceptre of a binding nationalism grows from the ethical and social pulse of the TRC as from reconciliation we move to a process of cleansing and healing. Crucially, this has tended to translate into a form of healing at the service of nationalistic unity. Hence, Freedom Park chooses to deal with 'divisive elements and pain in order to focus and celebrate commonalities that bring a nation together. A divided nation is not a nation. The purpose of reconciliation is to heal the divisions of the past.'[34] Yet, in contra-distinction, we may state that a nation is but a border, a terrain, a temporal mode of governance and a plurality of human differences – *never the essence of unity*.

These three phases informed an accumulative process, where layers of intention were added to form the complex and ambitious motivations of Freedom Park, as we have it today. The evolution of the Park is not the product of a unitary intention, and the project has involved a healthy degree of debate and tension.

Approaching the Site

Approaching Pretoria from the south via the N1 motorway, one catches an early glimpse of the Voortrekker Monument (see Figure 6.1), its solid

6.1 The
Voortrekker
Monument,
Gerard Moerdijk
(inauguration,
1949).
Photograph by
the author.

mass commanding a distant hilltop to one's left. This infamous symbol
of Afrikaner nationalism – designed by architect Gerard Moerdijk – was
created under the auspices of the Central People's Monument Committee,
a body formed by the Federation of Afrikaans Cultural Associations in
1931.[35] Continuing forward, the road drops to reveal the outskirts of Pretoria
and the Voortrekker Monument falls from view. Within minutes, a turn to
the left captures a dramatic view of Freedom Park situated on a hilltop to
one's right. From this vantage, the Sikhumbuto – a memorial for Freedom
Park – embraces the crest of the hill with its sweeping curve of low-lying
stonewalls and rising poles that reach to the sky (see Figure 6.2). Located
here at Salvokop, Freedom Park has initiated an explicit dialogue with the
apartheid legacy of the Voortrekker Monument.[36] One's approach into the
capital city (Pretoria) is literally framed by the contrasting presence of these
two monuments – the sensitive and ethereal expression of the Sikhumbuto
standing in measured contrast to the more dominating Neo-Classical mass
of the Voortrekker Monument. Explicit ideological differences parallel this
aesthetic contrast. Moerdijk, for example, claims that his design creates a
'tangible tribute' to the Voortrekkers who 'laid the foundation for a white
civilization … in the interior of Southern Africa … to tame nature, to conquer
the [black] savages and establish his state'.[37] The story of this undertaking is

represented in the 27 panels of the historical frieze that line the walls of the Hall of Heroes – the major interior space of the monument. The narrative for the frieze follows the Great Trek from Cape Town (1833) to the recognition of the Boer Republic (1852) – a carefully scripted dramatisation that reaches a climax when the boers triumphed against the Zulus at the Battle of Blood River on 16 December 1938. It is said that the boers had taken a sacred vow: '[h]ere we stand before the God of Heaven and earth to make a covenant unto Him, that if He will protect us and deliver our enemy into our hands, we shall observe this date as a day of thanksgiving like a Sabbath', and hence 16 December is a public holiday in South Africa, which was formerly known as the 'Day of the Vow', or 'Dingaan's Day'.[38] In post-apartheid South Africa, this holiday has been renamed 'the Day of Reconciliation', and Freedom Park is intended as a primary site of remembrance and national celebration.

The humanism of Freedom Park stands in marked contradistinction to the blatant racism of the Voortrekker Monument. And yet, despite this fact, there are some similarities between the two monuments that bear considering. At a superficial level, one cannot but wonder to what extent Freedom Park has wished to emulate the functional programme of the Voortrekker Monument – both being sited on a hill (a natural reserve), and including a shrine to fallen heroes, a garden of remembrance, a public amphitheatre, an archive and architecture that explores earthly forms of expression. Yet more importantly, Moerdijk notes the lack of historical precedent for his intended design: '[t]he Voortrekkers had developed no characteristic monumental architecture.'[39] Moerdijk would therefore maintain that his primary point of reference was the Bible '[l]ike Abraham, when he left Ur of the Chaldees to found a new state, he would have made his monument a religious one.'[40] The thinking among the intellectuals of Freedom Park is oddly similar in this respect in that authentic African forms of commemoration are deemed, primarily, to be

6.2   The Sikhumbuto settled at the crest of Salvokop, The Freedom Park. Courtesy of Graham Young.

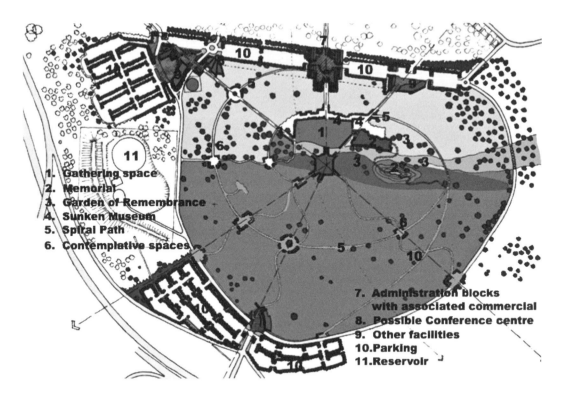

1. Gathering space
2. Memorial
3. Garden of Remembrance
4. Sunken Museum
5. Spiral Path
6. Contemplative spaces
7. Administration blocks with associated commercial
8. Possible Conference centre
9. Other facilities
10. Parking
11. Reservoir

6.3 Urban design framework for the Freedom Park, FPAA. Courtesy of GAPP Architects / Urban Designers.

spiritual, mythical, ritualistic, and without architectural precedent and as we shall see, much critical debate has been focused here.

UIA Competition Process and Brief

Revel Fox, a renowned architect from Cape Town, was appointed to the Freedom Park board to provide architectural advice in the early stages of this project. Unfortunately, his tragic death left something of a vacuum and I was not able to interview him.[41] The importance of Fox's involvement may be gleaned from Serote's words on the occasion of his memorial service held in December 2004: 'our compatriot, comrade, our friend, Revel … he smiles a delicate smile, and makes us laugh, as he strides into the horizon … we are here now searching, we miss Revel … come to Freedom Park, Revel, and rest.'[42] An interview with Barry Senior, principle of GAPP Architects and Urban Planners (GAPP), confirmed that Fox was already a member of the board in 2001, when a consortium of three architectural firms – GAPP, MMA Architects (MMA) and Mashabane Rose Associates (MRA), here abbreviated as Freedom Park Architects in Association (FPAA) and would later be called the Office of Collaborative Architects (OCA) – won the tender and were appointed to prepare an urban design framework for the site.[43] Their design, completed the same year, places commemorative spaces at the crest and to the northern leeside of the hill, with radiating axes that establish 'vistas' to

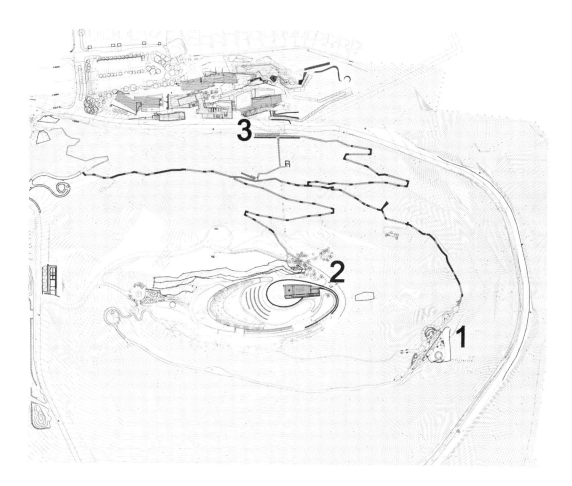

city landmarks that surround, and a 'narrative path' – also referred to as the 'spiral path' – that spirals up to support 'a journey of multiple narratives' (see Figure 6.3).[44] Construction for the site layout and infrastructure commenced soon after, under the direction of the FPAA, while the commemorative aspect – a memorial, a museum and a garden of remembrance – was to become the substance of a design competition (see Figure 6.4).

Initially, a local design competition was considered, but the idea for an all-Africa competition was later tabled and accepted by the trust.[45] However, the final decision would appear to have been influenced by the FPAA, whose PowerPoint presentation to the trust promoted the idea of a UIA-accredited International design competition and where the success of the Constitutional Court – which had involved an international competition – was cited as precedent for this choice.[46] In May 2002, the FPAA was asked to prepare a design brief,[47] and by November 2002 a UIA press release announced entry details for the intended competition.[48]

The design brief for the UIA competition takes its primary clue from the Urban Design and Developmental Framework.[49] Attached to the competition brief as Figure 1, the urban design defines three distinct zones: the base of the

6.4   Site plan of the completed project, depicting: 1) Isivivane (shrine), 2) Sikhumbuto (memorial), 3) //hapo (museum) The Freedom Park, OCA. Courtesy of the Office of Collaborative Architects: GAPP Architects / Urban Designers + Mashabane Rose Associates + MMA Architects.

hill being 'a public zone engaging with the inner city'; the crest is intended as the 'symbolic and sacrosanct aspect of Freedom Park' where the museum, memorial and garden of remembrance are to be situated; and finally the slope of the hill 'is a transitional space where ... journey takes place from the public to the sacrosanct, from the real world to the spiritual world'.[50] Competition entries are asked to consider the three primary architectural elements of the Park, namely: the museum; the garden of remembrance, which is to include interspersed sculptures and an amphitheatre as a space that will 'acknowledge national heroes and heroines and serve as a beacon of inspiration for present and future generations'; and finally, the memorial which is intended as 'the spiritual sanctum of the entire Freedom Park precinct, expressing a national human experience of heroism, sacrifice, human suffering and loss'.[51]

Key aspects of the Freedom Park Conceptual Framework – which as we have seen may be associated with Mbeki – inform the stated intension of the scheme.

Freedom Park must stand as a monument to our new found democracy founded on the values of human dignity, equality, human rights and freedom ... The precinct will narrate the story of South Africa's precolonial, colonial, apartheid and post-apartheid history and heritage over a period of 3.6 billion years ... Freedom Park will improve the accessibility of our heritage, arts and culture by adding the silent voices of South Africa's indigenous people onto the landscape.[52]

This clear statement of ideological intent, however, is not translated into architectural terms, and the leading question about architectural character is inadequately resolved by the brief. It is stated, for example, that '[t]he aesthetic and architectural character of the proposal must reflect that the complex is located in South Africa which has an artistic heritage and cultural context' and that 'the aesthetic must also be an expression of newness and innovation'.[53] Yet these suggestions, which are pretty much the only suggestions on offer, are overly wide and unclear – and especially so for an international audience – and surprisingly, no clarity is provided as to what these aesthetic intentions might entail. Senior, who worked on the brief, emphasised that the choice of words, as used here, had avoided a focused guidance on aesthetic matters because the client (FPT) was unclear as to what they wanted in architectural terms.[54] It was hoped, at this early stage, that the competition would throw up answers to these difficult questions but in fact, this was not to be the case. It should be noted that a late attempt was made to clarify the cultural agenda of the trust when during the second stage, a reading material pack was distributed to the contestants, including two speeches by Mbeki, one of which being Mbeki's influential 'I am an African' speech; a research paper entitled 'African Cosmology' by D.E.N. Mabogo; a document titled 'Freedom Park Trust Programme 2004' which includes discussion on matters relating to African cosmology, IKS, traditional African practices and symbols; the role of traditional healers, and so forth.[55] Yet the significance of this material, when used as a point of reference in contemporary design, is difficult to fathom.

Furthermore, since the contestants' designs had already been formed, the late inclusion of this subject matter is unlikely to have had an influence on the final designs.

Adjudicating the Competition

Adjudication of the first round commenced on 22 April 2003 – 17 July for the second – at the Sheraton Hotel in Pretoria.[56] The international panel of jurors met with Mbeki 'who spent some time with the jury' and who were also treated with a tour of the site, the Apartheid Museum by MRA (2001), and the Constitutional Court, which was under construction at that time.[57] The panel of jurors consisted of the chair and deputy chair of Freedom Park (Serote and Barbara Masekela – Masekela was replaced by Professor Julian Beinart in the second round), a further member of Freedom Park board (Revel Fox, who was appointed as chair of the jury), a UIA representative (Dr Raci Bademli who was replaced by Gerrit Burger in the second round), an American architect (Max Bond), a Nigerian architect (Olufemi Majekdumi), and finally a Spanish architect (Jodi Ferrando).[58] A non-voting panel of mostly South African advisors – consisting of a deputy jury, technical consultants, and a registrar (Hendrik Prinsloo, development manager for the Park) – were also party to most of the discussions.[59] Some 133 competition entries were received from across the world, 15 of which were disqualified, and an eventual five – plus two commendations – were selected to enter the second round.[60]

Unfortunately, I did not have much success with interviewing the international jurors, who proved difficult to contact. Revel Fox and Professor Bademli both passed away, while Bond, Ferrando and Beinart – from the USA – initially agreed to respond to email-based questions, but unfortunately did not their replies. I was, however, granted a substantial interview with Serote, received emailed comments from Bruger, and was able to speak to key members of the panel of advisors, which shed important light on their deliberations. And this situation is somewhat remedied by the existence of two detailed jurors' reports, as well as comprehensive minutes to the meetings of the jury – minutes to four meetings in the first round, and to three in the second – which throw light on the deliberations of the jury.

At the third meeting of the jury, on 24 April 2003 – including the panel of advisors – Masekela 'suggested that each member of the panel should define the criteria they will be using to judge the schemes'.[61] Some of the criteria mentioned are conventional, such as: relevance of the design idea, the quality of the architecture, the clarity of design intention, and so forth. Yet these sit alongside more particular criteria that look to address the unique circumstance of this scheme, hence: 'African Identity' and the proper 'abstract way to symbolize it' (Professor Beinart); '[t]he South-Africaness of the scheme' (Burger); a '[s]ense of the hill' and how this 'relates to nature (Africa)' (Bademli); 'Blending the environment to the scheme' (Ngobeni); '[i]mpact on landscape' (Saidi); '[m]ind

6.5 Design submission by OBRA, rendered perspective (2003). Courtesy OBRA Architects.

applied to environment' (Serote), and so on.[62] A fair degree of convergence is apparent here; however, the architectural correlate to these criteria would prove difficult to resolve and the adjudication was marked by fierce debate. Serote remembers that there was a pointed debate as to 'what is African' and as to how one might attempt to symbolise this.[63] He recalls, in this regard, how the international jurors had tended to support notions of 'universal expression', whereas the South African jurors wished to find a design that would speak with a more unique 'African voice'. Significantly, the majority of South African participants that were interviewed mentioned this same point of tension.[64] Unfortunately, I was unable to confirm this view with the non-South African members of the jury and therefore, the primary point that may be noted here, from a South African perspective, is the *perception* of a clear difference of view. The political sway of perception is, of course, very real.[65] Tunde Oluwa and Mphethi Morojele (of MMA), for example recall that the international jurors favoured a bold and monumental expression while Fox, in particular, strongly disapproved of this approach, and that on the last night a prolonged debate ensued, and the jury were clearly divided as to the desired outcome.[66] A further point that emerged from my interviews is the way South African participants wished to support a sensitive approach to landscape and environment, and significantly this commitment – which was emphasised by the brief, and in the juror's first round report – was here deemed to be in opposition to the more pronounced qualities of stand-out, iconic designs – an aspect to which we shall soon return.[67] In the end, the jury failed to agree on a winning scheme, and the final decision was to award the three schemes with a shared and equal second place – a judgement that was within the provisions of the competition brief.[68]

Design Submissions

We shall now consider the three, second-place schemes as a way to further clarify key areas of disagreement among the jury. The scheme entered by OBRA Architects from the USA positions five granary, tower-like forms on the crest of the hill. Four towers, grouped together and raised above the site by a common base, accommodate the museum with a nearby outdoor gathering space 'indented into shallow depressions', and a fifth solitary tower is used to accommodate the Witness Memorial, positioned 'in a clearing in the Sculpture Garden' to one side (see Figures 6.5–6.6).[69] The structure of the granary-like forms is 'conceived as a double shell of masonry and concrete with an air gap between to allow for passive cooling'.[70] According to the architects the 'ascending verticality from the summit of Salvokop Hill will take its place amongst the other landmarks to the south and balance the horizontal presence of Sir Herbert Baker's Union Buildings to the north'.[71] This project demonstrates a respect for African tectonic traditions, coupled with modern design innovation that is thoroughly forward looking, with the architects maintaining that 'Freedom Park will launch a new era … a time for re-constructing and renewal of culture and cultural recourses'.[72]

A section through the museum reveals how the curvaceous interior volumes are dramatically connected via spiralling ramps to 'facilitate a smooth flow of visitors' (see Figure 6.6).[73] The architects poetically explain that '[t]he ever changing chiaroscuro of light played out on the plastered walls of the galleries, the ramps reminding bodies of their own weight as they move through space, and the curved surface of the cavernous interior, subtly invoke a spiritual transcendence only understood with the whole body.'[74] The innovative quality of this design and the intellectual focus of the supporting documents inspire confidence – there is a lot to admire in this scheme. OBRA's submission, however, proved to be highly contentious. Minutes to the second meeting of the second round of adjudication record highly divergent views as to the appropriateness of this scheme: '[t]here is something uniquely organic about it in terms of African culture', 'the scheme evokes a sense of compatibility with its environment', '[t]he circular form implies gathering, continuity, equality', '[w]hen I look at this building it is almost foreign', 'I don't know what is African about this building? There is a building in Papua New Guinea that looks just like it', 'I don't want this to be known as the Black persons' version of the Voortrekker Monument.'[75] Significantly, Serote and Morojele both made comments similar to the last,[76] namely that when seen from a distance – as one does when approaching Pretoria – the height of these impressive towers would appear to compete with the imposing presence of the Voortrekker Monument. Post-apartheid architecture has to deal with a legacy of imposing, racist, colonial monuments, a circumstance that has resulted in a widespread aesthetic aversion to strong iconic expressions, propagated by monumental mass.

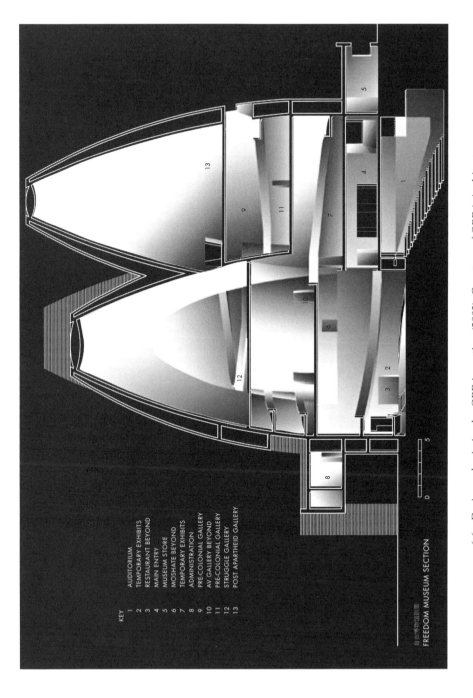

KEY

1	AUDITORIUM
2	TEMPORARY EXHIBITS
3	RESTAURANT BEYOND
4	MAIN ENTRY
5	MUSEUM STORE
6	MOSHATE BEYOND
7	TEMPORARY EXHIBITS
8	ADMINISTRATION
9	PRE-COLONIAL GALLERY
10	AV GALLERY BEYOND
11	PRE-COLONIAL GALLERY
12	STRUGGLE GALLERY
13	POST APARTHEID GALLERY

自由博物館剖面圖
FREEDOM MUSEUM SECTION

0   5

6.6   Design submission by OBRA, section (2003). Courtesy of OBRA Architects.

A further point of contention emerged from the architects' explanation of their Witness Memorial – and by inference the museum as well – an explanation, which it must be said, involves a rich and poetic layering of metaphoric intension:

[i]nspired by the African tradition of carving a grave from within a Baobab trunk as repository for the remains of important community members, The Witness Memorial can be seen as a hollowed-out tree trunk. Its voided interior 30 meters wide, and 20 meters in diameter … is more suggestive of a womb than a grave, a Sanctuary, to memorialize those who struggled to give birth to freedom.[77]

Here we have metaphoric reference to an African baobab trunk, a reference to African practices of memorialisation, a womb and a sanctuary. To this, we might wish to add that the towering forms are also reminiscent of African baskets, and that the iconic presence of the towers is softened by the use of fluid forms that allow for a sculptural relation to the landscape. However, mention of the baobab must have upset members of the jury concerned with ideas of indigenous authenticity. The jurors' report of the first round maintains that '[t]he imagery of the grove of baobab trees … was strongly questioned … it was pointed out that they are not indigenous to the site, nor would they survive if transplanted'.[78] Then later that 'Baobab trees do not grow in this region'.[79] Interviews with the panel of assessors underscored the perception held among the majority of South African participants that this scheme – and despite being championed by some – is fundamentally insensitive to the site. And ultimately, the final jurors' report would maintain that '[t]he unique shapes are not fully convincing nor are they perceived to be … appropriate'.[80]

The submission entered by a Hong Kong-based architect, Peter To Tai-Fai, stands in clear contrast to the former (see Figures 6.7–6.8).[81] The bold geometry of this partially subterranean design consists of a series of concentric circles with shifted centres that spiral inward towards an inner circular memorial wall – termed the 'Event Horizon' – where the space at the centre accommodates an open-air amphitheatre. With the insertion of this singular figure at the top of Salvokop, the architect's intention is 'to allocate all the functions at the crest instead of having them separately situated at different locations of the area'.[82] This choice of a circular geometry, positioned at the crest, is deemed to be 'logical' and 'appropriate,' indeed 'almost inescapable', allowing for an 'omni-directional character', one that will 'ornament the hill just like the decorative patterns around [pottery] or the decorations put over heads of indigenous Africans'.[83] Furthermore, the circle is chosen because it provides a 'spiritual symbol of completeness and holiness … one of the sacred forms [used] throughout the history of architecture worldwide', and as used 'in vernacular architectures … in Africa.'[84] It is worth noting here that vigorous debates as to the rounded nature of African architecture would occur at a later stage of the Park, as we are soon to see.

6.7   Design
submission by
Peter To Tai-Fai,
perspective plan
(2003). Courtesy
of Peter To Tai-Fai
(Hong Kong).

The circular plan is intended as a type of African 'Lukasa Map', but which is not indigenous to South Africa, 'a kind of mnemonic. Composed basically of a memory board covered with beads and cowrie shells … either signifying spirit capitals, or showing a migratory route'.[85] Translating this into the museum, the 'major spaces (the towns/regions) and times (at which events of historical significances happened) are mapped into the architecture (including the natural landscape),' whereby visitors who follow 'the designated routes … are actually conducting pilgrimage through the history of South Africa'.[86] This is achieved by placing exhibits around the circular plan in a physical/geographic relation to their place of origin. And the intended arrangement introduces an interesting museological twist whereby exhibits pertaining to colonial history are housed inside the building, 'like the conventional [Western] museums all over the world', while exhibits relating to indigenous peoples are 'spread all over the hill top … in the Garden of Remembrance'.[87] This scheme is insightful for its challenge to conventional, indeed colonial museology – a move that anticipates subsequent debates. Finally, the memorial is intended as an inner ring-like structure 'marking the Event Horizon', which is elevated at the top … to act as the visual focus of the whole development'.[88] The author derives his poetic concept of an 'event horizon' from the point of threshold that leads into a black hole where light and matter are absorbed and at which point neither can escape – a

metaphor for the 'unknown' substance of the future which will be presented at Freedom Park, a 'huge attraction that absorbs the past'.[89]

Comments recorded at the jurors' second meeting of the second stage are, once again, somewhat divided: for example, the saucer plan appears 'almost as though it has been dropped from space'; 'a hostile, alien presence'; whereas a different set of views find this scheme to be 'the most interesting spatial experience of anything here ... It doesn't compete with the Voortrekker Monument. It doesn't do anything serious to the skyline'; 'I believe this has the gem of a scheme, which properly handled architecturally, could become an outstanding piece of architecture'.[90] An important point of debate would appear to have centred on the embedded nature of the plan. The jurors' first round report explained that 'concern was expressed as to whether the scheme would present a sufficient iconic presence to those viewing it from the bottom of the hill'.[91] Then later, the second round report moved on to observe that '[t]he building is sufficiently sunken into the crest of the hill to limit its impact on the skyline whilst still, maintaining a definite presence.'[92] One may deduce that a degree of ambivalence existed among the panel as to how one might address the racist legacy of bold monumentality – such as the nearby Voortrekker Monument – how to subvert the familiar dominating gesture, yet preserve an adequate sense of iconic presence. And it should be remembered that similar questions were raised by the architecture of the Constitutional Court. In the final analysis, however, this design was deemed to be 'a self contained scheme' that relies upon 'abstract mapping techniques', and which has 'resulted in little consideration being given to the overall organization of the site'.[93]

The last of the three second-place submissions is that of Vladimir Djurovic and Imad Gemayel, architect and landscape designers based in Lebanon. This scheme is structured by a series of cross-axes that order the landscape to form a narrativised path (see Figures 6.9–6.10). The architect's explain their concept, which is 'about nature ... infused with the therapeutic power of the landscape, [Freedom Park] will create a sanctuary for reflection, forgiveness, and ultimately reveal the true soul of South Africa, the common home of all humanity'.[94] Entering from the northern side, visitors circulate via an urban piazza with administration buildings that settle at the foot of the hill. From here, it is possible either to take the spiral path, which moves around to the

6.8   Design submission by Peter To Tai-Fai, site model (2003). Courtesy of Peter To Tai-Fai (Hong Kong).

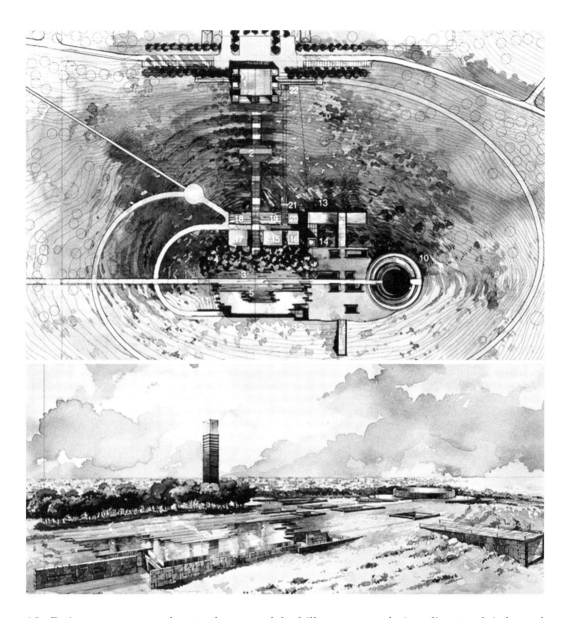

6.9   Design submission by Vladimir Djurovic and Imad Gemayel, rendered site plan and perspective (2003). Courtesy of Vladimir Djurovic and Imad Gemayel.

east and up to the crest of the hill, or to ascend via a direct path informed by an axis that runs in a north to south direction. Passing a 'commemorative space' dedicated to Mbeki and a 'panoramic terrace', the journey proceeds onto the 'gathering space' at the crest where '[a] breathtaking water basin, with a 57-meter-long infinity-edge further dramatizes the sensation of being on a panoramic mountaintop. Scattered in the centre ... is a stage of rocks ... The water surface acts as a perfect mirror to an ever-changing skyline, gatherings and performance.'[95] At this point, a primary cross-axis reorientates motion in a west-to-east direction passing a 'contemplation garden' and on to the memorial formed from a large cylindrical space sunk

6.10 Design submission by Vladimir Djurovic and Imad Gemayel, perspective elevation of the memorial (2003). Courtesy of Vladimir Djurovic and Imad Gemayel.

into the ground, and accessed via a pair of ramps that spiral down and back up again situated to either side (see Figure 6.10).[96] The architects explain that upon entering the central space

one is immersed in the vast purity of the circle, one is found completely surrounded by the names of the heroes and heroines that have sacrificed their lives for this ultimate cause, behind which a constant flow of water droplets fall as the endless tears and blood that were shed for this cause.[97]

Returning to the contemplation garden, the visitor may enter the subterranean museum, which follows a tunnel, the 'primordial shaft' that is 'burrowed though the hill' connecting from the south to the north side – 'the intention of this primordial shaft is to take us back to our essential beings, narrating the entire history of South Africa, from the beginning of time until the present …here the museum unfolds in a simple chronological layout'.[98] And finally, upon exit on the northern side, the experience culminates with an ascent up 'The Nelson Mandela Tower' which is intended as 'a permanent mark on the landscape' and 'a beacon of hope, a symbol of freedom and inspiration for a better future'.[99]

The landscaped nature of this scheme was widely appreciated by the South African members of the panel that I interviewed – Serote, in particular, spoke of the nature-sensitivity of indigenous architecture, and went on to comment that the 'landscape schemes' were the ones that moved in the right direction.[100] These comments are also supported by the reports of the jury – '[i]t is a sensible project that deals with all the elements in a way that does not impose on the hill.'[101] And 'the significance of nature in the creation of Freedom Park is admirable'.[102] Criticism, however, was focused on the tower which 'has to deal with the context of memorial towers, such as the Voortrekker Monument' and, comments recorded at the second meeting on the second round include: 'the scheme is much better without the tower', '[d]efinitely take the tower away'.[103] And yet, if the tower were to be removed, this scheme would lack a visible presence on the hill, and debates that featured with the previous scheme are likely to have ensued. Regarding the memorial, the use of a circular form was appreciated for its 'many resonances with an African past', but the pure and stark quality of the design was deemed to be 'too severe'.[104] Ultimately, the jury felt that the submission did not reach its full potential – '[t]he goal of achieving a complete synchronicity with nature has not been realized.'[105]

Post-Competition Arrangements

The UIA competition did not result in a winning scheme, but the process tabled concepts and questions that were to influence the eventual design of the Park. The immediate question that faced the board was how to move forward. In a personal letter to Serote, Fox lays down three possible paths of action, namely that: a discussion could be had with 'one or more' of the three finalists, or 'a second limited competition' with 'selected participants' could be established, or lastly, the trust could decide to extend 'the scope of the consulting team already appointed'.[106] Fox adds: '[i]n my opinion, the last option is the one in which the Board will have the most involvement.'[107] A complication with this last option was the fact that the principals of MMA – Moreojele and Oluwa, who were part of the architectural consulting team – had served as members of the non-voting panel of the jury. The UIA would maintain, however, that involvement on the non-voting panel did not preclude participation as a future consultant.[108] The tender proposal for a new consulting team was put out in early June 2004, and the Office of Collaborative Architects (OCA, a collaborative of GAPP, MMA and MRA) won the tender and was appointed as architects for the design of Freedom Park.[109]

The post-competition stage of the project was characterised by extended consultation with numerous public interest groups to ensure public ownership of the Park, as well as the involvement of traditional healers; commissioned research on African cultural practices, spirituality and mythology, IKS, and so forth; and intensive debate ensued as to how these concerns might influence the architecture of the Park.[110] Indeed, everything pertaining to the design was questioned and debated, and we shall refer to key points of discussion where pertinent to the formation of the Park.

The layout of Freedom Park as we have it today is fairly close to that defined by the early Urban Design Framework, although the spiral path now moves towards the east to symbolise life and regeneration – and not towards the west as was the case with the Urban Design Framework (see Figures 6.3–6.4).[111] Primary points of entry are positioned at the foot of the hill on the northern side where a public space collects visitors before directing them into the //apo (museum), then up the spiral path towards the Isivivane (a shrine) and onto the Sikhumbuto (a memorial) situated at the crest of the hill. Alternate paths of motion are also possible, leading more directly to the Sikhumbuto and/or the Isivivane. We shall now consider, in chronological order, the three primary architectural interventions that have shaped the Park – Isivivane, Sikhumbuto and //hapo.

Isivivane

Initially referred to as the 'boulders contemplation space', the design for the Isivivane commenced prior to the UIA competition and was not included

in the scope of the competition as it was always intended as part of the landscaping plan for the spiral path.[112] The UIA competition brief merely refers to 'narrative points' that are to be places along the spiral path, whereas documents supplied in the second round informed competitors as to the intentions for Isivivane.[113] Valorised by many as 'the very essence of Freedom Park' this sacred shrine is the symbolic 'final resting place of the spirits of those who died in the struggle for freedom' (see Figures 6.11–6.12).[114] At his address on the occasion of the handover of the Garden of Remembrance, Mbeki proclaimed:

6.11 Isivivane, Freedom Park. Photograph by the author.

[t]his is a place to which all our people of all colours, cultures, ages and beliefs, men and women, will come to pay their quiet tribute to those whose memory will never be extinguished, who will live on in every generation that lives, summoning each to be the standard bearers of the cause of the freedom of all humanity.[115]

A primary influence on the concept of the Isivivane comes from the anthropological research work of Professor Harriet Ngubane.[116] In her work on the 'African Understanding of the Concept of Memorial' – a research paper that was prepared for the Park – Ngubane states that

[t]he African concept of a memorial is not confined mainly in the commemorative buildings or portrayed through sculpture [as is the case in the West], but is spread out over various forms of cultural behaviour. A well-known structure that portrays memorial is a heap of stones along long distance pathways known as Isivivane.[117]

6.12 Isivivane with Lesaka in the mist, Freedom Park. Courtesy of Graham Young.

She does not comment any further on the Isivivane in this paper, but rather goes on to cite further examples of African customary practice that, in her view, signify types of memorialisation that are not tied, exclusively, to monumental form, for instance: burial sites designated by stones and a planted aloe, the practice of burying family members within the homestead such that their 'identity was embedded within the homestead precincts',[118] the naming of children as a commemorative event, the names of royal residences that 'reflect the area or aura connected with a historical event',[119] the position and importance of the grandmother's house in the homestead as a 'place where all the rituals are performed towards the ancestors ... [and as] a tangible structure on memory of the most important woman with regard to descendants as they are sons, daughters in law, great and great grand children to her.'[120] In each case the point is to show that African traditions of commemoration are not externalised in memorial objects, but are linked to rituals and systems of belief that are themselves embedded in daily forms of practice. The Isivivane at Freedom Park, therefore, is not conceived as a Western-style memorial or shrine, but rather is intended as a performative site of embodied memory, ritual and spirituality, and is infused with a wealth of over-determined symbolic references. The Isivivane is intended as a homestead, with the *lesaka*, or central core, as the burial site. A fine spay of mist, emitted from the floor of the *lesaka*, ensures an aura of mist and mystery (see Figure 6.12), a place where visitors can pay their respect to the spiritual resting place, a 'home' for those who sacrificed their lives for freedom. The Isivivane is not merely a symbolic representation – although it does include a representational function – but rather is deemed to be the actual resting place of the departed spirits of those who died, and is therefore considered to be a sacred place, one where the visitor must remove her shoes, and wash her hands on departure.[121]

In a prior workshop presentation, Ngubane developed further thought as to the significance of Isivivane. As already noted, the Isivivane is a heap of stones, situated at certain long intervals to mark the way along a distant journey. Ngubane, here, explains that in 'the indigenous African view of environment ... People recognise a symbiotic relationship between themselves and ecology, which, apart from flora and fauna, also includes the spiritual entities connected to the people in a given area.'[122] One's journey is no mere passage or departing, but rather provides opportunity for 'homage to the landscape and all that it contains. Placing a stone [upon Isivivane] ... is an act of leaving something behind which unites one with such land and its people, spirits, flora and fauna'.[123] From this, we may interpret the Isivivane to mark a journey in the life of the nation, a place where stones are left in an act of homage to the land, its people and the ancestral spirits of those who have departed – memorialisation is tied to the journey of life. This metaphor is suggestive for it highlights the individual, particular and transitory nature of the passage towards a common future. Interpretive literature published by Freedom Park, however, has tended to emphasise a more unitary conception, hence an official information brochure issued to visitors prefers to emphasise that the 'concept of Isivivane is derived from the verb viva, which means to come together in a group ... commitment to solidarity and unity of purpose'.[124] At the centre of the Isivivane is the *lesaka*, a seTswana word,

which in African culture ... [is used to describe] a circular structure (often a cattle byre) commonly found in South African villages where generation upon generation are buried ... This is the Contemplative palace inside the *Isivivane* where the fallen heroes and heroines are laid to rest.[125]

Eleven boulders encircle the *lesaka*, nine of which were selected from places of 'historical significance' within each of the nine provinces of South Africa, while the remaining two were selected to represent National Government and the international community.[126] Prior to departure, cleansing and healing ceremonies were performed over the boulders in each of the nine provinces, and further ceremonies were performed upon arrival at the Isivivane. These ceremonies were conducted in keeping with indigenous traditions where it is believed that a process of cleaning and healing is required before the newly deceased can reach the realm of ancestral spirits. To this end, 'rituals are performed by the living in order to help the spirit of the deceased to reach a full cycle of the spiritual life'.[127] At Freedom Park, these ceremonies are linked to the question of reconciliation and symbolic reparations for the human violations of the past because it is believed that the spirits of those who died for freedom must be cleansed and healed before coming to rest at the Isivivane.

Graham Young – landscape architect for the Isivivane – explained in an interview that the client was very clear about what they wanted, and that

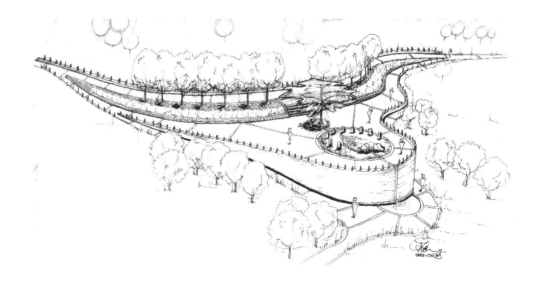

6.13　Early design sketch for the Isivivane, Freedom Park,
Graham Young (2003). Courtesy of Graham Young.

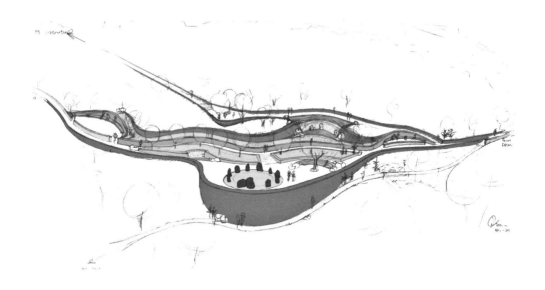

6.14　Rendered perspective for the Isivivane, Freedom Park,
Graham Young. Courtesy of Graham Young.

his design had evolved smoothly in response.[128] The Isivivane is a stylised landscape – not a building – and possibly, it is for this reason that the client's intensions were readily translatable. The physical locality of the Isivivane was determined in conversation with traditional healers, and Young emphasised that his first gesture was inspired by the site.[129] Young chose to fill up the slope of the terrain, bubbling it out to form an inhabitable terrace rather than cutting into the side of the hill, a move that is uncommon to indigenous practise, Young said.[130] An early sketch shows the *lesaka* at the centre of the terrace, with a curved line of boulders and trees that mark the boundary to a raised pathway. A later version of this idea introduces a single tree – a '*kgotla*' or meeting place – positioned between the *lesaka* and the steps that lead between the boulders (see Figure 6.13). This second sketch is included in the design concept brief for the Garden of Remembrance and the client's criticism is noted in this document, namely that the steps leading from the *kgotla* to the *lesaka* 'are too "western" and classically formal. Its location [the *kgotla*] should be reconsidered along with a more asymmetrical design of the steps.'[131] In the final design, the boulders encircle the *lesaka*; the *kgotla* is repositioned in an asymmetric fashion to the right; a fountain is added at the highest point of the site; and smaller threshold spaces are created to facilitate entry (the removing of shoes) and exit (the washing of hands), as well as bypass circulation routes (see Figure 6.14). The design is artfully conceived. Approaching from the north along the spiral path, one's motion is channelled via the sinuous stone walls. A sense of expectation is aroused, as the full measure of one's destination cannot be seen. On removing one's shoes, a quick curve to the left reveals the ring of stately boulders that gather together in the mist – a most memorable scene.

Sikhumbuto

Laid into the natural contours at the crest of the hill, the sweeping gestures of the Sikhumbuto curve to hold a central amphitheatre and sanctuary (see Figure 6.15). Presented as 'Freedom Park's major memorial element, the Sikhumbuto stands as a testimony to the conflicts that have shaped the South Africa we live in today.'[132] Formerly named Isikhumbuto, the concept for the Sikhumbuto is derived from this siSwati word – *ishikhumbuto* or 'memorial' – the precise meaning for which, however, differs from the English equivalent.[133] Isikhumbuto is said to involve a form of remembrance that brings together the living and the dead, 'a place of remembrance of those who have passed on and also a place of invoking help in the current and future affairs of … society'.[134] The living and the dead are here brought together by the programme that combines a memorial – a Wall of Names and sanctuary – with a gathering space intended for public events. These elements follow directly from the UIA design brief, yet the Sikhumbuto would acquire a new significance by virtue of its relation to the Isivivane. Upon completion of the Isivivane – at the handover of the Garden of Remembrance – Mbeki emphasised that

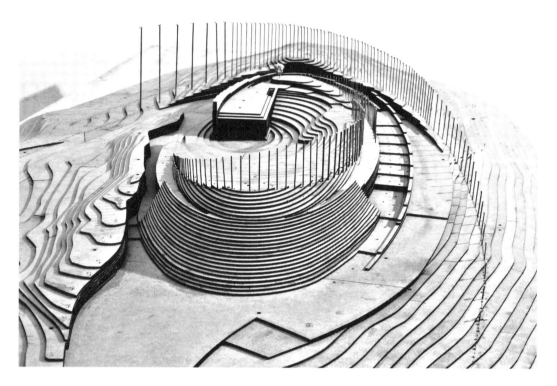

6.15 Model of the Sikhumbuto, Freedom Park, Marco Cianfanelli. Courtesy of Marco Cianfanelli.

'names … [would] be inscribed on Freedom Park'.[135] The Isivivane – which was derived from an African conception of memorialisation, one that is spiritual and embodied rather than representational and abstract – does not bear any names, and understandably so. Ramzie Abrahams – heritage manager for Freedom Park – and Serote independently noted that Mbeki's speech had emphasised the need to record names, and from this it became clear that a more conventional memorial was needed to supplement the Isivivane.[136] The inscription of names on a memorial wall is an aesthetic form that, clearly, resonates with Western historic practice. By combining Isivivane and Sikumbutho, Freedom Park – whether consciously or not – has moved to include African alongside Western forms of memorialisation. The combined effect is, perhaps, not dissimilar to that encountered at Mpumalanga where a domed Assembly and a symbolic tree stand side by side, a form of hybrid inclusion that speaks to the cultural legacy of South Africa's divided past. At Freedom Park, however, we have noted that nation-building is positioned alongside an ethical conversation with formerly subjugated belief systems and practices. From this, it may be observed that where the Isivivane facilitates a conversation with cultural practices that issue from the past – embodied and immediate – the Sikhumbuto initiates a more linear and representational narrative of the nation by inscribing the names of those who died in the eight conflicts that led up to South Africa's recent democracy.[137]

The early conceptual design of the Sikhumbuto was marked by a disagreement between the designers Morojele (of MMA) and Rose (of MRA) who, at one point, decided to present different schemes. Morojele kindly provided me with a PowerPoint presentation that was prepared to display the alternative schemes.[138] The first design option, prepared by Rose – whose work featured in the chapters on Kliptown and Kimberley – shows a linear and spiralling motion formed by an organic, ellipse-like geometry that holds a gathering space, positioned at the crest of the hill (see Figure 6.16). Approaching from the west, visitors circulate along the gentle curvature of the Wall of Names, moving in an easterly direction. The pathway sits on the southern side of the Wall of Names, and is cut into the contours of the landscape while the northern side of the wall is embedded into the landscape where the inner ground-plane of the Sikhumbuto is raised to meet the top of the wall. A series of cave-like display spaces – the 'Chambers of Conflict' – cut through the wall and into the filled earth on its northern side, the reference for which is gleaned from 'caves inhabited by traditional healers in the Ficksburg mountains'.[139] At its eastern end, the memorial wall makes a dramatic turn towards the northern side with entry into the central space of the Sikhumbuto, and it is at this tight turning point in the curvature of the wall that names relating to the liberation struggle are inscribed. At this juncture in the architects' presentation, reference is made to the 'passage of soaring walls' at Great Zimbabwe (see Figure 3.6).[140] A sanctuary is positioned to the north-western side in close proximity to a commemorative wild olive tree that was planted by Mbeki. Here, the space of the landscaped Sikhumbuto opens to the northern slope via a series of terraces that step down towards the museum that is situated at the foot of the hill.[141]

The second design option, prepared by Morojele, works from the idea that the entire hill is a monument, with the Sikhumbuto positioned at the convergence of a network of spiralling and radiating paths that lead up and connect back to the featured sites of the hill. The plan possesses a similarly organic, oval orientation only the precise layout is far less sequential and linear than was the case with the former design (see Figure 6.17). Three curved walls rise from the landscape to define an arrangement of 'overlapping spaces' that allow for multiple points of entry.[142] Morojele explained that his idea was to privilege a sense of gathering by inscribing names, exclusively, on the inside of the walls.[143] His design wished to avoid a fixed and prescriptive narrative, and a series of 'spatial pulls and different foci' was introduced to accommodate various groups of visitors who would be free to use the space in different ways such that 'no one person could own the entire space'.[144] The client, however, preferred the more sequential narrative of Rose's design, which was deemed to be more fitting to the victories of the liberation struggle – linear narratives are, largely, supportive of nation.[145] Morojele's design also introduced the idea of a stylised reed sculpture with a sequence of vertical, knife-like poles positioned toward the ends of two of the enclosing walls. The presentation includes a photograph taken by David Goldblatt of reeds that enclose the cattle briar at Mgungundlovu – the Place of

6.16   Early design for the Sikhumbuto, MRA (2005). Courtesy of the Office of Collaborative Architects: GAPP Architects/Urban Designers + Mashabane Rose Associates + MMA Architects.

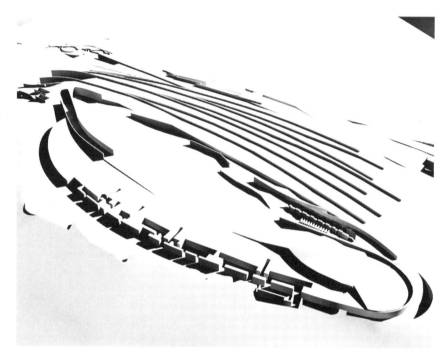

Dingaan – an image that inspired Morojele's design.[146] The client got excited about the prospect of a reed sculpture, and the final design would appear to have evolved from a combination of the reed sculpture and the more sequential aspect of Rose's plan.

The Sculpture of Ascending Reeds, as it is called, proved evocative for the client who was quick to associate it with Ngubane's anthropological reconstruction of an African creation mythology. According to Ngubane: '[t]he last item in creation was that of a human being (*umuntu*) who came out of a reed growing in a bed or reeds.'[147] Ngubane argues that the reed (*uhlanga*) 'represents motherhood', and notes that 'the chief mourner in cases of death is a married woman who is closely connected to the deceased through marriage'.[148] It is the mother that 'nurtur[es] the spirits of the newly deceased members of their husband's lineage to enable such spirits to reach the necessary maturity to enter into the fold of an ancestral spirit'.[149] And from this, it is clear that reeds may be associated with motherhood, and the rejuvenating passage of birth, of nurturing into life, and transition into the afterlife. As we have seen, the Sikhumbuto is intended as a memorial that brings together the living and the dead, the past and the future, and hence the reference to reeds provides a poetic, African symbol for this conception. Reaching from earth to sky, the reed poles may be understood to link an earthly life to the afterlife, and the sculpture is remarkable for having introduced a powerful, femininity to the symbolism of the Sikhumbuto.

On a more formal level, the repetition of vertical poles also engages the question of how to commemorate in the shadow of colonial and apartheid

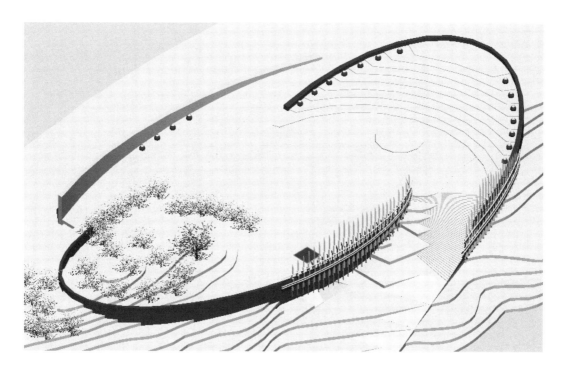

6.17 Early design for the Sikhumbuto, MMA (2005). Courtesy of the Office of Collaborative Architects: GAPP Architects/Urban Designers + Mashabane Rose Associates + MMA Architects.

monumentality. The reed poles have a clear presence on the hill, and successfully establish Freedom Park when viewed from afar. Yet, at the same time, the sculpture has enabled a dissolution of monumental mass (see Figure 6.2). Marco Cianfanelli, a South African artist who was invited to work on the reed sculpture, explains that the stainless steel poles tend to reflect the surrounding atmosphere such that the reed sculpture disappears at certain time of the day.[150] Indeed, the ethereal nature of the Sculpture of Ascending Reeds provides a welcome counterpoint to the more dominant presence of the nearby Voortrekker Monument.

Cianfanelli spoke at length about his interest in contextual forms of art, be they public or environmental.[151] He emphasised his concern for the reed sculpture to belong to the hill, and that, in his estimation, no clear-cut distinction should be made between the architecture, landscaping and sculpture of the Sikhumbuto. Electing to work closely with the design team, Cianfanelli gave input into the conceptualisation of the final design, and assisted with moulding and sculpting the terrain of the hill to form a 'seamless transition' with the surrounding site.[152]

Cianfanelli informed me that he experimented with numerous designs. An early sketch provided by the architects shows a line of poles growing taller toward the amphitheatre on the western side. This motion is sensible from the point of view of wanting to form a sense of closure to the space of the amphitheatre, but Cianfanelli adds that the client wanted a rising motion to the east as a gesture towards the rising of the sun.[153] The final design would appear to have evolved from a combination of both approaches, with

6.18 Swirling counter motion of the Sculpture of Ascending Reeds, Freedom Park, Marco Cianfanelli. Photograph by the author.

a dramatic countermotion formed by a sweeping gesture of reed poles that curve up to the west, set against a counter curve that builds towards the east. Cianfanelli explained that he was anxious to achieve the correct perceptual density in the distribution of the poles and that the apparent continuity of the curve in fact relies upon a measured variance in the positioning of the poles, which gradually tighten upon entry into the steeper portions of the curve to ensure a perceived fluidity of line.[154] The reed poles are formed from telescoping sections that taper with length before fanning back and out to an inverted cone at the tip where concealed lights illuminate the sculpture at night. Each of the almost 200 reed poles are geometrically unique in terms of spacing, height and profile, a complexity that was introduced by Cianfanelli to correct for perspective effects and ensure a sense of seamless transition as the reed poles draw their sweeping lines through space.

Moving up the hill from the Isivivane, the spiral path leads to the crest of the hill on the western side of the Sikhumbuto. From here, the parallel lines of the memorial walls – inscribed with names related to the eight conflicts – fan out and lead in an easterly direction around the southern edge of the raised gathering space of the Sikhumbuto. As one enters the tightened curve on the western-most side – a path that leads around to the sanctuary and into the gathering space at the centre – it is possible to turn back, 180°, and circulate

6.19   The Hall of Heroes, Freedom Park. Photograph by the author.

6.20   Sanctuary and amphitheatre at the Sikhumbuto, Freedom Park.
Photograph by the author.

via a curved stair that leads directly up and into the central gathering space of the Sikhumbuto. At the top, entry is dramatised by the swirling counter motion of the Sculpture of Ascending Reeds which flies overhead, rising this way to the east, now that way to the west (see Figure 6.18). The counter foci and vortices so formed have an almost giddying effect that is accompanied by the wind, the powerful light of day, and the embrace of the amphitheatre that rises to the western side. Moving forward to the west, it is possible to circulate back down to the cave-like interior of the Hall of Heroes tucked beneath the raised amphitheatre, where computer touchscreens provide biographical information relating to names that are engraved on the walls (see Figure 6.19). Ahead on the north-eastern side, the sanctuary which is half embedded in the landscape, emerges from the terrain as a focal point for the entire space (see Figure 6.20). Yet the semi-frontal form of the sanctuary does not have sufficient presence to hold the geometric force of the space that is focused upon it and as such, the presence of the sanctuary is perceived as an anticlimax. The architecture, at this point, seems undecided over questions of monumentality and of object focus, a situation that brings us back to the complex, and at times conflicted, circumstance of post-apartheid public designs.

//hapo

Finally, the third intervention at Freedom Park that we shall consider is the //hapo or museum. //hapo is a San word – the closest English equivalent for which is 'dream' – derived from 'the San people's philosophy that "a dream is not a dream unless it is shared by the community"'.[155] From the word //hapo, we may deduce that the museum is constitutive of a collective vision. The design process for the //hapo, however, proved highly protracted with sustained debate as to the appropriate form of expression.

We have noted that Freedom Park wished to establish an authentic expression, one that is tied to formerly marginalised types of indigenous knowledge and practice. In this regard, the dominant source of reference has been to natural phenomena – reeds, boulders, fire and water – derived from indigenous myths, rituals and traditions. These naturalistic references served well for the creation of the Isivivane and the Sikhumbuto, both of which are largely landscape or sculpturally based designs. The Isivivane proceeded without contention because the design was directly motivated by indigenous traditions. The Sikhumbuto, with its 'Western'-style wall of names, proved somewhat more contentious, and it is significant that the building elements of the Sikhumbuto are either buried into the landscape or downplayed. When it came to the museum, however, questions of building aesthetics could not be diverted into landscaping. And so here, in the context of this contemporary architectural intervention, the clients' favoured types of naturalistic reference would prove somewhat more difficult to resolve. Indeed, the role of architectural form was up for debate. Abrahams, heritage manager for the

Park, was to ask the question: '[i]s the conception of architecture-as-form a Western approach to design?'[156]

The museum is of course a Western, colonial building type and unsurprisingly, this fact generated a fair degree of critical thought and self-criticism. The approach that is adopted by the //hapo is one that emphasises performative aspects of display, 'different modes of depiction' which include 'story telling and the promotion of oral tradition, real and virtual displays of original artefacts'.[157] A leading concept is the idea that 'content must inform container', that the form of the architecture must be derived from a dialogue with the contents of the museums, material and mythical alike.[158] Rose explains this concept in another way, in that the primary question from the client has not been 'what is an African architecture, but rather, what is the idea behind the image', what is the link to indigenous knowledge, history and practice? Rose adds that, for him, the point has not been to repeat a traditional form, or to fix old notions, but to invent new forms of expression that take inspiration from indigenous traditions.

In the approved design brief, it was agreed that the //hapo plan would take its cues from the natural terrain of the site, yet this intention was not so easily resolved.[159] Rose, who worked extensively on the conceptual design of the //hapo, explained that he proposed three successive designs: an early linear design, followed by a second entitled 'The Unbroken Song', and a final design that is derived from the idea of boulders.[160] The first scheme, which began in early 2004, was derived from a photograph taken by Rose, depicting cracks and crevices in rocks that were found on the site. Rose explained that the linear plan was chosen to accommodate a narrative timeline, the building being embedded at the foot of the northern slope.[161] A central open space facilitates entry, and a 'crack' in the built mass, allows for an oblique circulation over the building and onto the spiral path that leads up the hill (see Figure 6.21).

A museological report, commissioned and prepared for the client by Thinc Design (from New York City) and Visual Acuity (from West Sussex, England), inspired a second attempt.[162] This document suggests three concepts that may inform the museum, namely the 'River of Time and Pool of Reflection', 'Themes and Variations' and 'Ripples on Water'.[163] The new design evolved from the first concept – '[t]he unbroken song of South African history forms the undulating spine … Along this slender 'river of time' would be situated circular spaces (the 'pools') that operate as special exhibit galleries, performance space, media presentation and primarily gathering spaces that can be utilized for in-depth storytelling and discussion.'[164] An early sketch shows a waving wall that is intended as the 'river of time' (see Figure 6.22). This scheme was developed in significant detail, yet at a certain point the design was to elicit strong criticism from certain members of the trust. Rose explains that the plan type had suggested a flat roof, which he chose to cover with grass to help the structure blend with the hill.[165] This decision was not well received by the clients who saw the grassed roof as suggestive of burial, a burial that is suggestive of death, and by inference an association that was deemed to be inappropriate.

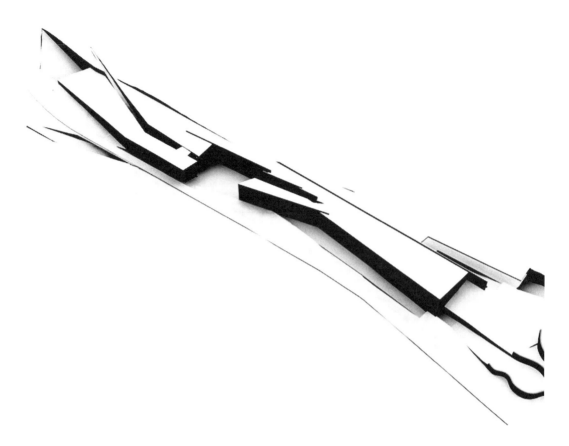

6.21 First design for the //hapo (2004). Courtesy of the Office of Collaborative Architects: GAPP Architects/Urban Designers + Mashabane Rose Associates + MMA Architects.

The design had also developed a somewhat angular, geometric expression that was strongly disliked by some. The angularity of the scheme sparked extensive debate as to the rounded nature of precolonial indigenous architecture. Prior to colonial contact, the indigenous architectures in Southern Africa were circular, rather than orthogonal, as is still evidenced in many traditional, rural homesteads in Southern African. And a preference for fluid, organic and rounded forms has been an ongoing topic of debate among the intellectuals of Freedom Park.[166] The preference for rounded forms may seem odd when viewed in the light of contemporary architectural aesthetics, but these matters are relative, and as such need to be understood in relation to their unique circumstance. And it must be said that simplistic distinctions of this kind – for example, as students of architecture my generation wished to think: angular-is-good, orderly-is-bad – often inspire highly original approaches to design. Ultimately, the proposition rounded-good, angular-bad is less interesting in terms of what it has to say about African design, yet more interesting in terms of what might be achieved by the use of these terms.

I tried to probe the notion of rounded architecture in my interviews. Serote was quick to point out that there were differing views among the members of the trust. His own view is that where the 'debate points to circular form alone,

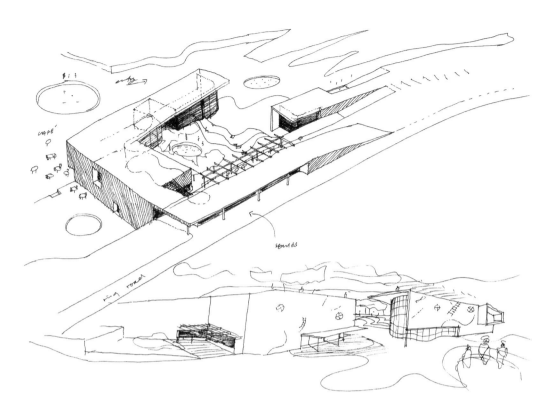

it impoverishes creativity', and he spoke in favour of free experimentation with a variety of forms.[167] At this point in the conversation, I changed my approach, asking why the consistent focus upon organic form at Freedom Park. To which, Serote replied that the aesthetics of the Park is derived from the African Creation Story, where it is said that we should be respectful of nature – organic architecture being the aesthetic correlate to this commitment.[168] Morojele feels that the concept of rounded architecture, as promoted by leaders of the Park, should not be understood in purely formal terms, but rather as a metaphor, one that wishes to learn from aesthetic qualities of indigenous settlements and that shows a sympathetic dialogue with the natural environment.[169] While Rose points out that the rounded forms of indigenous architectures are tectonic in origin, being derived from soft materials such as mud, grass and reeds, a pattern that requires careful, if not difficult, translation for a modern context.[170]

Rose's third design concept for the //hapo was derived from his visit to Credo Mutwa's healing garden at Kuruman in the Northern Cape. The trust sent a delegation to consult with Mutwa – an artist and traditional healer – on various conceptual matters relating to the Park, and Rose was among the eleven who made the trip.[171] Mutwa – who possesses the demeanour of a prophet – is renowned for his 'Holy Garden', a place that is believed to provide a 'healing atmosphere' for those who are sick.[172] The garden is

6.22   Second design for the //hapo. Courtesy of the Office of Collaborative Architects: GAPP Architects/Urban Designers + Mashabane Rose Associates + MMA Architects.

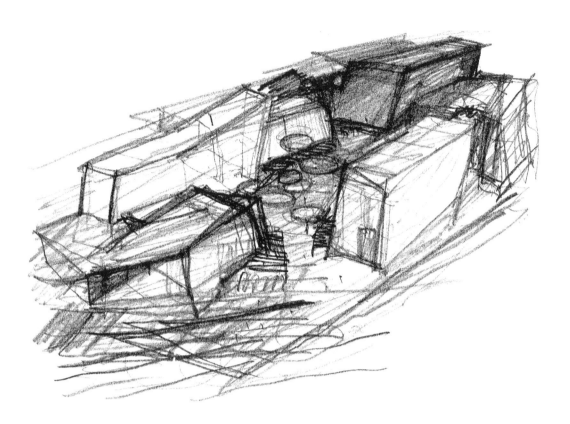

6.23   Third design, conceptual sketch for the //hapo Courtesy of the Office of Collaborative Architects: GAPP Architects/Urban Designers + Mashabane Rose Associates + MMA Architects.

full of plants and artworks made from 'cement, rocks or boulders, iron and steel. A colossal crucifix towers over the garden' and according to Mutwa, sculptural figures represent Jesus and his child, Jesus' wife (that is Mary Magdalene), Goliath and his wife, Joseph of Arimathea, and a boulder that represents the Hand of God is believed to generate 'more power than the other boulders'.[173] Rose explained that it was while sitting on the rocks in Mutwa's garden that he had the idea to make a museum from a collection of rock-like forms placed around a central outdoor space sited at the foot of Salvokop hill.[174] His sketch, drawn on the plane during the return flight, demonstrates the concept that would finally capture the clients' imagination (see Figure 6.23).[175]

Boulders featured prominently at the Isivivane, and the trust's commissioned research into the significance of boulders in indigenous practises and beliefs helps to explain their use here – a metaphor of building-as-boulder. According to research conducted by Dr Lynette Hlongwane: '"stones in all sizes and shapes, are the foundations of the earth. Africans believe that before there was soil, there was stone. So a stone is symbolic of the human mind which is undefeated and lasts forever."'[176] And from Matshilo Motsei's research, we learn that 'the rock is our home. In the beginning, African people lived in the colossal mountains where they constantly listened to the voice of silence … mountains and caves served as shrines for ancestral worship'.[177] And from

6.24
//hapo, model.
Courtesy of
the Office of
Collaborative
Architects: GAPP
Architects/Urban
Designers +
Mashabane Rose
Associates +
MMA Architects.

Mutwa, rocks 'were the first to be created … Rocks have powers … fire is born of rocks … stones are the bones of the earth'.[178] From this, we can see that boulders serve as a primal image of stability, of home, of the ancestors, of healing and of power.

In the final plan, seven boulder-buildings are joined in a 'J'-shaped formation, holding a central, outdoor space called the IKS Garden (see Figure 6.24) – 'an area in which indigenous knowledge is brought to the foreground through storytelling, objects, interpretation, artistic production and performance … the literal and spiritual heart of //hapo'.[179] The museum narrates a story of the seven epochs – the Ancestor Epoch, the Peopling Epoch, the Colonisation and Resistance Epoch, the Industrialisation and Urbanisation Epoch, the Nationalisms and Struggle Epoch, the Nation Building Epoch – with a boulder given to each.[180] Rose explains that the theatrical nature of the interior is created via contrasts of light and dark, and by a sequence of expanding and contracting spaces.[181] The boulders define tall and expansive volumes, whereas the connecting spaces that lead onto the next are small and compressed, with low ceiling heights. These tight connecting spaces are used to narrate the shift or rupture that occurs in the visitor's motion from one epoch to the next. Interior surface planes flow seamlessly from wall to ceiling to achieve a primal cave-like interior, with slots and cut-outs that provide dramatic lighting effects (see Figure 6.25). The story of the 'seven epochs' that connects our past with our future wishes to encapsulate the stability and healing power of natural boulders.

The building is constructed from a series of large steel-frame trusses that span across the full width of the structure to provide an uninterrupted space

6.25   Rendered interior perspective of the //hapo. Courtesy of the Office of Collaborative Architects: GAPP Architects/Urban Designers + Mashabane Rose Associates + MMA Architects.

for the interior (see Figure 6.26). The architecture is conceived as a double skin, with an inner and outer shell formed from a series of tilted and faceted planes that wrap to create building mass and space, and to conceal the structure. External wall planes lean in and out of vertical, while roof planes pitch up and down in a zigzag motion to achieve a shape that is reminiscent of boulders. The resulting mass has an impressive sense of grandeur and scale, yet it is one that settles carefully into the terraced contours at the foot of the hill. Treated as one seamless shell, the external skin is made from sheets of plywood that follow the geometry of the supporting steel trusswork beneath, and are clad with thin copper sheets. Internally, wall and roof surfaces are mostly made from dry walling that is fixed to secondary structural frameworks that hang down from the trusses above. This approach allows interior surfaces to be formed in a plastic and uninhibited fashion, creating the sense of a natural, cave-like interior, and in response to the museological requirements of the plan. These tectonic and structural resolutions confirm the *ideational* nature of this design. Architectural form at the //hapo is ideologically motivated, and metaphorically conceived in relation to the immovable strength and mythical significance of natural boulders.

Concluding Remarks

By way of conclusion, we shall consider the representational structure of this project in terms of Fanon's preoccupation with mask and skin – displaced versus natural presentations of identity. Freedom Park is in search of a deeply authentic and indigenous identity – a naturalness of the skin. In the early stages of the Park, design interventions were tied to nature, landscape and ritual and in so doing, the Park has wished to achieve an immediacy of presence. The Isivivane is intended as a performative site of embodied memory. It is direct and immediate – a space embodied by the presence of the deceased – yet it is also aesthetically abstracted, a symbol that invites memory and participation. Where the Isivivane attempts to create a unique and 'authentically' African form of memorialisation, the Sikhumbuto, by contrast, accepts a conventional Western typology – a wall of names – an approach that is more mediated and conceptual, rather than immediate and embodied. The realisation is, nevertheless, linked to indigenous themes and mostly by virtue of landscaping and the inclusion of the Sculpture of Ascending Reeds, while building elements are either sunken or downplayed. And we noted that when taken together, the Isiviane and Sikhumbuto allow for a hybrid mix of African and Westerns spatial types. The //hapo is, perhaps, the most adventurous structure at Freedom Park in that it attempts to unify aspects of the Isivivane

6.26   Structural framework of the //hapo, Freedom Park, OCA. Photograph by the author.

and Sikhumbuto – hence the immediacy of participatory exhibits, and storytelling derived from African oral traditions are housed within the more mediated spaces of a museum, itself a Western/colonial building type.

Prior comparison between the Legislature buildings at Kimberley and Mpumalanga revealed an opposition drawn between, on the one hand, a 'centred' representation tied to tropes of authenticity and tradition (Mpumalanga), and on the other, a 'de-centred' representation assembled from a multiplicity of fragments (Kimberley). The //hapo sits on the Mpumalanga side of this opposition, with its protection of tradition and its search for authenticity – an architecture of 'natural' skin. At Mpumalanga, however, the centred nature of the composition was achieved through the use of monumental geometry, whereas at the //hapo, centring occurs on a different register by virtue of the ideologies that motivate the design. The crucial point here is to note how the discourses that produced Freedom Park have wished to determine the essence of things. The Park has wished to promote the authenticity of indigenous forms to document and thereby to fix – through commissioned research – the significance of indigenous myths and practices, and ultimately to use this material as a motivation for the design of the Park. The seamless form of the //hapo, and the centred ideology that underpins it, are perhaps also a requirement of nationalism – a search for, and self-conscious representation of, the cultural genus of nation. The sceptre of national identity – which should not be conflated with cultural identities per se – is 'implied' in the previous chapters of this book, yet is now rendered *explicit* here at Freedom Park.

The //hapo is also similar to the Legislature at Mpumalanga in that the buildings' skin is also a mask, one that covers and hides the underlying structure, and in both cases the architecture is about the 'naturalness' of building skin, a skin that is also a mask. At Mpumalanga, African identity is mostly derived from material finishes and décor, while the actual form remains a somewhat conventional plan type. With the //hapo, however, a metaphoric relation to the mythical significance of natural boulders has inspired a truly contemporary and a highly original design. Architectural translation of the boulder concept has also required a fair degree of disguise – theatrical surfaces of copper and plasterboard that hide the structure. But it seems incorrect merely to describe this building as one that wears a mask, for architectural identity, here, infuses almost every aspect of the design – the plan, the building mass, interior space and tectonic resolution, each in their own way works to realise the metaphoric sense of a collection of boulders set in a healing garden. Yet the translation from idea into architecture is also a displacement. The //hapo is not the idea that gave it birth. The //hapo is the //hapo, a new, unique and futuristic architectural expression. From this, we might observe that this building is wearing a *new skin*, one that is motivated by the 'authenticity' of an old skin.

Notes

1   In her 'Position Paper', Callinicos explains that '[t]he Cabinet-approved Legacy Project has undertaken, to approve and facilitate the setting up of new monuments, museum programmes, plaques, outdoor art works, history trails and other symbolic representations … of our formerly neglected heritage'. Luli Callinicos, 'Position Paper: Freedom Park' (DACST, 2000), p 1.

2   FPT, 'Brief and Conditions: Architectural Competition' (Pretoria: FPT, 2003), p 5.

3   Callinicos, 'Position Paper: Freedom Park', p 1. Serote, CEO of the FPT, also emphasised this same point. Interview, Salvokop (September 2008).

4   Deborah Posel and Graeme Simpson (eds), *Commissioning the Past: Understanding South Africa's Truth and Reconciliation Commission* (Johannesburg: Witwatersrand University Press, 2001), p 5.

5   TRC, 'Truth and Reconciliation Commission of South Africa Report' (TRC, 2003), Vol. 6, Section. 1, pp 7–10.

6   Posel and Simpson (eds), *Commissioning the Past: Understanding South Africa's Truth and Reconciliation Commission*, p 3.

7   TRC, 'Truth and Reconciliation Commission of South Africa Report', Vol. 6, Section 1, p 3.

8   Postscript to the Constitution of the Republic of South Africa, Act 200 of 1993.

9   The commission called for reparations for victims, of which five distinct kinds were noted: urgent interim reparation, individual reparation grants, symbolic reparations (in other words 'exhumations, tombstones, memorials or monuments', the category to which the Freedom Park belongs), community rehabilitation programmes, and institutional reform. TRC, 'Truth and Reconciliation Commission of South Africa Report', Vol. 6, Section 2, pp 94–5.

10   Interview, Johannesburg (August 2008).

11   Callinicos, 'Position Paper: Freedom Park'. FPT, 'Freedom Park Conceptual Framework' (Pretoria: FPT). Three-Person Committee and Heritage Department, 'Vision for the Design Brief' (Pretoria: FPT, 2004). The Three-Person Committee – consisting of Professor Harriet Ngubane, General Masondo and Dudu Bogatsu – are a core group of intellectuals that provided leadership during the formative stages of Freedom Park.

12   Callinicos, 'Position Paper: Freedom Park', p 1.

13   Ibid. p 2.

14   Ibid.

15   Ibid.

16   FPT, 'Freedom Park Conceptual Framework', p 5.

17   Ibid. p 6.

18   Ibid. p 7. The selected timescale of 3.6 billion years, beginning in the vicinity of Barberton, is surely derived from Mbeki's public citation of John Reader's book *Africa: A Biography of the Continent*. Citing Reader, Mbeki states: 'The Barberton Mountain Land is built of layers of sediment that were eroded from a pre-existing landscape and deposited in a marine basin … Some of the earliest-known forms of life evolved in the waters above; as they died, the remains of

these microscopic organisms sank to the bottom and were fossilised as the ooze was transformed to chert. They are preserved there still – the earliest-known evidence of life on Earth, 3.6 billion years old, in Africa … The fossils preserved in the 3.6 billion-year-old cherts of the Fig Tree formation are the relics of single-cell bacteria. They comprise the earliest-known evidence of life on Earth, marking the transition from a sterile to an ultimately fertile world.' Thabo Mbeki, 'Address at the Presidential Reconstruction Programme Launch' (Kruger National Park: 2001), cited from: John Reader, *Africa: A Biography of the Continent* (London: Hamish Hamilton, 1997), pp 18–19. And regarding the origins of human life in Africa, see also: Donald Johnson and Blake Edgar, *From Lucy to Language* (Johannesburg: Witwatersrand University Press, 1996); Charles Brain, *The Hunters or the Hunted: An Introduction to African Cave Taphonomy* (Chicago: The University of Chicago Press, 1981).

19   FPT, 'Freedom Park Conceptual Framework', pp 7–20. Regarding the concept of 'African Renaissance', see: Thabo Mbeki, 'The African Renaissance, South Africa and the World' (United Nations University, 1998).

20   Thabo Mbeki, 'The African Renaissance Statement of Deputy President Thabo Mbeki' (SABC, Gallager Estate: 1998).

21   Thabo Mbeki, 'Speech at His Inauguration as President of South Africa' (Union Buildings, Pretoria: 1999).

22   Thabo Mbeki, 'Address at the Third African Renaissance Festival' (Durban: 2001).

23   FPT, 'Brief and Conditions: Architectural Competition', pp 5–6.

24   My interviews underscored this precise understanding: Ramzie Abrahams (heritage manager for Freedom Park), Pretoria (August 2008); Professor Yonah Selleti (former heritage manager for Freedom Park), Pretoria (September 2008); Mphethi Morojele (of MMA), Johannesburg (September 2005).

25   Benedict Anderson, *Imagined Communities* (London: Verso, 2003), pp 11–12.

26   Anderson suggests that the modern nation is a form of 'imagined community', Ibid.

27   Although Serote was CEO at the time of the UIA competition, his vision and leadership for the Park came into its own after the failed outcome of the international competition.

28   Three-Person Committee and Heritage Department, 'Vision for the Design Brief', p 8.

29   Ibid.

30   Ibid.

31   The term 'living heritage' used here is made with reference to the National Heritage Act of 1999, which promotes the preservation of living heritage, defined as 'the intangible aspects of inherited culture', which may include 'cultural tradition, oral history, performance, ritual, popular memory, skills and techniques, indigenous knowledge systems', and so forth. National Heritage Resources Act 25 of 1999.

32   Callinicos, 'Position Paper: Freedom Park', p 5.

33   Three-Person Committee and Heritage Department, 'Vision for the Design Brief', p 8.

34   Ibid. p 9.

35   Board of Control of the Voortrekker Monument, 'The Voortrekker Monument Pretoria: Official Guide' (Pretoria: Board of Control of the Voortrekker Monument, ca 1950), p 24.

36   Interviews held with Gadd (August 2008, Johannesburg), the first CEO of Freedom Park, and Dr Sifiso Ndluvu (July 2008, Pretoria), a historical researcher for the Freedom Park, confirmed this intended relationship. Further reasons given for the choice of site was due to its visibility (interview with Gadd, and interview with Serote, September 2008, Salvokop) and the fact that the land had belonged to Transnet (South Africa's major transport company) and could be acquired at a reasonable price (interview with Gadd). Serote stated that Thabo Mbeki selected the site (interview with Serote).

37   Board of Control of the Voortrekker Monument, 'The Voortrekker Monument Pretoria: Official Guide' pp 29–30.

38   Riana Heymans and Salomé Theart-Peddle, 'The Voortrekker Monument Visitor's Guide and Souvenir' (Pretoria: Voortrekker Monument and Nature Reserve, 2007), p 35.

39   Board of Control of the Voortrekker Monument, 'The Voortrekker Monument Pretoria: Official Guide', p 32.

40   Despite this statement by Moerdijk, the architecture of the Voortrekker Monument appears to be modelled on the Völkerschlachtdenkmal in Leipzig, completed in 1913, a building that Moerdijk was familiar with. Ibid. pp 32–5.

41   I was, however, granted an opportunity to study files, relating to Freedom Park, held at Fox's office (Revel Fox and Partners, Cape Town, July 2009). The material was helpful, but few insights as to Fox's involvement could be gleaned from these papers.

42   Mongane Wally Serote, poem dedicated to Revel Fox in, 'Proceedings at the Memorial Service for Revel Fox held at the Cape Town International Convention Centre on 20 December 2004' (Cape Town: Revel Fox and Partners, 2004).

43   Interview with Barry Senior, Johannesburg (August 2008). Interview with Clive Richards of GAPP, Johannesburg (July 2008).

44   FPAA, 'Final Draft Urban Design and Development Framework' (Johannesburg: FPAA).

45   FPT, 'Freedom Park Project Management: Interim Progress Report with Specific Reference to the Architectural Competition' (Pretoria: FPT, 2002), p 3.

46   Interview with Senior, Johannesburg (August 2008). FPAA, 'Freedom Park, National Legacy Project: Update on the Architectural Design Competition' (Pretoria: FPT).

47   GAPP and MMA, letter to Hendrik Prinsloo, project manager for the Freedom Park (Pretoria: FPT, 14 May 2002).

48   UIA, 'UIA Press Release: International Competition for the Design of Freedom Park in Pretoria, South Africa' (Pretoria: FPT, 2002).

49   FPAA, 'Final Draft Urban Design and Development Framework'.

50   FPT, 'Brief and Conditions: Architectural Competition', p 16.

51   Ibid. pp 23–4.

52   Ibid. pp 7–8.

53   Ibid. p 18.

54   Interview, Johannesburg (August 2008).

55   FPT, 'Architectural Competition Instructions for the Second Stage Competitors' (Pretoria: FPT, 2003).

56   FPT, 'Freedom Park Architectural Competition: First Stage Jury Report' (Pretoria: FPT, 2003), Preamble, p 1.

57   Ibid. Preamble, p 2.

58   FPT, 'Minutes of the First Meeting of the Second Stage of the Freedom Park Architectural Competition – 17 July 2003 at the Sheraton Hotel' (Pretoria: FPT, 2003); FPT, 'Brief and Conditions: Architectural Competition', pp 27–8.

59   The deputy jury consisted of four members in the first round and two in the second. The team of technical consultants consisted of three members in the first round, and seven in the second. FPT, 'Freedom Park Architectural Competition: First Stage Jury Report', Preamble, p 1. FPT, 'The Report of the Jury on the Second Stage of Freedom Park Architectural Competition' (Pretoria: FPT, 2003).

60   FPT, 'Freedom Park Architectural Competition: First Stage Jury Report', Preamble, p 2.

61   FPT, 'Freedom Park Architectural Competition: Third Meeting of the Freedom Park Jury' (Pretoria: FPT, 2003), p 2.

62   Ibid. pp 2–3.

63   Interview, Salvokop (September 2008).

64   Ibid. Interview with Oluwa and Morojele, principals of MMA, Johannesburg (August 2008). Interview with Morojele, Johannesburg (September 2005, August 2003). Interview with Senior, Johannesburg (August 2008).

65   Burger was the only international member of the jury who responded to my emailed questions, yet unfortunately, his memory regarding the matter was unclear. Interview via email (July 2008).

66   Interview, Johannesburg (August 2008).

67   Interview with Serote, Salvokop (September 2008); Interview with Oluwa and Morojele, Johannesburg (August 2008); Interview with Morojele, Johannesburg (August 2003); Interview with Ngobeni, Johannesburg (August 2008); Interview with Prinsloo, Pretoria (September 2005); Interview with Senior, Johannesburg (August 2008). The brief states that the design must be 'environmentally sensitive' and 'all landscaping must be indigenous'. FPT, 'Brief and Conditions: Architectural Competition', p 18. In the jurors' first round report concern is raised as to the 'consequences of the scheme's impact on the natural environment'. FPT, 'Freedom Park Architectural Competition: First Stage Jury Report', Round one adjudication, p 2.

68   The jurors' final report explains that 'while each of these proposals has very positive qualities none … would satisfy the expectations and requirement of the Freedom Park Trust'. FPT, 'The Report of the Jury on the Second Stage of Freedom Park Architectural Competition'; FPT, 'Brief and Conditions: Architectural Competition', p 33.

69   OBRA, 'Freedom Park Pretoria, South Africa, Architectural Report' (Pretoria: FPT, 2003).

70 Ibid.

71 Ibid.

72 Ibid.

73 Ibid.

74 Ibid.

75 FPT, 'Minutes of the Second Meeting of the Second Stage of the Freedom Park Architectural Competition Held at 09:00 on Friday 18 July 2003 at the Sheraton Hotel' (Pretoria: FPT, 2003), pp 3–4.

76 Interview with Serote, Salvokop (September 2008); Interview with Morojele, Johannesburg (August 2003).

77 OBRA, 'Freedom Park Pretoria, South Africa, Architectural Report'.

78 FPT, 'Freedom Park Architectural Competition: First Stage Jury Report'. Report on Winning Entries, p 2.

79 Ibid. Instructions for the second stage competitors, p 3.

80 FPT, 'The Report of the Jury on the Second Stage of Freedom Park Architectural Competition'.

81 To Tai-Fai's written report is not always so easy to follow – one may assume that English is not the author's native tongue – and for which reason a degree of paraphrasing has been required.

82 Peter To Tai-Fai, 'Freedom Park, Salvokop, South Africa: The Event Horizon of the Future of South Africa' (Pretoria: FPT, 2003), p 3.

83 Ibid. p 2.

84 Ibid. pp 2–3.

85 Ibid. p 3.

86 Ibid.

87 Ibid. pp 5–6.

88 Ibid. p 5.

89 Ibid. pp 3–5.

90 FPT, 'Minutes of the Second Meeting of the Second Stage of the Freedom Park Architectural Competition Held at 09:00 on Friday 18 July 2003 at the Sheraton Hotel', p 5.

91 FPT, 'Freedom Park Architectural Competition: First Stage Jury Report', Report on Winning Entries, p 1.

92 FPT, 'The Report of the Jury on the Second Stage of Freedom Park Architectural Competition'.

93 Ibid.

94 Vladimir Djurovic and Imad Gemayel, 'Freedom Park: Report' (Pretoria: FPT, 2003).

95 Ibid.

96 Ibid.

97   Ibid.

98   Ibid.

99   Ibid.

100 Interview, Salvokop (September 2008).

101 FPT, 'Freedom Park Architectural Competition: First Stage Jury Report', Report of Winning Entries, p 1.

102 FPT, 'The Report of the Jury on the Second Stage of Freedom Park Architectural Competition'.

103 Ibid. FPT, 'Minutes of the Second Meeting of the Second Stage of the Freedom Park Architectural Competition Held at 09:00 on Friday 18 July 2003 at the Sheraton Hotel', p 6.

104 FPT, 'The Report of the Jury on the Second Stage of Freedom Park Architectural Competition'.

105 Ibid.

106 Revel Fox, letter to Wally Serote (Cape Town: Revel Fox and Partners, 13 August 2003).

107 Ibid.

108 Revel Fox, letter to Hassan Asmal (Cape Town: Revel Fox and Partners, 20 August 2003).

109 FPT, 'Minutes of the Second Phase Planning Committee, Held on the 07 May 2004' (Pretoria: FPT, 2004), p 2.

110 Interview with Serote, Salvokop (September 2008).

111 FPAA, 'Final Draft Urban Design and Development Framework'; OCA '!Ke E: /Xarra //Ke: Stage One Report Appraisal and Project Definition' (Johannesburg: OCA, 2004), p 14.

112 FPT, 'Garden of Remembrance: Design Concept' (Pretoria: FPT, 2003).

113 FPT, 'Brief and Conditions: Architectural Competition'; FPT, 'Freedom Park Trust Programme 2004: Second Draft' (Pretoria: FPT, 2003).

114 OCA '!Ke E: /Xarra //Ke: Freedom Park Architectural Brief' (Pretoria: OCA, 2004), p 18; Three-Person Committee and Heritage Department, 'Vision for the Design Brief', p 7.

115 Thabo Mbeki, 'Address at the Ceremony to the Hand over of the Garden of Remembrance, Freedom Park' (Salvokop: 2004).

116 Professor Harriet Ngubane completed her PhD at Cambridge University, and is perhaps best known for her book *Body and Mind in Zulu Medicine*. Ngubane passed away in October 2007. Harriet Ngubane, *Body and Mind in Zulu Medicine* (London: Academic, 1977).

117 Harriet Ngubane, 'Research Paper on the African Understanding of the Concept of Memorial' (Pretoria: FPT, 2003), p 1.

118 Ibid.

119 Ibid. p 2.

120 Ibid. p 3.

121   Although based upon indigenous practices and beliefs, the primary symbols, if we may call them that, which are used here – namely water, soil, mist, fire and stone – might be described as 'archetypical' and are chosen to facilitate a wider spiritual significance. It should be noted that 'various faith based organisations' – African, Buddhist, Christian, Islamic, etc. – were welcomed, and indeed participated in the cleansing and healing ceremonies held at the Isivivane. FPT, 'African Cosmology: The Story Behind the Boulders, Soil, Cleansing and Healing Ceremonies', *Freedom Forever* 1, no. 1 (2004).

122   Harriet Ngubane, 'The Role of Research in the Indigenous Knowledge Sector of Freedom Park: Youth Workshop on Freedom Park – Pretoria' (Pretoria: FPT, 2003), pp 4–5.

123   Ibid. p 5.

124   FPT, 'The Freedom Park: Isivivane', in an official tourist brochure (Pretoria: FPT).

125   Three-Person Committee and Heritage Department, 'Vision for the Design Brief', p 3.

126   Some soil and a tree were also donated from each of the nine provinces. FPT, 'The Freedom Park: Isivivane'.

127   Harriet Ngubane, 'An African Perspective on the Management of Life and Death and Its Implications for Nation Building and Reconciliation in South Africa' (Pretoria: FPT), p 4.

128   Interview, Pretoria (August 2008).

129   Ibid.

130   Ibid.

131   FPT, 'Garden of Remembrance: Design Concept' (Pretoria: FPT, 2003).

132   FPT, 'Freedom Park: Sikhumbuto', in an official tourist brochure (Pretoria: FPT).

133   Ibid. Three-Person Committee and Heritage Department, 'Vision for the Design Brief', p 3.

134   Ibid. Also see: FPT, 'Freedom Park: Sikhumbuto'.

135   Mbeki, 'Address at the Ceremony to the Hand over of the Garden of Remembrance, Freedom Park'.

136   Interview with Serote, Salvokop (September 2008). Interview with Abrahams, Pretoria (August 2008).

137   The eight conflicts are: precolonial wars, genocide, slavery, wars of resistance, the South African War, the First World War, the Second World War and the South African liberation struggle.

138   OCA, 'Freedom Park: 23-03-2005' (Johannesburg: OCA, 2005).

139   Ibid.

140   Ibid.

141   The wild olive tree is positioned on the existing landscaped roof of the sanctuary announced by a commemorative plaque that reads, 'MOTHO KE MOTHO KA BATHO. Unveiled by the President of the Republic of South Africa, Thabo Mbeki, 16 June 2002'.

142 OCA, 'Freedom Park: 23-03-2005'.

143 Interview, Johannesburg (August 2009).

144 Ibid.

145 Ibid.

146 Ibid. OCA, 'Freedom Park: 23-03-2005'.

147 Harriet Ngubane, 'An African Creation Story' (Pretoria: FPT, 2003), p 1.

148 Ibid. p 5.

149 Ibid. p 5.

150 Interview, Johannesburg (October 2008).

151 Ibid.

152 Ibid.

153 Ibid. I was able to find a PowerPoint presentation, prepared by the architects, that showcases two early designs, one rising to the west while the revised design rises towards the east. OCA, '2006-04-13' (Johannesburg: OCA, 2006).

154 Interview, Johannesburg (October 2008).

155 Three-Person Committee and Heritage Department, 'Vision for the Design Brief', p 3.

156 Interview, Pretoria (August 2008).

157 OCA '!Ke E: /Xarra //Ke: Stage One Report Appraisal and Project Definition', p 21.

158 Interview with Abrahams, Pretoria (August 2008).

159 '[t]he topography of the northern slope will to a large extent determine the shape of the exhibit floor, which is likely to be more linear in nature, along the East West orientation'. OCA '!Ke E: /Xarra //Ke: Stage One Report Appraisal and Project Definition', p 23.

160 Interview, Johannesburg (August 2008).

161 Ibid.

162 Tom Hennes, Blair Parkin, and Mike Shakespear, 'Draft Report on a Consulting Visit by Thinc and Visual Acuity' (New York and London: Thinc Design and Visual Acuity, 2004).

163 Ibid. pp 28–35.

164 Ibid. p 28.

165 Interview, Johannesburg (November 2009).

166 For instance, I happened upon the following statements, scattered across a range of documents obtained from the Freedom Park archive. From Serote: '[o]ne of the most prominent forms in African society is the circle. Round houses, circular homesteads; circular kraals; circular formations of Lekgotla etc. … how does the above, innovate modern architecture'? From Ngubane: 'things should be in a circular nature and sharp objects should be avoided'. Credo Mutwa: '[a] round building is a friendly building and signifies that all sitting in a round house are equal.' And from Thinc and Visual Acuity: 'Freedom Park should *free the*

voices and knowledge that has resided here for thousands of years … This will affect
… the *design* of the architecture … including an emphasis on curvilinear spaces
and rounded surfaces'. Mongane Wally Serote, 'Brief on Iks and Freedom Park
– Discussion Document' (Pretoria: FPT); FPT, 'Minutes of the Second Phase
Planning Committee Held on 18 June 2004 at 15:00' (Pretoria: FPT, 2004); FPT,
'Notes on the Consultative Meeting between the Freedom Park Trust Delegation
and Credo Mutwa Held on 11 April 2007 in Kuruman (Northern Cape)'
(Pretoria: FPT, 2007), p 7; Hennes, Parkin, and Shakespear, 'Draft Report on a
Consulting Visit by Thinc and Visual Acuity', p 15.

167   Interview, Salvokop (September 2008).

168   Ibid. In her African creation story, Ngubane notes the chameleon's 'ability to
camouflage and merge with [the] immediate environment minimises individual
prominence and underlies unity, similarity and cohesiveness … patience,
caution and compromise are well represented by … the chameleon … [who]
symbolises the core of social values which form the basis of African *ubuntu'*.
Ngubane, 'An African Creation Story', pp 3–4.

169   Interview, Johannesburg (August 2008).

170   Interview, Johannesburg (August 2008).

171   From the minutes to the consultation, we learn of Mutwa's views regarding:
spirituality, 'everything is God … Africans do not believe in God, they do know
that God does exist and that everything is God'; regarding ubuntu, 'I don't
exist, you don't exist, we are one'; regarding the environment, 'Humankind was
created to protect the environment and animals' and so forth. FPT, 'Notes on the
Consultative Meeting between the Freedom Park Trust Delegation and Credo
Mutwa Held on 11 April 2007 in Kuruman (Northern Cape)', pp 1–5.

172   Ibid. p 2.

173   Ibid. p 2.

174   Interview, Johannesburg (August 2008).

175   Ibid.

176   Hlongwane's research is based upon interviews with some 32 participants
including 'traditional healers/doctors, academics, Government officials, African
philosophers/thinkers, traditional African priests, and general citizens'. The
above citation is quoted from participant 'DK'. Lynette Hlongwane, 'The
Significance of Boulders and Water in African Traditions' (Pretoria: FPT), p 5, 7.

177   Motsei's research is based upon ten in-depth interviews with 'key informants'
including six 'traditional healers', 'a spiritualist, a historian, and a curator of an
indigenous museum'. Matshilo Motsei, 'Sacred Rocks, Ancient Voices: Spiritual
Significance of a Rock and Water in African Healing' (Pretoria: FPT), p 6, 15.

178   FPT, 'Notes on the Consultative Meeting between the Freedom Park Trust
Delegation and Credo Mutwa Held on 11 April 2007 in Kuruman (Northern
Cape)', p 5.

179   FPT, 'Freedom Park: //hapo', in an official tourist brochure (Pretoria: FPT).

180   Ibid.

181   Interview, Johannesburg (November, 2009).

Conclusion

Identity and Difference

Postmodern perspectives in contemporary critical philosophy have wished to oppose grand and totalising narratives of history, polity and society. The last grand narrative to have affected our field of study was, arguably, the modern movement in architectural design. Modernist theory and practice was premised on a singular perspective, which believed it could capture architecture in its totality. For instance, the modern movement promoted a homogeneous concept of functionalism, which was supposed to be valid for all circumstances. The realisation that functionality is in fact complex, multiple, divergent, and open to social contestations, seldom occurred to modernist thought. In contrast to this reductionism of the singular project in design, I believe we must today re-imagine architecture and society as a wide field of expanding and, at times, unstable differences. *We need a differential conception of architecture.* In presenting this book, I do not claim to know the 'Truth' of the matter, whatever that could mean, but rather, I have wished to propose a considered reading, one that hopes to engender further thought and study. Architecture is a complex medium, one that registers wide-ranging significance on multiple levels. It is doubtful whether a singular view, such as the perspective argued for here, could hope to capture the greater fullness of architecture's social significance. It is certainly not my intention to silence other, equally valid, perspectives.

The *leitmotif* of Fanon's thought, in *BS*, is the irresolvable question of black identity. An implication of this proposition is that non-closure must surely feature on both sides of the colour bar – a point that Fanon hardly develops – meaning that white histories and subjectivities are equally unresolved and the discursive divides that separate white from black are, ultimately, arbitrary and unstable – unstable, not impotent, and despite the best efforts of colonial power. For Fanon, the promotion of a positive black identity is staged in response to the demeaning stereotypes of the colonised world. Fanon searches for an authentic expression of a black-self in the poetics of Negritude, but ultimately the deepest questions of racial and cultural identity remained open-ended: '[n]o attempt must be made to encase man, for it is his destiny to be set free.'[1]

The question of an African identity in design cannot and should not be answered in a singular or definitive sense. Instead, following the suggestion of Ernesto Laclau, I believe we would do well to concentrate 'attention on the multiplicity [of the phenomenon] itself', a multiplicity of symbolic resonances which exist to enrich the scope and substance of a collective, African imaginary.[2] To support a unitary movement, or a coherent Style, would be to promote a static concept of contemporary African architecture – one that falls short of Fanon's more fluid conception of the subject. For this reason, I have preferred to emphasise the displaced complexity of different post-apartheid imaginations which, in their various ways, have each made meaningful contributions to an emerging African imaginary in South Africa. Yet no one design should be taken to represent a definitive position – hence we should speak of African expressions and identifications, not Identity and not Style. The projects presented by this book are, in most cases, exemplary with respect to this general orientation, and key architectural themes include: an expanded contextualism which crosses various histories, timescales and imaginations; cosmopolitan and open-ended narratives; new imagery and spatial types which de-throne colonial symbols of power; as well as forms of public transparency through the creation of inclusive public spaces and participatory discourses.

Hybrid Representation

In closing, I wish to comment on my findings with respect to the hybrid character of the buildings under consideration. It may be noted that my criticism has relied on a distinction drawn between modern, or contemporary design, and more particular forms of African expression. This theme was introduced in Chapter 2, where the adjudication for the Legislature at Mpumalanga made a distinction between the so called 'contemporary statement' in design versus a more 'responsive' approach to design, one which included 'vague reference to Africa and local context'. Similar distinctions were made throughout the book. A crucial question now emerges as to the precise relation that exists here between the terms of this distinction – between the words 'modern' and 'Africa'. The question may be formulated as follows: do we mean to support a binary that sets Africa off against the modern? Do my interpretive ideas of 'foreign elements', and the duplicity of mask and skin, rely upon a closed distinction of Africa against the modern? The short answer is no. It was not my intention to suggest a relation of this kind, and to read this book in this way would be to misrepresent the hybrid character that I have wished to uncover. With hindsight, it is now possible to clarify the structure of hybrid representation that has emerged from the theoretical and empirical study of this study. The logical form of the hybrid formation that I have appealed to requires a double motion of *appropriation* and *inclusion* to render a complex figure which is also a subversion of the dominant – not a synthesis, but a layering of the form, an inclusion of difference and a resistance to closure.

In Chapter 2, I argued that the purity of the modern can be opened to form a new hybridity: White Skin, Black Mask. This hybrid formation provides a non-pejorative conception of the modern because it must be acknowledged that the modern is often defined in static opposition to the premodern, to traditional or even notions of the uncivilised and the savage. A hybrid conception of the contemporary involves both an appropriation of the modern and a subversion of its exclusionary purity through the inclusion of formerly silenced narratives. If I have appeared to support the African side of the equation, then this was so, because there was never any doubt as to the thoroughly assertive position of the modern with respect to the case studies of this book. It will be remembered that in Chapter 1, Fanon's diagnosis does not involve a clear-cut binary because the masks of identity that he uncovers, at times, retain the effects of reversal, where the undecided status of 'authentic' identity destabilised the stasis of the binary relation. The play of mask and skin is a 'both-and' and an 'in-between', not an 'either-or'. In the architectural terms of post-apartheid public designs, we may state that achieving inclusivity has required themes of African material tectonics, climate, landscape, patterns of dwelling, long-surviving figures, types and symbols including imaginaries of the prehistoric and the precolonial, cultural metaphors and handcraft, both modern and traditional – elements and imaginations that have been layered onto the architectural object. The distinction of mask and skin – for instance, understood as architectural structure and surface treatment – was not intended as a closed binary, but rather as an interpretive device for studying the complex, hybrid relations that have occurred between distributions of formerly excluded elements.

In the introductory chapter, two avenues of enquiry were set out: the first operating on an architectural level where I was concerned to understand how aesthetic representation 'relocates' architecture with respect to 'established codes', and the second operating on a social level where I wished to look at forms of participation and identification. We shall now consider how the structure of hybrid representation relates to these two themes.

The theme of skin and mask (of given and subverted forms of identity) was gleaned from Fanon and used to study architectural order derived from building structure (a key aspect of modern design) in relation to surface articulation, especially with respect to the inclusion of what I have termed 'foreign elements', which showcase formerly excluded narratives. I was careful to emphasise that Fanon's terms should not be reduced to questions of architectural aesthetics, and that my translation of these terms was merely heuristic, and not ontological. The four case studies worked with different relations of mask and skin, and I emphasised the positive plurality that emerges from these different approaches to design. However, from the point of view of the structure of hybrid representation as introduced above, it is also necessary to clarify relations between signifiers of the 'modern' and of 'Africa' that are implied by each instance.

At Mpumalanga, we saw that African décor was used to disguise a prototypical, contemporary, office-building plan. The building is wearing a mask, yet in doing so, the project also wishes to present an 'authentic' image of identity. A centred representation of this kind is not without merit, and I have welcomed the timely contribution of this impressive design. Nevertheless, it must be stated that the choice of dressing the modern with African signifiers has tended to cast a closed relation of Africa versus the modern without a play of disruption or reversal. The Northern Cape Legislature, by contrast, took a more dispersed approach to the symbolisation of Africa through the use of a cosmopolitan field of reference. The saturated quality of the built presentation has meant that Africa is not tied to some authentic beginning in a premodern or precolonial past but rather the dispersed substance allows the symbolisation of Africa to float across a range of timescales – from the precolonial to the contemporary – and across different imaginative referents. Fragments of mask and skin were placed in close proximity such that the representation flickers in between – the mask could be the skin and the skin might just as well be the mask. Our binary of Africa versus the modern is disrupted, and we are brought closer to Fanon's preoccupation with an unresolved and fluid conception of identity.

The Constitutional Court operates in a similar vein through the hybridising of diverse and disaggregated elements. Unlike the Northern Cape Legislature, however, the modernistic aspect of the court also attempts to reconcile, or to synthesise, the diverse elements of the composition, to unify the diversity of post-apartheid society through forms of inclusive sympathy. Nevertheless, totality fails and the project is richly layered with complex and inviting traces of difference that transcend static duality. At Kliptown, duplicities of mask and skin do not necessarily result in a progressive hybrid, for in this case the one seems in denial of the other, and the symbolisation of Africa is domesticated as a contrived surface patina.

Finally, Freedom Park is similar to the project at Mpumalanga in that both are primarily concerned with tropes of authenticity and the centring of representation that has resulted from this approach is one that privileges tradition. But it may also be observed that where the Mpumalanga Legislature involves the disguise of a fairly conventional building plan, Freedom Park has wished to challenge established typologies. At the //hapo, in particular, we appear to have a near inversion of the complex at Mpumalanga for where Mpumalanga hinges upon the disguise of an African mask, the //hapo uses African mythology as the justification for an assuredly contemporary expression in design. In terms of our binary of Africa and the modern, Africa now provides the myths and metaphor that inspire the contemporary spirit of this design. Yet despite this apparent inversion, duplicity is maintained as the image is not identical to the idea, and the work is surely not the mythology that has sought to authenticate it.[3]

The second critical theme concerned forms of participation and identification, which relate to the aforementioned structure of hybrid representation because the involvement in the development process requires an appropriation and disruption of the established autonomy of professional protocol in design. Our binary now concerns the relation between intentions of the professional team, and the views or contributions made by others, including the client, artists and crafters, member of the public, and so forth. At Mpumalanga, for instance, a difference of interpretation emerged as to the correct reference for an African space of assembly. Notably, this issue would not have occurred had the architects been closed to ad hoc forms of discussive participation that were sparked during the development of the design. This difference of view was ultimately resolved through the inclusion of a pair of incommensurable symbols, a dome and a tree. And at Kimberley, the inclusion of artworks by Van den Berg added a spontaneous element that, crucially, has supplemented the dispersed and cosmopolitan character of this design. These projects prefigure the more developed forms of participation that featured in subsequent chapters.

At Constitution Hill, the historic nature of the site allowed for easy metaphoric translation – the prison is to the court as the past is to the future. A public discourse on rights was disseminated through media, and the documenting of people's memories was used as a key element in the programming of Constitution Hill. The architecture of the court furthered this participatory aspect, primarily through the inclusion of crafted elements, which have successively democratised the imaginative context of the project, opening the more usual autonomy of architectural representation to a much wider public audience. The Walter Sisulu Square of Dedication was, initially, set to evolve out of research into the historic nature of the site and the voices of the local community. Unfortunately, this visionary process was dropped in favour of a highly formalised design, one which fails to appreciate the complex 'authenticity' of the site. An architecture of the grand gesture has been welcomed by the institutions who wish to promote their developmental agenda for Kliptown, but the programme and resulting design are trapped in a stubborn loop of professional autonomy, and the scheme has unfortunately failed to raise processes of inclusion above bread-and-butter issues of the day. Regrettably, we are stuck with an inflexible distinction of professionals versus the people. Positioning the Walter Sisulu Square of Dedication as sister to the Constitutional Court throws up many unexpected questions with regard to the effectiveness of participatory narratives. Ironically, questions of discursive participation are more successful at the Constitutional Court, where the design is screened off from the everyday life of the city that surrounds whereas at Kliptown, questions of participation seem complicated by circumstances of poverty and the actual role that architecture has played remains contested and uncertain.

Freedom Park commemorates silenced and subjugated aspects of South Africa's history – the lives of those who suffered in the conflicts of the past and homage to indigenous cultural practices. Development of the park involved extensive participation from various movements and interest groups – women, youth, unions, faith-based organisations, and so forth. But the leading influence on the park was derived from commissioned research into indigenous practices and forms of knowledge – work that has imparted poetic, mythical, cyclical and spiritual qualities to the narratives of the park. This ethical orientation is also co-joined to a master narrative of nationhood and national identity – a motion that privileges notions of origin, of continuity, of social cohesion and the linear passage of time. In this, the park shows a complex and unresolved duality formed between its ethical and nationalistic aspect. The crucial point about highlighting this tension is not to say no to nation, but rather to sound alarm against the exclusionary tendencies that are entailed here. An encouraging aspect of the park, however, issues from the richness and poetic density of the mythologies it has appropriated – narratives that may be mobilised against the closure of nation. As to whether this indeed will be the case, only time will tell.

Notes

1   Frantz Fanon, *Black Skin, White Masks* (London: Pluto Press, 1986), p 230.

2   'Perhaps the death of *the* Subject (with a capital "S") has been the main precondition of this renewed interest in the question of subjectivity. It is perhaps the very impossibility of referring any longer the concrete and finite expressions of a multifarious subjectivity to a transcendental center that makes it possible to concentrate our attention on the multiplicity itself' – Ernesto Laclau, cited in John Rajchman (ed.) *The Identity in Question* (London: Routledge, 1995), p 93.

3   It will be remembered that the leading question at the //hapo has not been 'what is an African architecture?' but rather, 'What is the idea behind the image?' – which is to maintain a disjunction, a duality of image to idea.

Bibliography

CHAPTER 1

Berman, B., Eyoh, D. and Kymlicka, W. (eds) (2004). *Ethnicity and Democracy in Africa*. Oxford: J. Currey.

Bhabha, H.K. (1994). *The Location of Culture*. London: Routledge.

Fanon, F. (1967). *The Wretched of the Earth*, translated by Constance Farrington. London: Penguin.

—— (1986). *Black Skin, White Masks*. London: Pluto Press.

Fenton, S. (1999). *Ethnicity: Racism, Class and Culture*. Basingstoke: Macmillan.

Gibson, N.C. (2003). *Fanon: The Postcolonial Imagination*. Oxford: Polity Press.

Gordon, L.R., Sharpley-Whiting, T.D. and White, R.T. (eds) (1996). *Fanon: A Critical Reader*. Oxford: Blackwell.

Harris, R. and Rampton, B. (eds) (2003). *The Language, Ethnicity and Race Reader*. London: Routledge.

Hegel, G.F. (1949). *The Phenomenology of Mind*, translated by J.B. Baillie (2nd Edition, Revised). London: George Allen and Unwin Ltd.

King, A. (ed.) (1996). *Re-Presenting the City: Ethnicity, Capital and Culture in the Twenty-First Century Metropolis*. Basingstoke: Macmillan.

Lokko, L.N.N (ed.) (2000). *White Papers, Black Marks: Architecture, Race, Culture*. Minneapolis: University of Minnesota Press.

Malesevic, S. (2004). *The Sociology of Ethnicity*. London: Sage.

Noble, J. (2007). 'White Skin, Black Masks: On Questions of African Identity in Post-Apartheid Public Architectural Design, 1994–2006'. PhD Thesis, University College London.

Norberg-Schulz, C. (1985). *The Concept of Dwelling: On the Way to a Figurative Architecture*. New York: Rizzoli.

Rajchman, J. (ed.) (1995). *The Identity in Question*. London: Routledge.

Read, A. (ed.) (1996). *The Fact of Blackness: Frantz Fanon and Visual Representation*. London: Institute of Contemporary Arts.

Taylor, C. (1994). *Multiculturalism: Examining the Politics of Recognition*, edited by Amy Gutmann. Princeton: Princeton University Press.

Young, I.M. (2000). *Inclusion and Democracy*. Oxford: Oxford University Press.

CHAPTER 2

Adell, S. (1994). *Double-Consciousness/Double Bind: Theoretical Issues in Twentieth-Century Black Literature*. Chicago: University of Illinois Press.

'An Ancient Beauty Revived' (1994). *The Sub Contractor: The Official Journal of the Federation of Associations of Sub Contractors of South Africa*, 6(6): 16–25, 35.

'Assessors Report on the Architectural Competition of the Riverside Government Complex' (1997). Johannesburg: Meyer Pienaar Tayob Schnepel.

Bhabha, H.K. (1994). *The Location of Culture*. London: Routledge.

B.I. Associates (1997). 'Consultants Practice Information Requirements: Mpumalanga Provincial Legislature and Administration Buildings'. Johannesburg: B.I. Associates.

—— (1997). 'Preliminary Competition Brief: Mpumalanga Provincial Legislature and Administration Buildings'. Johannesburg: B.I. Associates.

—— (1997). 'Detailed Competition Brief for Mpumalanga Provincial Legislature and Administration Buildings'. Johannesburg: B.I. Associates.

'Carved Plaster Shines in Prestigious Projects' (2005). *Concrete Trends: Official Journal of the Cement and Concrete Institute*, 8(1): 14–15.

Collinge, J.-A. (1994). 'Tone Down City Hall, Designers Are Told', *The Star*, 25 October 1994, p 2.

Constitution of the Republic of South Africa, Act 108 of 1996.

Department of Arts, Culture, Science and Technology (DACST) (1998). 'Cultural Industries Growth Strategy: The South African Craft Industry Report'. Pretoria: Department of Arts, Culture, Science and Technology.

Department of Sport, Recreation, Arts and Culture (2000). 'Purchasing of Art Works for the Riverside Government Complex and Legislative Assembly'. Nelspruit: Department of Sport, Recreation, Arts and Culture.

'Down by the Riverside' (1997). *The South Africa Quarterly Report*, January/March, p 49.

Du Bois, W.E.B. (1989). *The Souls of Black Folk*. New York: Bantam.

'Emnotweni Casino, Nelspruit' (2000). *Planning*, March/April, 168, pp 56–9.

'Fifty Two Million Rand Emnotweni Sun Hotel Opens in Nelspruit' (2002). *SA Builder*, November/December, 945, p 45.

Giesen, M. (1998). 'Riverside Mall, Nelspruit', *Planning*, November, pp 42–5.

Gilroy, P. (1993). *The Black Atlantic: Modernity and Double Consciousness*. London: Verso.

Hartley, R. and Shaw, L. (1994). 'The PWV Is Seeing Red over the Colours of Colonial Opulence', *The Sunday Times*, 30 October 1994, p 7.

Huffman, T.N. (1998). 'Cattle for Wives', *Arena*, 5(16): 2–5.

—— (1998). 'Presidential Address: The Antiquity of Lobola', *South Africa Archaeological Bulletin*, 53, pp 57–62.

Kawash, S. (1997). *Dislocating the Color Line: Identity, Hybridity, and Singularity in African–American Narrative*. California: Stanford University Press.

Khosa, M.M and Muthien, Y.G. (1997). 'The Expert, the Public and the Politician: Drawing South Africa's New Provincial Boundaries', *The South African Geographical Review*, 79(1): 1–11.

Legislative Assembly Art Committee (2000). 'Artwork Procurement Budget'. Pretoria: Meyer Pienaar Tayob Schnepel.

Lubisi, S.W. (2004). 'Official Dedication of the Mpumalanga Provincial Government and Legislature Buildings'. Nelspruit: Mpumalanga Provincial Government.

Malan, C. and McInerney, P. (eds) (2001). *The Making of an African Building: The Mpumalanga Provincial Government Complex*. Johannesburg: MPTS Architectural Library.

Mathiane, N. (1994). '"Rainbow Building" to Be Toned Down', *Business Day*, 25 October 1994, p 1.

MDS Architecture (1998). 'Riverside Mall: Nelspruit, Mpumalanga', *Architect and Builder*, December, pp 10–13.

Meyer Pienaar Tayob Schnepel (n.d.). 'Mpumalanga Provincial Legislature'. Johannesburg: Meyer Pienaar Tayob Schnepel.

—— (1997). 'Mpumalanga Provincial Legislature and Administration Buildings: Design Report'. Johannesburg: Meyer Pienaar Tayob Schnepel.

—— (2000). 'Riverside Government Administration Complex and Legislature: Report'. Johannesburg: Meyer Pienaar Tayob Schnepel.

Moleko, K. (1991). 'Seven Heavens: A Jumma Masjid in Maseru'. University of Natal.

Norberg-Schultz, C. (1985). *The Concept of Dwelling: On the Way to a Figurative Architecture*. New York: Rizzoli.

Rapoo, T. (2000). 'Reflections on Provincial Government in South Africa since 1994', in Y.G. Muthien, M.M Khosa and B.M. Magubane (eds) *Democracy and Governance Review: Mandela's Legacy 1994–1999*. Pretoria: Human Sciences Research Council, pp 89–105.

Schapera, I. (1955). *A Handbook of Tswana Law and Custom*. London: Oxford University Press.

Steering Committee (1999). 'Progress Report 01/10', 55. Nelspruit: Department of Public Works.

Taljaard Carter Ledwaba Architects (n.d.). 'Riverside Park Urban Design Framework for Phases 1 (Government Boulevard) and 2 (Along North South Boulevard)'. Johannesburg: Taljaard Carter Ledwaba Architects.

CHAPTER 3

Beaumont, P. (2004). 'Wonderwerk Cave', in D. Morris and P. Beaumont (eds) *Archaeology in the Northern Cape: Some Key Sites*. Kimberley: McGregor Museum, pp 31–6.

Britz, B. (1985). 'Secretariat for Bophuthatswana Government, Mmabatho (1978–83)', *UIA International Architect*, 8, pp 30–1.

Comrie, H. (1998). 'Detail Models'. Kimberley: Department of Public Works.

Comrie, H. (1998). 'Submission Drawings'. Kimberley: Department of Public Works.

Elliott, P. (1998). 'New Legislature Buildings for the Province of the Northern Cape: Report on Architectural Proposals'. Cape Town: Paul Elliott Architects.

'Government Square, Mmabatho' (1984). *Architecture SA*, May/June, pp 34–41.

Hall, S. (1988). 'New Ethnicities', in K. Mercer (ed.) *Black Film, British Cinema*. London: Institute of Contemporary Art, pp 27–31.

—— (1990). 'Cultural Identity and Diaspora', in J. Rutherford (ed.) *Identity: Community, Culture, Difference*. London: Lawrence & Wishart, pp 222–37.

Hoo, S.K. (2003). 'Govt Got Land for Free', *Diamond Fields Advertiser*, 2003, p 11.

Horner, J. (2004). *Kimberley Drawn in Time*. Kimberley: Kimberley Africana Library.

Independent Development Trust (n.d.). 'Northern Cape Legislature Project'. Cape Town: Hirsch Fish.

—— (1997). 'The New Legislature Buildings for the Province of the Northern Cape: Architectural Competition Brief – Format, Rules and Information'. Kimberley: Department of Public Works.

'Kimberley Mine: The Big Hole' (2004), in D. Morris and P. Beaumont (eds) *Archaeology in the Northern Cape: Some Key Sites*. Kimberley: McGregor Museum, pp 67–9.

Luis Ferreira da Silva (n.d.). 'Northern Cape Legislature: Kimberley, South Africa'. Johannesburg: Luis Ferreira da Silva.

—— (1998). 'Architectural Report: The New Legislature Buildings for the Northern Cape'. Johannesburg: Luis Ferreira da Silva.

Macroplan (1995). 'Evaluation of Additional Sites: On Which to Erect the Northern Cape Provincial Legislature Buildings'. Kimberley: Department of Public Works.

Maggs, T. (2004). 'Dithakong', in D. Morris and P. Beaumont (eds) *Archaeology in the Northern Cape: Some Key Sites*. Kimberley: McGregor Museum, pp 37–43.

Malan, C. and McInerney, P. (eds) (2003). *Building an African Icon: The Northern Cape Provincial Government Complex*. Johannesburg: MPTS Architectural Library.

Mashabane Rose Associates (1997). 'The New Legislature Buildings'. Johannesburg: Masabane Rose Associates.

—— (1998). 'Northern Cape Legislature Competition: Architectural Competition Entry, Stage 2, Document A'. Johannesburg: Masabane Rose Associates.

Mercer, K. (1988). 'Diaspora Culture and the Dialogic Imagination: The Aesthetics of Black Independent Film in Britain', in M.B. Cham and C. Andrade-Watkins (eds) *Blackframes: Critical Perspectives on Black Independent Cinema*. Cambridge, MA: MIT Press, pp 50–61.

Plaatje, S. (2005). *Mhundi*. Johannesburg: Penguin.

'The New Legislature for the Province of the Northern Cape: Report by the Panel of Judges on the Adjudication of the Competition' (1998). Johannesburg: Herbert Prins.

Urban Solutions (1997). 'Urban Design Rationale: Northern Cape Legislature'. Johannesburg: Urban Solutions.

Van Schalkwyk, J. (ed.) (n.d.). *Kimberley: The City that Sparkles*: Kimberley: JVS Publication.

CHAPTER 4

'A Beacon of Light Hope and Celebration' (1998). *Worx News*, 3(4): 1, 3.

Alfreds, L.-A. (1998). 'Total Transformation for Jo'burg's Old Fort', *The Star*, 9 April 1998, p 3.

'Architectural Competition for the Constitutional Court: Report by the Jury on the Conclusion of the Judging of the Constitutional Court Building' (1998). Pretoria: Department of Public Works.

Brink, E. (2000). 'Our History in the Making: The Johannesburg Fort 1893–1983'. Johannesburg: South African Heritage Resource Agency.

Chaskalson, M., Kentridge, J., Klaaren, J., Marcus, G., Spitz, D. and Woolman, S. (eds) (1999). *Constitutional Law of South Africa*. Kenwyn: Juta.

Competition Steering Committee (1998). 'Minutes of the Special Meeting of the Competition Steering Committee Meeting, Held on 13 March 1998'. Johannesburg: South African Heritage Resource Agency.

Constitution of the Republic of South Africa, Act 32 of 1961.

Constitution of the Republic of South Africa, Act 110 of 1983.

Constitution of the Republic of South Africa, Act 200 of 1993.

Constitution of the Republic of South Africa, Act 108 of 1996.

Constitutional Court of South Africa (2004). 'The Constitutional Court of South Africa: The First Ten Years'. Johannesburg: Constitutional Court of South Africa.

'Constitutional Court: Report by the Competition Jury on the First Stage of the Competition' (1997). Pretoria: Department of Public Works.

Cox, A. (2003). 'Old Fort – A Place of Pain and Tears', *The Star*, 25 November 2003, p 12.

Currie, I. and de Waal, J. (2005). *The Bill of Rights Handbook*. Lansdowne: Juta.

Department of Public Works (1997). 'Brief and Conditions: Competition for the New Constitutional Court of South Africa'. Cape Town: Department of Public Works.

—— (1997). 'New Constitutional Court: Minutes of the Meeting Held on 5 January 1997'. Johannesburg: South African Heritage Resource Agency.

Du Rand, J. (n.d.). 'Description of the Foyer Experience'. Durban: Jane du Rand.

—— (n.d.). Submission Drawings. Durban: Jane du Rand.

Gerdes, P. (ed.) (1999). *Geometry from Africa: Mathematical and Educational Explorations*. Washington DC: Mathematical Association of America.

Holm Jordaan and Holm (1997). 'Report'. Pretoria: Holm Jordaan and Holm.

Japha, D. (1997). 'Constitutional Court: Draft Brief'. Johannesburg: South African Heritage Resource Agency.

—— (1997). 'Draft Competition Brief for the New Constitutional Court Building of South Africa'. Johannesburg: South African Heritage Resource Agency.

Japha, D. and Japha, V. (1996). 'Preliminary Notes on the Proposed Competition for the Constitutional Court'. Johannesburg: Albie Sachs.

Johannesburg Development Agency (n.d.). 'National Artwork Competitions for the New Constitutional Court Building'. Johannesburg: Johannesburg Development Agency.

Kaplan, L. (2004). 'Past in Present Tense', *Mail and Guardian*, 8–15 April 2004, p 17, 19.

Lamberti, T. (1998). 'Mandela Names Winning Architects', *Business Day*, 9 April 1998, p 3.

Law-Viljoen, B. (ed.) (2006). *Light on a Hill: Building the Constitutional Court of South Africa*. Johannesburg: David Krut Publishing.

Ledwaba, L. (2004). 'Fortress of Past Pains', *Thisday*, 15 March 2004, p 8.

Lefort, C. (1988). *Democracy and Political Theory*. Cambridge: Polity Press.

Levin, L. and Rorke, P. (n.d.). 'Constitution Hill National Artworks Competition: A Proposal for the Sunscreens'. Johannesburg: Lewis Levin.

Liebenberg, J. (1998). 'General Notification to Participants', Pretoria: Department of Public Works.

Mandela, N. (1995). *Long Walk to Freedom: The Autobiography of Nelson Mandela*. London: Abacus.

Mokwena, S.K. (2004). 'Inside Number Four', *Mail and Guardian*, 12–18 March 2004, p 6.

Ntsobi, M.P. (2005). 'Privatisation of Prisons and Prison Services in South Africa'. Masters Thesis, University of the Western Cape.

OMM Design Workshop and Urban Solutions (1998). 'The New Constitutional Building of South Africa'. Durban: OMM Design Workshop and Urban Solutions.

O' Toole, S. (2004). 'Hanging Judge', *Sunday Times Lifestyle*, 22 February 2004, p 6.

Pearce Partnership (1998). 'The Constitutional Court of South Africa: Second Report'. Zimbabwe: Pearce Partnership.

Planning and Design Consultants (1997). 'Report'. Johannesburg: Planning and Design Consultants.

—— (1998). 'Report: Second Round'. Johannesburg: Planning and Design Consultants.

—— (1998). 'Second Round Submission Drawings'. Johannesburg: Constitution Hill Archive.

Preamble to the Constitution of the Republic of South Africa, Act 200 of 1993.

'Registrar's Summary and Comments on the Proceedings of the Panel of Assessors 10–17 November 1997'. Johannesburg: South African Heritage Resource Agency.

Rickard, C. (1997). 'Gates to Open on a New Era of Democracy', *Sunday Times*, 26 October 1997, p 16.

Rondganger, L. (2003). 'Symbol of Oppression Becomes Tool of Freedom', *The Star*, 24 June 2003, p 9.

Sachs, A. (2004). 'Every Picture Tells a Story', *Mail and Guardian*, 27 February–4 March 2004, p 2.

Segal, L., Martin, K. and Cort, S. (eds) (2006). *Number Four: The Making of Constitution Hill*. London: Penguin Books.

Snell, J. (1997). First Round Submission Drawings. Johannesburg: Constitution Hill Archive.

—— (1998). Second Round Submission Drawings. Johannesburg: Constitution Hill Archive.

South Africa Act 1909 (9 Edw. VII, c 9).

'Strong Constitution' (2002). *Sowetan*, 19 June 2002, p 21.

University of the Witwatersrand History Workshop (2004). 'History Workshop Report: Buildings, Hospital Hill'. Johannesburg: University of the Witwatersrand History Workshop.

CHAPTER 5

Birch (1994). Letter to the Manager, Stocks Construction Pty, 22 December 1994. Johannesburg: South African Heritage Resource Agency.

Bremner, L. (2004). 'Reframing Township Spaces: The Kliptown Project', *Public Culture: Society for Transnational Cultural Studies*, 16(3): 521–31.

City of Johannesburg (2002). 'Joburg 2030: Full Report'. Johannesburg: City of Johannesburg.

De Jager, J. (1996). Letter to Stocks and Stocks, 15 March 1996. Johannesburg: South African Heritage Resource Agency.

The Freedom Charter of South Africa (1975). Helsinki: World Peace Council 1975.

'Freedom Square Architectural Competition: Report by the Judges', Johannesburg, 2002.

Freedom Square Project Implementation Team (1997). 'Freedom Square Project: Business Plan'. Johannesburg: Lindsey Bremner.

'Heads of Agreement between City of Johannesburg Metropolitan Municipality Herein Represented by the City of Joburg Property Company (Proprietary) Limited (Council) and Jada's Economic Stores (Proprietary) Limited (Jada) Registration No. 61/00509/07' (n.d.). Kliptown: Jada's Economic Stores.

Johannesburg Development Agency (2002). 'Freedom Square Precinct: Architectural Competition Brief'. Johannesburg: Johannesburg Development Agency.

—— (2004). 'Kliptown Development Business Plan'. Johannesburg: Johannesburg Development Agency.

Kliptown Our Town Trust (n.d.). 'Kliptown Our Town Museum'. Kliptown: Kliptown Our Town Trust.

Kruger Roos Architects and Urban Designers (2002). Submission Drawing. Cape Town: Kruger Roos Architects and Urban Designers.

Lapping, B. (1986). *Apartheid: A History*. London: Paladin.

Lodge, T. (1983). *Black Politics in South Africa since 1945*. London: Longman.

Luthuli, A. (1962). *Let My People Go: An Autobiography*. London: Collins.

Manto Management (2004). 'Greater Kliptown Development Project: Social Development Needs Assessment Report'. Johannesburg: Manto Management.

Martinson, W. (1995). Letter to the Chief Executive Officer, Greater Johannesburg Transitional Metropolitan Council, 9 October 1995. Johannesburg: South African Heritage Resource Agency.

Meyer Pienaar Smith Architects (1991). 'Kliptown Dust Bowl Project: Proposed Soweto Shopping Centre'. Johannesburg: Meyer Pienaar Smith Architects.

Mashabane Rose Associates and Bremner (2002). Submission Drawings. Kliptown: Kliptown Our Town Museum.

National Monuments Council (1996). 'Discussion in Respect of Proposed Development of Shopping Centre at "Freedom Square", Kliptown'. Johannesburg: South African Heritage Resource Agency.

—— (1998). 'Minutes of Meeting, Re. Freedom Square'. Johannesburg: South African Heritage Resource Agency.

—— (1998). 'Proposed Provincial Declaration as a National Monument: Freedom Square, Kliptown, Johannesburg'. Johannesburg: South African Heritage Resource Agency.

—— (1999). 'Minutes of a Workshop of the Johannesburg Plans Committee: Northern Region on a Conservation Policy for Freedom Square, Kliptown, Soweto'. Johannesburg: South African Heritage Resource Agency.

—— (1999). 'Minutes of the Second Workshop on Developing a Conservation Policy for the Conservation and Development of the Freedom Square Precinct'. Johannesburg: South African Heritage Resource Agency.

'News in Camera' (2002). *Sowetan*, 27 June 2002, p 2.

Paragon Architects, Comrie Wilkinson and Green (2002). Submission Drawings. Johannesburg: Paragon Architects, Comrie Wilkinson and Green.

Prins, H. (2003). 'Conservation Policy for the Core Area Kliptown, Soweto'. Johannesburg: Herbert Prins.

Rodd, D., Krige, S., Brink, E. and Khanye, T. (1998). 'Freedom Square, Kliptown, Johannesburg: Survey of Historical Significance and Architectural Heritage'. Johannesburg: South African Heritage Resource Agency.

SAPA (2003). 'Turning a Sod for Sisulu'. *Sunday Times Metro*, 29 June 2003, p 2.

Scott Wilson Kirkpatrik Urban and Regional Planners (1997). 'Greater Kliptown Development Framework Plan: Final Report'. Johannesburg: Scott Wilson Kirkpatrik Urban and Regional Planners.

South African Heritage Resource Agency (2002). 'Proposal for the Development of the Freedom Square (Walter Sisulu) Precinct, Kliptown, Soweto: Comments by the SAHRA Advisory Committee'. Johannesburg: South African Heritage Resource Agency.

StudioMAS (2002). Submission Drawings. Johannesburg: StudioMAS, 2002.

—— (2003). 'Kliptown Urban Design Framework'. Johannesburg: StudioMAS.

—— (2003). 'Presentation to Project Team July 2003'. Johannesburg: StudioMAS.

—— (2003). 'Report of the StudioMAS Presentation Made to SAHRA on the Walter Sisulu Square of Dedication Precinct, 14 August'. Johannesburg: Herbert Prins.

—— (2003). 'SMME Development Opportunity'. Johannesburg: StudioMAS.

—— (2003). 'Texture Presentation'. Johannesburg: StudioMAS.

Suttner, R. and Cronin, J. (1986). *Thirty Years of the Freedom Charter*. Johannesburg: Ravan Press.

Van Onselen, G. (1995). 'And the People *Did* Govern', *Sunday Times Metro*, 25 June 1995, p 3.

CHAPTER 6

Anderson, B. (2003). *Imagined Communities*. London: Verso.

Board of Control of the Voortrekker Monument (ca 1950). 'The Voortrekker Monument Pretoria: Official Guide'. Pretoria: Board of Control of the Voortrekker Monument.

Brain, C. (1981). *The Hunters or the Hunted: An Introduction to African Cave Taphonomy*. Chicago: The University of Chicago Press.

Callinicos, L. (2000). 'Position Paper: Freedom Park'. Pretoria: Department of Arts, Culture, Science and Technology.

Constitution of the Republic of South Africa, Act 200 of 1993.

Djurovic, V. and Gemayel, I. (2003). 'Freedom Park: Report'. Pretoria: Freedom Park Trust.

Fox, R. (2003). Letter to Hassan Asmal, 20 August 2003. Cape Town: Revel Fox and Partners.

—— (2003). Letter to Wally Serote, 13 August 2003. Cape Town: Revel Fox and Partners.

Freedom Park Architects in Association (n.d.). 'Final Draft Urban Design and Development Framework'. Johannesburg: Freedom Park Architects in Association.

—— (n.d.). 'Freedom Park, National Legacy Project: Update on the Architectural Design Competition'. Pretoria: Freedom Park Trust.

Freedom Park Trust (n.d.). 'Freedom Park: //hapo', in an official tourist brochure. Pretoria: Freedom Park Trust.

—— (n.d.). 'The Freedom Park: Isivivane', in an official tourist brochure. Pretoria: Freedom Park Trust.

—— (n.d.). 'Freedom Park: Sikhumbuto', in an official tourist brochure. Pretoria: Freedom Park Trust.

—— (n.d.). 'Freedom Park Conceptual Framework'. Pretoria: Freedom Park Trust.

—— (2002). 'Freedom Park Project Management: Interim Progress Report with Specific Reference to the Architectural Competition'. Pretoria: Freedom Park Trust.

—— (2003). 'Architectural Competition Instructions for the Second Stage Competitors'. Pretoria: Freedom Park Trust.

—— (2003). 'Brief and Conditions: Architectural Competition'. Pretoria: Freedom Park Trust.

—— (2003). 'Freedom Park Architectural Competition: First Stage Jury Report'. Pretoria: Freedom Park Trust.

—— (2003). 'Freedom Park Architectural Competition: Third Meeting of the Freedom Park Jury'. Pretoria: Freedom Park Trust.

—— (2003). 'Freedom Park Trust Programme 2004: Second Draft'. Pretoria: Freedom Park Trust.

—— (2003). 'Garden of Remembrance: Design Concept', Pretoria: Freedom Park Trust.

—— (2003). 'Minutes of the First Meeting of the Second Stage of the Freedom Park Architectural Competition, Held on 17 July 2003 at the Sheraton Hotel'. Pretoria: Freedom Park Trust.

—— (2003). 'Minutes of the Second Meeting of the Second Stage of the Freedom Park Architectural Competition, Held at 09:00 on 18 July 2003 at the Sheraton Hotel'. Pretoria: Freedom Park Trust.

—— (2003). 'The Report of the Jury on the Second Stage of Freedom Park Architectural Competition'. Pretoria: Freedom Park Trust.

—— (2004). 'African Cosmology: The Story Behind the Boulders, Soil, Cleansing and Healing Ceremonies', *Freedom Forever*, 1(1): 10–11.

—— (2004). 'Minutes of the Second Phase Planning Committee, Held at 15:00 on 18 June 2004'. Pretoria: Freedom Park Trust.

—— (2004). 'Minutes of the Second Phase Planning Committee, Held on 7 May 2004'. Pretoria: Freedom Park Trust.

—— (2007). 'Notes on the Consultative Meeting between the Freedom Park Trust Delegation and Credo Mutwa, Held on 11 April 2007 in Kuruman (Northern Cape)'. Pretoria: Freedom Park Trust.

GAPP Architects and Urban Designers and MMA Architects (2002). Letter to Hendrik Prinsloo, project manager for the Freedom Park, 14 May 2002. Pretoria: Freedom Park Trust.

Hennes, T., Parkin, B. and Shakespear, M. (2004). 'Draft Report on a Consulting Visit by Thinc and Visual Acuity'. New York and London: Thinc Design and Visual Acuity.

Heymans, R. and Theart-Peddle, S. (2007). 'The Voortrekker Monument Visitor's Guide and Souvenir'. Pretoria: Voortrekker Monument and Nature Reserve.

Hlongwane, L. (n.d.). 'The Significance of Boulders and Water in African Traditions'. Pretoria: Freedom Park Trust.

Johnson, D. and Edgar, B. (1996). *From Lucy to Language*. Johannesburg: Witwatersrand University Press.

Mbeki, T. (1998). 'The African Renaissance Statement of Deputy President Thabo Mbeki', South African Broadcasting Corporation, Gallagher Estate.

—— (1998). 'The African Renaissance, South Africa and the World'. United Nations University.

—— (1999). 'Speech at His Inauguration as President of South Africa', Union Buildings, Pretoria.

—— (2001). 'Address at the Presidential Reconstruction Programme Launch', Kruger National Park.

—— (2001). 'Address at the Third African Renaissance Festival', Durban.

—— (2004). 'Address at the Ceremony to the Handover of the Garden of Remembrance, Freedom Park', Salvokop.

Motsei, M. (n.d.). 'Sacred Rocks, Ancient Voices: Spiritual Significance of a Rock and Water in African Healing'. Pretoria: Freedom Park Trust.

National Heritage Resources, Act 25 of 1999.

Ngubane, H. (n.d.). 'An African Perspective on the Management of Life and Death and Its Implications for Nation Building and Reconciliation in South Africa'. Pretoria: Freedom Park Trust.

—— (1977). *Body and Mind in Zulu Medicine*. London: Academic, 1977.

—— (2003). 'An African Creation Story'. Pretoria: Freedom Park Trust.

—— (2003). 'Research Paper on the African Understanding of the Concept of Memorial'. Pretoria: Freedom Park Trust.

—— (2003). 'The Role of Research in the Indigenous Knowledge Sector of Freedom Park: Youth Workshop on Freedom Park, Pretoria'. Pretoria: Freedom Park Trust.

OBRA Architects (2003). 'Freedom Park Pretoria, South Africa, Architectural Report'. Pretoria: Freedom Park Trust.

Office of Collaborative Architects (2004). '!Ke E: /Xarra //Ke: Freedom Park Architectural Brief'. Pretoria: Office of Collaborative Architects.

—— (2004). '!Ke E: /Xarra //Ke: Stage One Report Appraisal and Project Definition'. Johannesburg: Office of Collaborative Architects.

—— (2005). 'Freedom Park: 23-03-2005'. Johannesburg: Office of Collaborative Architects.

—— (2006). '2006-04-13'. Johannesburg: Office of Collaborative Architects.

Posel, D. and Simpson, G. (eds) (2001). *Commissioning the Past: Understanding South Africa's Truth and Reconciliation Commission*. Johannesburg: Witwatersrand University Press.

Postscript to the Constitution of the Republic of South Africa, Act 200 of 1993.

Reader, J. (1997). *Africa: A Biography of the Continent*. London: Hamish Hamilton.

Serote, M.W. (n.d.). 'Brief on Iks and Freedom Park – Discussion Document'. Pretoria: Freedom Park Trust.

—— (2004). Poem dedicated to Revel Fox, in 'Proceedings at the Memorial Service for Revel Fox, Held at the Cape Town International Convention Centre on 20 December 2004'. Cape Town: Revel Fox and Partners.

Three-Person Committee and Heritage Department (2004). 'Vision for the Design Brief'. Pretoria: Freedom Park Trust.

To Tai-Fai, P. (2003). 'Freedom Park, Salvokop, South Africa: The Event Horizon of the Future of South Africa'. Pretoria: Freedom Park Trust.

Truth and Reconciliation Committee (2003). 'Truth and Reconciliation Commission of South Africa Report'. Truth and Reconciliation Committee.

Union Internationale Des Architects (2002). 'UIA Press Release: International Competition for the Design of Freedom Park in Pretoria, South Africa'. Pretoria: Freedom Park Trust.

CHAPTER 7

Fanon, F. (1986). *Black Skin, White Masks*. London: Pluto Press.

Rajchman, J. (ed.) (1995). *The Identity in Question*. London: Routledge.

Index